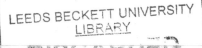

Film in Contemporary China

FILM IN CONTEMPORARY CHINA

Critical Debates, 1979–1989

Edited by
GEORGE S. SEMSEL
CHEN XIHE
and
XIA HONG

Foreword by John Lent

PRAEGER

Westport, Connecticut
London

Library of Congress Cataloging-in-Publication Data

Film in contemporary China : critical debates, 1979–1989 / edited by
    George S. Semsel, Chen Xihe, and Xia Hong; foreword by John Lent.
        p.   cm.
    Contains articles translated from Chinese.
    Includes bibliographical references and index.
    ISBN 0–275–94048–9 (alk. paper)
    1. Motion pictures—China. 2. Motion pictures—Philosophy.
    I. Semsel, George Stephen. II. Ch'en, Hsi-ho. III. Xia, Hong.
    PN1993.5.C4F5 1993
    791.43′0951—dc20   92–28522

British Library Cataloguing in Publication Data is available.

Library of Congress Catalog Card Number: 92–28522
ISBN: 0–275–94048–9

First published in 1993

Praeger Publishers, 88 Post Road West, Westport, CT 06881
An imprint of Greenwood Publishing Group, Inc.

Printed in the United States of America

The paper used in this book complies with the Permanent
Paper Standard issued by the National Information Standards
Organization (Z39.48–1984).

P

In order to keep this title in print and available to the academic community, this edition
was produced using digital reprint technology in a relatively short print run. This would
not have been attainable using traditional methods. Although the cover has been changed
from its original appearance, the text remains the same and all materials and methods
used still conform to the highest book-making standards.

For Milo and Mary Semsel

Contents

Foreword

John Lent

The word that best characterizes Chinese cinema of the 1980s is change. It was so in 1985 when the editor of *World Cinema* in Beijing insisted that George S. Semsel "note the date of this interview, . . . because even after a year, many things change here."[1] It is so today, as theorists sift through many options concerning the direction of Chinese film.

The accelerated transition that Chinese film theorists have experienced often-times has left them full of uncertainty, confusion and contradiction. At a dizzying pace, they have witnessed the shift of filmmaking from a propaganda, educational and political tool to an entertainment vehicle. There have been other changes as well.

For a while in the early 1980s, a concern for technology abounded in Chinese film. As Chen Xihe says in this volume, issues of form, style and expressive skills dominated; concurrently, a change in ideology also took place, with much criticism of Maoist thought. By the mid–1980s, Chinese traditional film theory, which pays attention to story and narrative, gave way to Western notions that image and photography were equally, if not more, important.

The Western influences were accepted in stages. Early in the decade, Chinese filmmaking was affected by Western traditional film theory. However, this changed too, especially after 1985, when a half-dozen American film professors went to China for varying stays. At decade's end, Western modern film theory, with an emphasis on the relationship of film to society and culture, was in vogue.

As the chapters in this volume indicate, the theorists are not of one mind on any issue, which is not to suggest that they should be. However, as at least one writer states, the unevenness and contradictions have left the field of Chinese film theory chaotic.

Listen for a while to the questions and concerns expressed in dialogues among the theorists. Granted, entertainment films should be encouraged, as the viewing of them provides a release—or as one speaker says, serves as an anti-repressive mechanism—but how many should be produced? A dozen or so, as is proposed by one theorist? More? Fewer? What about their expense? Does the mass production of entertainment films mirror the present trend toward consumerism in China, or is it a contributing factor to that trend? And what about entertainment films in relation to art cinema? Do entertainment films not have the task of improving themselves as art; do they not need more "exploration"? Hao Dazheng seems to think they do, stating, "Popular movies provide the cultural foundation and financial support of refined films" (see chapter 10).

All right, some agreement is reached that there must be linking of entertainment and art films. But which should be emphasized first? Simple, that which represents the most urgent need, one speaker argues. Then who should set the tastes for film? Theorists and critics who think they are more intelligent than the rest of society? Have they not harmed nonexperimental film by their overestimation of experimental film? By ignoring the nonexperimental film, have they not encouraged the public to dislike the experimental?

Other important concerns can be heard by listening to the theorists. Some, especially Zhong Dianfei, believe a "renewal of social concepts" is film's main role; most feel that individual desire should be explored in film, unlike before, when everything had to be subordinated to the needs of society. Some criticize the trend of anti-tradition in the films of the late 1980s; they believe entertainment films as a type of popular culture have a responsibility to reflect traditional culture. These are but a sampling of the many pivotal questions and issues raised by these leading film theorists of China.

The editors of this volume have provided a provocative and comprehensive mix of viewpoints in these dialogues and essays, which point to the significant changes in Chinese film theory during the latter half of the 1980s. As the editors say in their introduction, many of the essays have been "highly influential" in Chinese film production and theory. Coupled with a previous work edited by Semsel, Xia Hong and Hou Jianping,[2] this volume helps fill a major scholarship gap. It is important primarily because it allows Chinese film personnel to speak for themselves in their own language, using their own cultural and scholarly traditions.

More translation work of this type is called for, to complement (or offset) the many works on the subject by outside scholars, who have varying degrees of familiarity with Chinese culture.

NOTES

1. George S. Semsel, "China," in *The Asian Film Industry*, John Lent, ed. (London: Helm, 1991), p. 11.

2. George S. Semsel, Xia Hong and Hou Jianping, eds., *Chinese Film Theory: A Guide to the New Era* (New York: Praeger, 1990).

Preface

Li Tuo
Translated by Fu Binbin

A continuation of *Chinese Film Theory: A Guide to the New Era*,[1] this book is the second collection of translations designed to introduce the contemporary film theory of the People's Republic of China. Since the New Chinese Film Movement has aroused increasing interest among scholars, not only in mainland China, Taiwan, and Hong Kong, but in many countries of the West as well, the publication of such a book is obviously appropriate at this time. Its publication again reminds those who study Chinese film that in their research into the films of mainland China produced during the 1980s, attention should be paid not only to the film texts themselves, but also to the ways in which Chinese critics interpret these texts and how and in what context their theoretical discourse is produced. In this regard, I believe this book will provide abundant information.

In contemporary mainland China, a close relationship between film theory and film criticism exists. A number of scholars have even proposed that, at least on the mainland, theory preceded practice in the New Film Movement, that the movement was precipitated by new cinematic concepts and new film criticism. It is the former, they claim, which created the latter. Other critics, both in Taiwan and on the mainland, believe that the innovative movement in Taiwan films, represented by Hou Xiaoxian and Yang Dechang, should also be considered an important part of the New Chinese Film Movement, and that the new films on both sides of the Taiwan Straits should be taken as part of the same trend. Though this is an over-simplification, if taken as metaphor, their suggestion reflects to no small degree the importance of film theory and criticism in the development of the movement.

If Hollywood, with its massive industry, perpetuates the mainstream ideology of capitalism through its production of filmic commodities, then in socialist China, the system of film production itself is part of the national apparatus. The

Chinese film industry, as a state-run enterprise in which the Communist Party and its administration are the most important components, has never glossed over its responsibility to promote the mainstream ideology for the nation. Among the various forms of literature and art, film is the only production department that is strictly brought into line with state policies. Therefore, the birth of a "new film" inevitably becomes a revolt against the mainstream ideology, and the film encounters serious difficulties, under tremendous repression and resistance. The new films that have emerged could hardly have done so if film theory and criticism had not searched and found crevices on the theoretical level and broadened them with various strategies, so as to create large enough openings to allow discourse to confront the mainstream ideology. Had this not taken place, Chinese film artists would not only lack a language with which to express their implicit wishes, but also would be brought immediately back into line as soon as their deviation was detected. The advantage of this discourse was vividly exemplified by what happened in the debates in the early 1980s over the modernization of film language and the new concept of film. The "new" cinematic concepts and modes provided by critics were immediately taken by a group of film directors as weapons against the official standards for film, enabling them to wedge themselves onto the screen, which had been filled with socialist films, and thereby create a small space for their new films. Although the space was not large, the turbulent sounds and colors within it opened a new era for Chinese film.

If the activity of Chinese film theory and criticism in the early 1980s was mainly manifested through its influence upon filmmaking, toward the middle of the decade and later, the alliance between theory and practice became comparatively loose. By that time, film theory had already established its own independent discourse and could confront the mainstream ideology directly. This was partly due to the participation of a group of young critics who gave great impetus to the field of film study and criticism, but even more important was the new situation which emerged in the realm of ideology.

Since Deng Xiaoping advocated reform in 1978, two developments have been profoundly changing China. First, the rapid development of a market economy seriously challenged the state-planned economy which is the basis of a socialist country. Second, unprecedented activity of various "heretical" thoughts and theories emerged under the name of the "emancipation of the mind" and the gradual collapse of the mainstream ideology. Around 1985, these two interwoven developments gave theoretical circles in mainland China a "freedom" they had never had before. Although the government launched one political movement after another to fight the "freedom of the bourgeoisie," the mainstream ideology could only sustain its dominant position on the surface. Underlying this situation, every field of scholarship, including philosophy, history, and aesthetic theory, became a haven for marginal discourses which continually conflicted with the authoritarian central discourse. Consequently, new and intricate power structures formed, not only between the central and marginal discourses, but also between the different marginal discourses. In this chaotic game, film theory and criticism, at the forefront of the ideological struggle, became very active.

Debates and conflicts were everywhere. Traditional critics, who still adhered to the Maoist ideas about literature and art, opposed the young people clinging to the "new theories" of Louis Althusser, Jacques Lacan and others. Critics who argued that the primary task of film criticism was to advance film practice debated those who promoted film criticism as an activity of "reading" according to a certain theoretical framework. Those against the production of entertainment films opposed those who saw them as the solution to the dwindling audience. However, no matter how chaotic and intricate these conflicts, the revolt against and subversion of the mainstream ideology remained the primary concern.

Film theory and criticism in the 1980s in mainland China can only be understood in this historical context. The translation and study of foreign theory, for instance, be it the enthusiastic endorsement of André Bazin and Seigfried Kracauer in the early 1980s or the more recent studies of narrativity or deconstruction, exerted a tremendous influence upon the development of contemporary Chinese film theory. (Even after the June 4, 1989, incident in Tiananmen Square, the Chinese periodical *Contemporary Cinema* published a special issue specifically discussing Jacques Derrida and post-structuralism). However, unless we put them into the aforementioned context, we will scarcely discern, hidden behind the enthusiastic recommendations, translations and studies, the use of these "modern" theoretical discourses to resist Mao Zedong's speech to the Yanan Forum on Literature and Art (1942). The emphasis upon and fascination with Western theories was, to a large extent, a strategy in the fierce struggle for the power of discourse, though the participants themselves were often unaware of it. Another example can be found in the discussion of "entertainment" films, especially in the explorations into the psychological and sociological principles of making them. (The term "entertainment," in fact, serves as a euphemism for "commercial.") The motives for these discussions and research, of course, came on the one hand from the commercial pressures upon film in the flourishing market economy; on the other, film theory seized the opportunity to open a room for discourse for itself.

These strategies raised unforeseen problems. Hollywood commercial movies and the entire discursive system in which they are produced, whether in the United States or any other Western country, are organic components of capitalist ideology. Once imported into mainland China, they constituted a serious threat to the mainstream ideology, as incompatible with it as oil with water. By drawing upon them, film critics in mainland China placed themselves in peril, for they needed to find a way to draw a line of demarcation between themselves and the Hollywood ideology. This question might have been avoided, but for a variety of reasons, had it not been sharply addressed, it might not have developed into a direct and deep discussion for a fairly long time. That would have been a great pity.

Another important issue, which has not attracted enough attention in the development of film theory in mainland China, is that no matter what spectacular achievements it gained in the 1980s, or what rich, interesting materials it has provided its researchers, contemporary film theory and criticism in mainland China, generally speaking, remains comparatively naive.

Film theory and criticism in mainland China, unable to progress in as lively and vigorous a fashion as it did before June 4, 1989, has entered into a depression, which I do not believe will last long. Perhaps this temporary depression will prove, in the end, beneficial, leading people to a sober reflection on past experience. The kind of relationship Chinese film theory and study should establish with Western theories should be a major consideration. As I pointed out earlier, to foster a strategic opposition to the mainstream ideology, theorists and critics had to rely largely on Western theoretical discourses for support, but in so doing, they neglected to handle the relationship between themselves and the ideology of Western capitalist countries. As a result, they unconsciously brought themselves into interpretations based on relationships between the "First World" and the "Third World." This was an embarrassing dilemma, for it meant they had to surrender their own subjective position in order to oppose the hegemony of imperialist discourses.

This was not new to Chinese intellectuals. Ever since the May Fourth Movement in 1919 which led to the formation of the Communist Party, generations of Chinese have been trapped in this dilemma. On the one hand, they want to realize a Western-style modernization; on the other, they want to resist imperialist aggression. It is primarily because of the fierce political, military, and economic conflicts between imperialists and their colonies, between capitalist countries and weaker, under-developed countries, that people cannot easily locate the struggle for power on the discursive level. China in the 1980s was engulfed in waves of modernization, making it even more difficult for people to pay attention to such an issue.

However, there are indications that an awareness of the need to oppose the hegemony of the First World discourse is already taking shape. The recent debate over Third World film criticism in the theoretical circles of mainland China is one indication. Triggered by Zhang Jingyuan's 1989 translation of Fredric Jameson's article "Third World Literature in the Era of Multi-national Capitalism,"[2] a discussion began to develop about the way to reveal how the language of capitalism in Western, First World countries controls and represses the Third World through a "superculture," and how the Third World should seek its own position, to oppose the hegemony of Western discourse.

Interestingly enough, the most representative presentation of this discussion was conducted by a theoretical magazine. The Chinese periodical *Film Art*, in its first issue of 1991, published a group of articles by Zhang Yiwu, Liao Shiqi, Zhang Jingyuan and Dai Jinhua which elevated the debate to new heights. When Zhang Yiwu called for the establishment of a "Third World discourse" independent of Western theoretical discourse in order to seize the power to interpret the world, Zhang Jingyuan criticized Zhang Yiwu's opposition to the authoritarianism of Western culture, arguing that it would only lead to another kind of hegemony, such as "Sino-centralism." In contrast, Liao Shiqi insisted that since the formation of a world market is now inevitable, the establishment of a "mutual discourse," shared by both First and Third World countries is also unavoidable.

If the debate in *Film Art* had continued, it might have been interesting indeed, but after the release of this issue, *Film Art* ceased publication because, so it was claimed, it was "financially inadequate." Perhaps the magazine's closing symbolizes the long and difficult road contemporary Chinese film theory and criticism still has to travel. Despite such setbacks, however, it is no longer possible for either Chinese film or Chinese film theory to take the road of retrogression. The diverse contradictions and conflicts represented in the translations published here, as well as the emotions and wishes permeating every one of them, have not ceased to exist.

Semsel, an American scholar and professor of film and one of the leading figures in the study of Chinese film, recognizes that an important task at this time is to make available to the West the writings of filmmakers and scholars in China. Until this has been done, Western scholars will be crippled in their research, and the work of their Chinese colleagues will remain unknown outside their native land.

Chinese Film: The State of the Art in the People's Republic, by Semsel, and the subsequent *Chinese Film Theory: A Guide to the New Era* systematically introduced the Chinese film world to the West and already have had a significant influence both in China and abroad. The current volume furthers this effort.

In conclusion, I wish to commend my two friends, Che Xihe and Xia Hong, for their contributions to this book. Both are outstanding scholars of the younger generation in the theoretical circles of mainland China, whose emergence in 1985 brought fresh life to film theory and criticism. Both of them have already done much for the benefit of China. This book should be seen as a welcome continuation of their past efforts.

I have also taken pleasure in reading this book for a personal reason. It has brought me memories of past years and the many people and events that made them lively and bright. These events have been among the most interesting experiences of my life.

NOTES

1. George S. Semsel, Xia Hong, and Hou Jianping, eds., *Chinese Film Theory: A Guide to the New Era* (New York: Praeger, 1990).

2. *Contemporary Cinema*, no. 6 (1989).

Acknowledgments

We would like to thank the authors translated here for their kind permission to translate and edit their fine articles. The work would not have been possible without their wholehearted endorsement and cooperation. Our gratitude also to Anne Davidson, our editor at Praeger, for her concern throughout this project, and to John Lent and Li Tuo for their interest in our work. Finally, we would like to express our appreciation to Rosemary Semsel and the Ohio University School of Film for their continuing support.

Introduction

When, after 1979, China formally launched its modernization program and reform movement, and established a full diplomatic relationship with the United States, Chinese society was largely concerned with technological and ideological development. In terms of technological development, the government renewed policies from the past and new achievements of the West were introduced, in an all-out effort to advance the "four modernizations" of industry, agriculture, the military, and science and technology. Toward this development, both the Chinese authorities and the civilian population took a positive and unreserved attitude. In terms of ideological development, however, the situation was more complex. At the December 1978 meeting of the Third Plenary Session of the Eleventh Communist Party Conference, Mao Zedong's thoughts concerning class struggle and continuous revolution under socialism were abandoned. China's new leaders, headed by Deng Xiaoping, established the leadership of the Party and the socialist system as the final boundary for expanding ideology, while on the other hand, the population demanded more democracy and freedom.

Technological and ideological development were also embodied in Chinese film studies, though during the early 1980s, concern for technological development dominated. This began with a challenge to the traditional concept of film as recorded drama and with an appeal for the modernization of film language, following debates, first over the literary quality of film and over the new concept of film. These debates inspired studies into the unique nature of the medium and discussions on its nationalization.[1] These developments, which focused on technology and dealt primarily with issues of form, style and expression, strongly and directly influenced production and made deep changes in the film form and style of China.

Significant changes in Chinese film also took place on the ideological le' during this time; however, these changes were not caused by the development of film studies, but primarily by the more general ideological developments in Chinese society. A major subject of films made during this period was criticism of Mao's ideology and policies, and sometimes the ideology and policies of the Communist Party, which had dominated Chinese society for thirty years (1949–1979).

In the latter half of the 1980s, Chinese film studies shifted from technological to ideological concerns, from matters of ontology to the relationship of film to society. The following developments became more prominent:

1. In 1985, the call for new social concepts.
2. Beginning in 1985, the Fifth Generation and the Xie Jin "model."
3. In 1986, the recognition and review of traditional film aesthetics—Yingxi—from the perspective of culture and philosophy.
4. From 1987 to 1989, the discussion on the position and function of the entertainment film in Chinese culture and film.
5. From 1988 to 1989, the debate on the position and nature of Chinese film theory in the New Era (1979 to 1989).

Of these developments, discussions on the issue of culture, as expressed in the works of the Fifth Generation, and on the entertainment film are directly related to the two most important film movements after the mid-1980s: the study of Yingxi and the debates over film theory in the New Era are explorations of the philosophy and methodology of film theory itself, both traditional and contemporary. The common concern of these studies is ideology. They search, examine, redefine or reorient the ideological nature of film as a product of culture.

In addition, the focus of many historical and critical works shifted from form and style to ideology and culture. In the late 1980s, the interest in pure theory was gradually replaced by an historical and critical perspective. This also can be considered one aspect of the shift, because film scholars and filmmakers no longer considered film an eternal art isolated from society and culture, but a form closely connected to both. Therefore, more than ever before, they began to examine film in terms of the conditions of society and culture. The following research reflects this concern: Hu Jubing and Yao Xiaomong on the film policy of the Communist Party during the 1950s, Shen Jiming and Zhou Yongping on the film audience in China during the 1980s, Hu Ke on the women directors of the 1980s, Li Yiming and Dai Jinghua on Chinese films of the 1950s and 1960s (the classic film period of the Communist Party) from a new position and Zhang Wei on the relationship of Chinese film to traditional Chinese culture.[2]

These developments radically changed Chinese film, in terms of ideology as well as in terms of form and style, and at the same time, they re-featured Chinese film theory itself. Only through the contributions of theory, for example, were the works of the Fifth Generation more widely recognized, understood, and developed further. Similarly, the entertainment film, through the direct influence of theory, reached its peak in the late 1980s. Through this process, Chinese film theory itself came out from under the shadow of political ideology and became an independent matter, with new approaches and methodologies.

THE HISTORICAL BACKGROUND

The development of Chinese film theory during the 1980s was deeply rooted in the history of the nation. Following the establishment of the People's Republic in October 1949, all aspects of Chinese society on the mainland, including film, came under Communist Party rule. The film industry was nationalized soon after 1949, and the Ministry of Culture set up the Film Bureau, with two main divisions, one concerned with film production and the other with distribution and exhibition. With this, Mao's slogan, "Politics takes command!" came into full play. The entire industry was required to serve whatever purposes the Party dictated, and film became a propaganda tool of the political authorities. This situation, carried to the extreme during the Cultural Revolution, continued until 1978. During the 30-year period, Chinese film theory was required to follow strictly the official ideology, and its major function was to maintain the control of the official ideology over film production. Consequently, the ideological nature of film and its relationship to political authority received the most attention and became the most important issue in film studies. As a matter of fact, this issue was not studied academically, but was simply addressed according to Mao's principle about the arts ("All arts are political tools and must submit to the Party's leadership.") Discussion and doubt were not allowed; questions or challenges could lead one into serious political trouble. Issues of film form and style occupied little space and, in most cases, were predetermined by the political aesthetic of socialist realism.

After 1979, the new political authority relaxed its control of the arts, replacing the policy of "art should serve politics" with "art should serve socialism and the people." At the same time, most Chinese filmmakers, who had long detested the political influence over film and film studies, were eager to change the situation. With this background, film studies in China were reoriented toward a new, de-politicized direction, shifting from political/ideological issues to technical/stylistic issues. Many Chinese film scholars began to investigate the nature of film as a singular art and to treat film and film phenomena from the perspective of pure technique/aesthetics. Declaring that "film is film," distinct from political propaganda and also from the other arts, they believed that neither the general principles of art, including those of drama and literature, nor the general principles of politics could capture the essence of the medium.

In the mid-1980s, the demand for further political reform and ideological freedom in Chinese society increased daily, not only breaking with Mao's dogma, but going much further. As economic and technical reform progressed, the old political and ideological systems became increasingly significant obstructions of continued development. People realized that economic reform could not go further within the traditional political and ideological structures, and that to advance, China needed to undertake political reform as well. At this juncture, several perceptive film scholars, including the former chairman of the Society of Chinese Film Criticism, Zhong Dianfei, turned to the ideological issues of film and called for "the renewal of social concepts." This was the turning point for Chinese film studies in the 1980s, as more attention began to be paid to the relationship of film to society and to its ideological nature. This was not a return to pre-1979 perspectives. While film was again approached from an ideological point of view, its position in relation to the dominant ideology was no longer submissive, but critical.

THE INFLUENCE OF THE WEST

On one hand, the development of Chinese film theory during the 1980s was based in its national roots; on the other hand, it took place under the strong influence of international developments, in which Western film theory played an important role. During the 1950s and 1960s, Western film theories were scarcely known in China and had little influence on Chinese film and film theory. What was massively introduced and had strong influence on China was Soviet film theory. Then, during the Cultural Revolution, China totally closed its doors to the outside. In 1979, China began to open to the outside, especially to the West. Western film theories and theorists, both traditional and contemporary, began to be introduced on a large scale. This introduction came primarily through two major Beijing journals: *World Cinema* and *World Art and Aesthetics*. The China Film Press also published dozens of books of Western, mostly classical, film theory. In the early 1980s, China went through a period of de-politicization. The slogan, "Film is a tool of politics," was replaced by the belief that "Film is art," which corresponded with the emphasis of traditional Western theories on the aesthetic characteristics of the medium. Consequently, traditional rather than contemporary Western theories, especially the works of André Bazin and Seigfried Kracauer, evoked the greatest response from Chinese film circles.

In the summer of 1984 and for several subsequent summer seminars, five groups of prominent American scholars were invited to Beijing by the Society of Chinese Film Workers to give presentations or lectures. Bill Nichols, Brian Henderson, Nick Browne, Janet Staiger, Ann Kaplan and Vivian Sobchack were among them. They centered their presentations on semiotics, structuralism, psychoanalysis, feminism, Marxism and ideological theory and criticism. In addition, in the fall of 1986, Browne, a professor from UCLA, gave a series of lectures at the Beijing Film Institute on the history of Western film theory. Participants in these seminars included filmmakers, scholars and writers from all over China. Through their presentations and lectures, some of which were eventually published, contemporary Western film theory became comprehensible and useful to Chinese film scholars. Dr. George S. Semsel, a professor of Film at Ohio University, also spent a year working and lecturing in Beijing at the China Film Export and Import Corporation, as a foreign expert. At the same time, the two most important film magazines in China, *Contemporary Cinema* and *Film Art*, began to publish important works of modern Western film theory.

The introduction and study of Western film theory reached a peak in the mid-1980s. The theories which focused on ideological issues produced the strongest influence on Chinese writers, for at the time the whole trend of Chinese social thought began to shift toward political and ideological problems. Chinese intellectuals were looking for the means by which to criticize the old political and ideological system and to construct a new position for themselves. These theories offered them a weapon.

The influence of Western film theory on Chinese film theory can be seen clearly from three points of view: (1) the methodological, (2) the cultural and philosophical, (3) the political and aesthetic. In terms of methodology, Western film theory brought a scientific spirit to Chinese film theory, a point made in the later 1980s by radical scholars engaging in the debate on the nature and position of new Chinese film theory.

In the West, film theories following Christian Metz are generally considered scientific, not only because they employ the methods of linguistics and psychoanalysis, but also because, rather than advocate one kind of practice, they seek a comprehensive understanding of the medium, to explain how film works, how it generates meaning. In contrast, the theories of Bazin and Kracauer are usually considered forms of aesthetic theory. In China, however, all Western theories, including those of Bazin and Kracauer, are considered scientific. To understand this, we must know the traditional concept of film in China, as well as understand the indigenous culture and philosophy. This is the context in which Western film theories were presented and by which Chinese scholars reacted to them.

One of the major characteristics of the traditional Chinese concept of film is that most attention in film theory is devoted to the narrative level. It does not deal significantly with *image*, the basic unit of film material, or *photography*, the basic method of filmmaking, but with *story*, the larger unit of film, and *narrative*, the method of storytelling. Therefore, traditional Chinese film theory defines film as a kind of drama (Yingxi) or literature (novel). This approach is closely related to traditional kind of philosophical and cultural reasoning in China, which is synthesis, not analysis. The whole always comes first; the individual always comes last. For example, when addressing an envelope in China, one begins first with the country and then proceeds, in order, to province, city, street, building and finally the name of the addressee. The order of social priority is from state or family to individual, never from individual to family or state.

The photographic ontology of Bazin and Kracauer led Chinese scholars to see film from another perspective, to define it from the image/photography level, claiming that to do so was scientific and accurate, whereas to defin the story/narrative level was primitive and inaccurate. In the discuss as art in the early 1980s, the theories of Bazin and Kracauer advance(

on the level of technique/form and provided new energies by which the movement in film theory could break through the old concepts of film. Of course, their theories offered not only a new methodology, but also a new aesthetics for Chinese film. Their realist aesthetics were so popular that their theories became guidelines for the New Realist Aesthetics Movement of Chinese film in the early 1980s. What should be noted, however, is that Chinese film and film theory absorbed these theories only in terms of technique, and did not include the assumption of ethics.

Though their methodology was still affirmed in the late 1980s by Chinese scholars, by the mid-1980s, the aesthetic influence of Bazin and Kracauer began to decline, and contemporary Western theories replaced it. Like traditional Chinese film theory, the latter pay close attention to issues of politics and ideology, but at the same time, Western theories deal with these issues from a totally different position and approach. This points directly to another major characteristic of Chinese traditional film theory: the strong color of politics and morality. Traditional Chinese film theory has always had practical political and ethical ends, constantly attempting to find out what film should be politically and ethically. This characteristic is related to the basic spirit of traditional Chinese culture, which mainly takes an ethical and moral, rather than a physical and cognitive, attitude toward the world. For example, the aesthetics of Confucius emphasized the role of aesthetic enjoyment in moral and political education, while those of his near contemporary, Plato, followed an epistemic approach. Confucius focused on the relationship between art and morality, between art and good behavior, and evaluated art in terms of "perfection in both beauty and virtue." In contrast, Plato stressed the relationship between art and truth, between art and knowledge, and saw art as fundamentally mimetic. After 1949, the traditional Chinese aesthetic was combined with the political principles of the Communist Party to produce a kind of political aesthetic which served the dominant ideology.

After 1979, most scholars and filmmakers abandoned this politicized film aesthetic, drawing first upon Bazin and Kracauer in turning from politics to art. However, by the mid-1980s, when political and ideological issues demanded direct confrontation, they took the matter beyond the theories of Bazin and Kracauer. The radical film writers in China, searching for a new approach to politics and ideology, saw the potential of contemporary Western theory to direct them away from issues of aesthetics toward issues of ideology, and to enable them to treat film with a scientific and cognitive attitude. Western studies of film ideology did not deal with film from a particular ideological position, but scientifically investigated and analyzed film as an ideological practice. This approach offered Chinese scholars the possibility of dealing with the issue of ideology independently and critically; at the same time, it provided them a certain protection, because science and modernization were the official policy.

Obviously this change was not only in the significance of methodology, but also in the significance of politics. In the context of Chinese culture, "scientific" and "cognitional" first mean a spirit of independent and objective thinking, liberated from theological or political dogmas. Therefore, it is assumed that they are opposed to the dominant politics and ideology. As a matter of fact, the same thing had already taken place, in the influence of Bazin and Kracauer on Chinese film theory of the early 1980s. Consequently, in terms of political influence, Western film theory encouraged Chinese film theory to eliminate the influence of the dominant ideology in the early 1980s and, now, to confront the dominant ideology directly, with a new stance.

In the theoretical literature, the influence of contemporary Western film theory can be seen in the debate over film theory during the New Era, from 1988 to 1989. Some of the more radical film scholars openly took the contemporary Western film theories as their guideline and labeled Chinese mainstream film as an ideological myth. In their discussion of the entertainment film, Chinese scholars, drawing upon Sigmund Freud, redefined the entertainment film as a revolutionary concept, and reestablished its position in contemporary Chinese culture. This discussion overwhelmingly affected the aesthetics of Chinese film in the late 1980s. In addition, modern Western film theory widely encouraged a position critical of the dominant ideology in the historical and critical works in China of the late 1980s.

Developments in Chinese film theory during the 1980s were no longer the products of a closed culture, but the results of a dynamic process, a dialogue, between the national and international cultures; this has become a basic characteristic of all of contemporary Chinese society.

This book, a collection of recent literature, documents the major developments and issues of Chinese film theory during the second half of the 1980s. Many pieces in this book were highly influential in Chinese film theory, as well as in the film production in their time. Articles discussing Xie Jin's films from a cultural and ideological perspective are excluded, because they already have appeared in Section V of *Chinese Film Theory: A Guide to the New Era* In addition, one important development of film studies in the late 1980s, a work dealing with the ideological and political issues of Chinese film from a historical and critical perspective, briefly mentioned earlier, was not included for the sake of brevity.

Through the works in this collection and the one that preceded it, Western readers can trace the rise of a national literature dealing with film, at a time when ideological views were being increasingly questioned or, as in the USSR, abandoned as failures. The relationship of this thinking to the Tiananmen Square massacre should be noted. The relationship of film to culture, and the questions surrounding the way a nation considers outside influences, are also important.

NOTES

1. Regarding the development of Chinese film studies in the early 1980s, see George S. Semsel, Xia Hong and Hou Jianping, eds., *Chinese Film Theory: A Guide to the New Era* (New York: Praeger, 1990).

2. Hu Jubing and Yao Xiaomong, "The Policies of New China and its Discourse," *Contemporary Cinema*, vol. 1 (1989); Shen Jiming and Zhou Yongping, "The Film Audience in the Ten Major Cities," *Contemporary Cinema*, vols. 2 and 4 (1985); Hu Ke, "Female Directors and the Feminine Consciousness," *Contemporary Cinema*, vol. 4 (1986); Li Yiming, "Xie Jin's Films and Chinese Film History," *Film Art*, (Feb. 1990); Dai Jinghua, "History and Narrative," *Film Art*, (Feb. 1990); Zhang Wei, "How Traditional Culture Dominates Chinese Film," *Film Art*, (Oct. 1985).

Part I

The Call for New Social Concepts

By the end of the 1970s, Chinese film theory had rid itself of direct control by political ideology and made great progress in the study of the ontology and characteristics of the medium. By the mid-1980s, the assumption that film is primarily a tool of propaganda had been replaced by the concept of film as an autonomous art form. In a new development, Chinese film was treated as a kind of ideology in itself, and its social relationships were studied once again. The first sign of this transition was the publication in 1985 of "On Innovation in Social and Cinematic Ideas" by Zhong Dianfei, then chair of the Society of Film Criticism.[1] In his article, cinematic concepts refer to ideas about form and style, whereas social concepts refer to ideology and the social values of film.

Zhong reaffirmed the mainstream of Chinese film theory since 1979, though he emphasized the relationship between film and society. "Our cinema," he wrote, "in a period of major social reform, must undertake the renewal of social concepts as its main task. Whether or not a film captures the spirit of our times does not depend on its depiction of reform, but on its perceptions of society as seen through the eyes of a reformer."[2]

A second, highly influential article was "on the Modern Consciousness of Filmmakers" (1985), by Wang Zhongming, who sharply criticized the conservative social concepts of otherwise new and progressive directors, who were radically pursuing new ideas of cinema. In his article Wang maintained that "in production, the modernization of ideology has certainly not attracted sufficient attention when compared to that given the modernization of our understanding of film. However, modernizing ideology should be considered an extraordinarily urgent agenda confronting any progressive filmmaker."[3]

Both papers turned to the issue of ideology, which before 1979 had been the major focus of Chinese film studies. However, the attitude toward ideology was not the same as it once had been. Before 1979, Chinese film studies followed the official principles of ideology (pro-socialism and pro-Party leadership) and applied them to film analysis. Zhong and Wang, in their writings, established their own ideological principles, which were dedicated to radical reform and a full reopening of China to the outside world and which strongly criticized the traditional, often official, ideology. Yet in terms of methodology, both remained traditional. In order to deal with the ideological issues of film, they followed a sociological approach, according to which they attempted to construct a new set of ethical rather than scientific principles. In their studies, the issues of content and reform were treated separately, creating a new ideological criticism based upon the indigenous Chinese culture. This criticism was radically different from the ideological theory and criticism that would develop in China in the late 1980s, which was obviously influenced by the West.

In 1957, Zhong Dianfei himself had been criticized by Mao. He was condemned as a rightist and sent to a labor camp, where he remained for twenty years. At the end of the 1970s, he came back into the public eye and soon became chair of the Society of Film Criticism, while Wang, a recent college graduate, chaired the Beijing Society of Young Film Critics.

NOTES

1. Zhong Dianfei, "On Innovation in Social and Cinematic Ideas," *Film Art*, February 1985.

2. Ibid., p. 8.

3. Wang Zhongming, "On the Modern Consciousness of Filmmakers," *Film Aesthetics 1983*, Zhong Dianfei, ed. (Beijing: Culture Association Publishers, 1983).

Innovation in Social and Cinematic Ideas
A Foreword Given at the First Annual Meeting of the Learned Society of Chinese Film Criticism, Dalian 1984

Zhong Dianfei
Translated by Fu Binbin

All I can offer you today is at best a foreword. An annual meeting without a general report is still an annual meeting; however, film theory is no longer film theory without being closely integrated with practice. To segregate subject from object, and separate theory from practice, is the root of dogmatism. In this regard, literature and art are no exception. Last year I published an anthology of film aesthetics, *Cinematic Aesthetics: 1982*,[1] in an attempt to approach certain things that happened in filmmaking the year before in terms of aesthetic insights. The book was generally well received, I was told, except in academia, where some claimed the work could hardly be considered aesthetics. I was also dissatisfied, but remain confident, because as an abstraction of certain cinematic phenomena, the book lacked insight. The articles touched on specific issues and made significant generalizations, but failed to elevate them, in a rigid sense, to the level of aesthetics. This reveals our lack of theoretical preparation and mastery.

If this is so, why do I remain confident? It's because cinematic aesthetics is a new discipline, in the world and in China. It is derived from related disciplines, such as film history, theory and criticism. Film aesthetics cannot fully develop without the interaction of many non-cinematic sciences, such as philosophy, the social and natural sciences, anthropology, the study of art, the psychology of literature and art, information theory and futuristics. If aesthetics is interdisciplinary, then film aesthetics is even more so.

In recent decades, Chinese film theory has developed fully in terms of sociology or politics. Even today we can hardly think of cinematic issues without

---

NOTE: Several subheadings not in this speech have been added, for readability.

first considering a political point of view. As an aesthetic consciousness, concept and experience, this habit, whether consciously or subconsciously, affects our aesthetic judgment, what we usually call a nod or shake of the head.

The task of cinematology is to promote or normalize film culture. The old slogan, "Entertainment through education," admits that film entertains, but makes education its purpose. Education for cultural knowledge, administered by the Ministry of Education, comes first, and aesthetics, considered the responsibility of literature and art, is mostly seen in its influence on structure, as well as its aspirations to the beautiful. This function of film cannot be replaced by politics, philosophy or the social sciences. Education which bores cannot lead to healthy development of the mind and is not good in the long run.

Film may have been around for more than eighty years, but it did not control the rise and fall of a nation. The frightening criticism of *The Story of Wu Xun* (1950), given serious thought, might be considered harmful rather than beneficial. A good deal of political dissent in China came from film. Doesn't that teach us something? Those who study film history know that the left-wing films of the 1930s contributed, as did the progressive films from the Kuomindang area of the 1940s, but what ousted the empire of Chiang Kaishek was the mighty legions of communism, a million strong, who marched to the South. I am not saying film is useless, but I do not think it is capable of regulating the rise and decline of a nation.

A lesson from the facts tells us that when something is overly exaggerated, it loses its value. Film is neither infinitely great nor insignificant, but merely a pleasant variation in cultural life, enough to bring people, after an intense day of hard work, to split their sides with laughter, sigh, weep, become lost in thought, boil with rage or be overcome with grief. Moreover, the same film can be felt in different ways. Those who feel joy can be happy, those who feel sad can grieve. There's nothing wrong with that. Art is democratic, and so is film. It may be temporarily workable to force a definition upon film, but in the long run that goes nowhere, as we learned not too long ago from the Gang of Four.

BACK TO REALITY FROM THE OTHER SHORE

On what, then, should we focus our first annual meeting? I think we should focus mainly on innovation, in our ideas, in our attitudes toward life and in our ideas about film.

It seems to me that socialism in China is reawakening. The wave of reform now sweeping the country is a great new beginning, in which Marxism inherits ideologically the tradition of *The Communist Manifesto* and redefines the road it takes. If we fail to recognize this or underestimate it, our cinema will not keep up with the times, and there will be no true emancipation of the mind. I do not think emancipation of the mind is merely a decorative phrase, but I do not consider it a scientific notion, either. The theory of communism is a scientific, not religious dogma. Its vitality lies in this.

It is unfortunate that some of our comrades take communism as religious dogma, and therefore see it only as an explanation of the world on the other shore and consider the world we inhabit as a purgatory. They talk about "contrasting past misery with present happiness" to indicate the progress of society, and shut out our basic desire to improve and beautify our lives in the guise of "opposing the corrosive influence of bourgeois ideology." Poverty is cherished, wealth depreciated. Looking only to the past to see social development greatly restricts the progress of productive forces and defames communism and socialism.

The social consciousness once based in the momentary comfort of the peasants and the feudal closed-door policy must be renewed. This is a cardinal question related to subjects of film and portrayal of characters, and to whether or not the direction of our film art can meet the demands of modernization and better promote its construction. China needs to change. Not only must its economic system change, but also its concept of people. In this age of electronics and information, the remnants of militant communism and feudal ideals ought to be replaced by new, multi-disciplinary, multi-dimensional, and multi-level concepts of science and dynamics. The age of pastoral feudalism must be brought to an end; the traditional idea of self-perfection must be discarded and the concept of a utopian society overthrown. The curtain of a dynamic new phase has already been drawn. If we film artists have not realized this, then all our cinematic techniques, be they long or short takes, lip synchronization or sound-image counterpoint, wide screen or artificial wide screen, will not be sufficiently effective to push our society forward and represent the new situation and the spirit of the age.

Concepts of value, morality or right and wrong, in the most general sense, even if we draw upon their classical definitions, cannot help but be reexamined by the facts of life. Do we not say that when looking at a question, we should see the nature of it? Do we not call ourselves socialist realists? Then where does the nature of things lie? Should reality satisfy the mind, or should the mind correspond to reality?

THE HOLY FAMILY HAS ABUNDANT DESCENDANTS

Here we are talking about attitudes toward life, social concepts and ideas about film. But we are not conceptualists. Conceptualists take ideas as independent entities, operating in almost the same way as the will of God. Therefore, even what was considered effective in the many years of revolutionary practice and thus is difficult to abandon should be changed in method or style in accordance with changing historical tasks. *The Last Choice* (1983) is, of course, a film about reform; however, what it wants to reform is the thinking and style of the leadership, to make it more typical of the 1950s. That doesn't fit today.

As has been pointed out, the time of Newton's dynamics could only create a philosophy of dualism: action and reaction, motion and stasis, good and evil, beautiful and ugly, cause and effect. But the age of information has produced a philosophy of "multi": multi-levels, multi-dimensions, multi-effects, multi-causes and single effect, single cause and multi-effects. In the time of Newton, we remained comparatively superficial in our understanding of the forms of matter. The discovery of motion theory made it possible for humans to be multi-structural, multi-lateral, multi-dimensional and multi-leveled in their recognition of the objective world. If this were not so, we could hardly imagine unifying China and Hong Kong under two coexistent systems. To sigh vainly over the degeneration of the morals and the loss of primitive simplicity in human minds, or to go for productive forces and admit that the changes in the material world will inevitably lead to variations of every aspect of life, whether or not one can bear the sight of them, is of no importance. And it is even more unnecessary to criticize the new changes in favor of the past. The human head contains many hard layers, the precipitate of tradition. The Chinese have more layers than other people, since their tradition has been weathering for 5,000 years; the Americans have less, because they only have a history of 200 years. Egypt, also thousands of years old, has more precipitate in its people's minds; thus its women are still required to wear veils.

Matters of conception and morality are even harder to define. For more than 30 years, we have promoted the idea of "equality in poverty," but now, to be conspicuously rich, and a "10,000-yuan family," is encouraged. After the award is issued on the stage, however a fight usually breaks out offstage. In *The Last Choice*, when the girl gets rich raising rabbits, the people around her turn green with envy. Some want her to lend them money or to take away her rabbits. The leader of the work brigade even takes away the queen doe she used for breeding. All she can do is cry. We can call this a miniature of contemporary China. The idolizing of the literati and officialdom is deep-rooted in Chinese intellectuals, ingrained as far back as the Warring States period. Do not think that the reform touches only ordinary cadres and business leaders. Are intellectuals naturally in tune with reform? The aloofness of intellectuals from politics and material pursuits is a fatal weakness in itself, and there are other weaknesses as well.

MORALITY, BUT NOT MORALIZATION

Considering men and women, right and wrong, and morality, we only know that "the States of Yan and Zhao are famous for their numerous, vehemently tragic heroes," but too few of us know that "the people in Yan entertain their guests with their wives." In the Ming Dynasty, as described in *Jin Ping Mei* (ming dynasty novel), entertaining guests with wives was replaced by entertaining them with servants. In the reign of Emperor Wu of the Han Dynasty, the Emperor sent his daughter, Princess Xijun, to the remote kingdom of Wusun to marry

King Kunmo. The aged Kunmo wanted to marry Xijun to his grandson. Xijun refused, and reported this to the Han imperial government. The response was, "Follow the local customs." Morality is not immutable. Even now, after thousands of years, we still do not have an absolute concept of morality and ethics, do we? Our uniformity is only a uniformity on the screen. If our films were less uniform, we might be in more accordance with the realities of life.

The winds of reform and open-mindedness, together with economic shock waves, will surely shake the old rules and precepts. We do not favor bourgeois self-expression, which would make film an object for the salon. However, we are also against rejecting innovation in our attitudes toward life, whether the rejection is in the name of tradition, or even of revolution. Without innovation, we would lose our basis for choosing and processing subject matter and judging characters. I have been working on an article about the film *Life* (1984), and after five revisions, I still have not finished it. Why is it so difficult? Because it concerns a sociological evaluation of the characters, mainly of Gao Jialin. The conflict, centered in the love affair between Gao Jialin and Liu Qiaozhen, illustrates the contradiction between the traditional idea, "Take root in the countryside," and the comparatively open idea, "Don't be afraid to be a bean sprout in the city." In the long run, we must make a choice between medieval tenderness and social benefits, between present and future, the emotional and the rational. Qiaozhen is lovely and moving. Even the yellow earth of North Shaanxi weighs heavily on my emotional world. But in the progress of society, emotions can play a positive role only in specific times. Once beyond certain limitations, they become a regressive force and prevent us from seeing new things in the bud, even make us the antithesis of the new.

One road before Gao Jialin leads to a warm and cozy *kang* with a wife and children. Qiaozhen will surely be a good "old lady." That is the road all previous generations followed, a "golden road" that has been encouraged and approved. But Gao Jialin refuses. As he tells his father and his grandfather, Deshun: "You have your way of life, I have mine. I don't want to live a life like yours, spending my whole life digging on the mountains of the Valley of the Gao Family!" He not only goes to town, to Nanjing, but even wants to go "to the United Nations." What an unrestrained and far-ranging soul! All Qiaozhen can tell him is, "That old sow in your family just gave birth to twelve piglets. One was crushed to death by the sow and there were eleven left. But one was dead the next day." The possibility of a marriage between Gao Jialin and Liu Qiaozhen does exist, since the magic of love may make them forget everything else, but what would the rest of their lives be like? Wouldn't it be better for Qiaozhen if they parted now, when the raw rice has not been cooked, rather than seek a divorce after some eight or ten years?

Qiaozhen is a tragic figure, and the direct cause of her tragedy is Gao Jialin, but isn't Gao Jialin also tragic? His reasons are more complex. The most basic is that our society has not created a broader space for its younger generation.

We need a sober-minded understanding of the present situation, to put our weight, film, on the side of open-mindedness and reform, instead of where the outmoded and outworn is cherished and the old is used to negate the new.

THERE IS NO SIMPLE ARITHMETIC ON THE SCREEN

The noble nature of an artist is first of all revealed in a keen ability to observe, perceive and contemplate the time in which the artist lives. An artist cannot simply perceive, endure and yield to the pulses of the time without insightful contemplation.

Truth is simple as long as our attitude toward it is selfless. However, in terms of filmmaking, the truth that "everything is for the development of the forces of production" is simple in practice. Why not? I still hold by an old opinion: our object is neither the production process nor the product, but productive human beings, alive with diverse needs and interests. Film, once led into minute, boring technical descriptions that even scriptwriters and directors cannot fully understand, becomes a perversion of production and humanity. What is on the screen should be always and only the human not the production itself. In 1983, the senior research fellows at the Academy of Social Sciences and the Academy of Sciences held a get-together, and at the meeting, Lu Jiaxi noted that the two academies had originally been a unit and were later separated. As a matter of fact, the artificial separation of natural from social sciences affects the development of both. Kant was a philosopher, but the hypothesis of the formation of the solar system that he proposed in 1755 greatly advanced the progress of the natural sciences, especially the theory of the universe. Thus it can be said that the social sciences equip the natural sciences with wings and make them fly. At the same time, the advancement of the natural sciences, with their explorations of the material world, influences powerfully the opening of the spiritual world. I know little or nothing of the two areas, but I have insisted that portrayal of a one-dimensional human is not only impossible, but also unnecessary. A multidimensional person is able to undertake single tasks, but a one-dimensional person could not undertake complicated work.

Today, an open-minded view of the world, society and life is essential to social progress. China exists in the world, and an individual is an individual in the 1980s and 1990s. The Sino-Japanese 21st Century Committee just closed its first conference. I need not mention how such global thinking will influence human perspectives. China now has the open mind and boldness of vision it has lacked for the past 35 years.

WE HAVE SPUN A COCOON AROUND OURSELVES AND NOW WE SHOULD HAVE THE COURAGE TO BITE IT OPEN

If Chinese film is to gain a foothold in the world and assert an influence upon world cinema, we need, of course, to do many things. But if we are not open-minded in terms of ideology, even if all we are trying to describe is an alley, a small village, a neighborhood factory, a son and his father, or a husband and his wife, we cannot do a good job, and what we work out will be of little significance. Those who consider Gao Jialin in *Life* an ungrateful man do, indeed, consider the Valley of the Gao Family a closed society.

In our lives there are things we cannot stand. Things frowned upon are not all good or bad; appraisal and judgment is needed. If we fail to view newborn things, for the moment unfamiliar, with a progressive, open-minded eye, our criticism will be left behind with the times and become a barrier to social progress. However, we do not admire only the new. We are socialists, who yield for the good of the entire society. Individualism, decadent and declining, is actually not new, but old and stale.

In a time of tremendous social reform, our film must take as its primal issue, innovations in our attitude toward life. Whether a film has the spirit of the times does not lie in whether or not it describes a reform, but in whether it looks at everything in society with a reformer's eyes. Last November we flew from Osaka to Shanghai. The empty hall of the airport looked especially desolate at dusk. We bought some food tickets, but the waitresses were too lazy to serve us; on the contrary, they gathered in a corner chatting. Their topic might have been Gue Kaimin and Li Xiuming [young film stars], who were with us. You see, we have airplanes, the airport, and the large concourse, but we lack a state of mind compatible with these trappings of modernization.

I think the opinion of Heng Wen [a politician of the East Jin Era 300–400 A.D.] is quite right: "Idle talk harms the country." If a few people want to idly gossip, let them. Perhaps such people, as one ingredient of society, cannot be saved. But if people all over the country talked idly and derided those who are earnest and down to earth, and criticized them as "only pulling the cart without watching the road" and "using production against politics," the country certainly would be harmed.

TROUBLES CAUSED BY THE "DIVORCE": THE OTHER MAJOR ISSUE IN OUR CONCEPT OF FILM

Innovation in our concept of cinema is also a major issue to be discussed here. My "theory of divorce" has caused many more disputes than I anticipated, and I want to say something about it while I have the opportunity.

First, I raised this issue totally out of my own free will. I was inspired by *Ji Hongchang* (1979), in which the mise-en-scène can be said to be completely obedient to convention. I think that Chinese film, in its current phase of development, is still in the same low situation. This is generally worth noticing, for otherwise film, as an independent art, could not develop very well. Consequently I was interpreted as saying that "drama," as I described it, really meant the stage. This is true. But let me say now that this is an issue concerning not only directing, but also scriptwriting, acting and lighting.

Second, traces of dramaturgy do exist in our films; this is nothing strange. It can be said that the problem began with Zheng Zhengqiu [a producer/director, one of the originators of Chinese film]; that is, the problem was brought into film from "civilized" drama. The left-wing film activists of the 1930s were also dramatists. This was the case with filmmakers even after the founding of the Republic. Few of the comrades from the liberated areas had engaged in film-making, or even seen any films. To me, film was also a new art. Therefore, it is quite natural for our film to have some of the old habits of drama and traces of the stage. In the past 30 years, we have been busy with various political campaigns, using film for political ends, and have been too busy to attend to the art itself. This is natural enough, but the problem has had to be raised, and once it was, comrades from the drama circle reacted strongly. Some even found such terms as "cinematic thinking" or "cinematic consciousness" offensive. Actually, a second, sober-minded thought will make one realize that every form of art has had to find its own identity. Drama itself is no exception. Artists undertaking filmmaking not only need a cinematic consciousness, but also need to fully engage in cinematic thinking in order to create really high quality films.

In China, I am afraid it was Lao She who first noticed the difference between drama and film. At the end of 1923, when the Mingxing Film Company released *The Story of an Orphan Rescuing His Grandfather* (1923), Lao She, in his review in *Shen Bao*, wrote, "The entire movie is rich in the flavors of the shadowplay, and actions typical of the new dramatizations are reduced."[2] The idea of divorcing film from drama was initiated in those comments.

Third, under the Republic, the stage itself has changed a great deal. This is a fact. But the stage is still the stage. This is also a fact. Drama is a stage art and can be nothing else. In addition to the aesthetics of the cinema, the aesthetics of drama should also be developed. That all forms of art develop their own aesthetic systems is an important condition for the flowering of Chinese art.

Fourth, every discipline has its lower and higher levels. Things in conflict on the lower level might be inseparable and harmonious on the higher. In geometry, all lines converge at infinity; military science, developed on the higher level, intersects with political science. The separation of film from drama is both necessary and inevitable—otherwise it would be difficult to develop film. Nevertheless, film and drama share some common principles. Consequently, the "theory of divorce" serves only as a figure of speech by which to promote the progression of film itself. Over a long period of time, the expression will be impractical. Once there has been a general awakening of the cinematic consciousness and the number of people who have studied film has increased and the level of the audience risen, the expression will naturally lose its significance.

HARPING ON THE OLD REFRAIN ABOUT THE BOX OFFICE

Nowadays, the topic most frequently appearing in discussions is not the divorce, but the box office. A matter of income, the box office is also closely related to the cinematic concept discussed here. A high box office value indicates a large audience, and a large audience shows that a film is liked. Films welcomed by the audience are, generally speaking, good, but not without exception. This is why the study of the audience is a part of cinematic aesthetics. The income of film has become an important question, which indicates that it has epoch-making significance. I want to make two points about this.

First, the movement of a film does not end with its completion, nor does it begin with the onset of production. The audience comes into existence when a film is in an embryonic stage, because the subject matter is a route to the audience. This issue is simpler and more understandable to the capitalist producer. Losing the audience means losing everything. We consider box office value a forbidden territory, primarily because film has been used as an instrument of propaganda for many years and profits or losses have not been an issue. High or low box office value has had almost nothing to do with filmmakers. Even today, the reform of the film industry faces numerous difficulties. Actually, the situation is much more beneficial to those who profit by other people's toil, and extremely unfair to those who work hard.

Film needs to win a larger audience. In the creative process, from establishing the framework, choosing the subject matter and handling the mise-en-scène, to acting, audience psychology ought to be considered. Audiences should be inspired, and thus encouraged to identify with the film. In this regard, the release of *Country Couple* (1983) was a good omen. The debate it aroused did much to reveal how a film extends into the audience. It showed that its creators did not draw conclusions for the characters, Tao Chun and Yu Musheng, but instead left the conclusions up to the audience. This does not mean the filmmakers had no ideas of their own.

Life, just recently completed at this writing, has a similar nature. I could not help but experience an intense struggle in my mind from the first time I saw the film to the time I finished my article on it. At the beginning, I found myself in full sympathy with Liu Qiaozhen, but finally I felt even more for Gao Jialin. This was the result of the struggle between the emotional and the rational. Emotions are important; however, in a time of great social change, the rational is needed most. Someone who is totally dominated by emotions tends to indulge in the past, and consciously or subconsciously forgets the present. Losing the present means a loss of the future.

The box office inspires us not to forget our audience, but to make a serious effort to understand it. For 35 years, we have turned our eyes primarily up, to the political climate. The opinions of artists have generally been someone's statements printed in official documents. Under such circumstances, no matter how hard one tried, it was impossible to develop a film style, school of film, or individuality. *The Legend of Tianyun Mountain* (1980) and *A Corner Forsaken by Love* (1982) began to break through this situation, but even today, we can hardly say that it has fundamentally changed. A product of the mind, film must be active and aggressive, rather than passive and defensive.

Second, the film audience has gradually broadened in scope. This is a change worth noticing. From serving workers, peasants and soldiers, film has gone to serving all the people. Even in a unified country, however, individuals are not in unity. They are different in profession, education, interests and nationality, and within those, they differ in age, sex and so on. The movie that can overcome all the differences and be enjoyed by everyone is certainly the movie we are looking for, but such a movie, in fact, is not a common sight. What is common is for the various people to choose the movies they would like to see. The release of *A Heartbroken Death* (1981) best represented the issue. People of higher cultural and artistic accomplishments considered it a "mournful symphony," while others thought Juansheng was a bad guy who caused Zijun's death. If the success or failure of a film is to be judged only by majority rule, however, then films such as *A Heartbroken Death* and *My Memories of Old Beijing* should never have been made.

Of course, we must not accommodate such an attitude. We encourage the arts loved by the common people and generally consider film a popular art form which should respect the interests of the majority. At the same time, we must not discriminate against highbrow art. It is unwise to leave any group of people in a vacuum in cinematic culture. Also, even popular films must be improved. It would not be proper if in their entire lives the masses had only *Heavenly Marriage* (1955) (a regional Chinese opera) to see.

Cinematic entertainment, technology and knowledge are what we all need. Humans always look forward to unknown terrain, hoping to have a chance to satisfy their curiosity. We Chinese have always had lofty aspirations and have been so serious that we have become solemn. Once Huo Yuanjia [hero of a television martial arts serial made in Hong Kong] fought his way here, we were taken by surprise, and his theme song echoed everywhere in the streets. If our own films had been as full of the joys and sorrows of life, and as flavorful, the situation would have been different.

Let us now turn to film criticism.

WHO CAN SEE FIVE MOVES AHEAD IN A CHESS GAME?

In China, those who can really comment on films are not critics, but politicians and administrative officials. There is nothing wrong with this. Criticism needs great foresight, and answers for the content of films drawn from the sum total of social life. It is not merely, as one of the articles to be read at this meeting suggests, that we need film critics who know audiovisual art. Film criticism has, of course, more than one function, but its social function, the result of theory and its guide, is the most fundamental. The problem is that this has been neglected for many years. Some have attacked a film for a single fault without considering its other aspects; some have quoted out of context; others have followed the traditional path of trivialization and deviated far from the real topic. Such criticism has often left those being criticized dumbfounded. Last year, (1984) when

Guangxi Film Studio produced *One and Eight*, a critic called it a eulogy for brigands. When the situation got out of hand, to defend the movie became tantamount to defending brigands. The other reviewers, including myself, found it difficult to do anything for the film, because to defend it meant, after all, to go too close to the gate of hell.

To seize on a single shot or single sentence and make an issue of it is the worst critical method. In terms of criticism, one must have strategic insight, which means discrimination in the face of reality. Reality is reality, whether you like it or not. The circle of realist theory has continued to shrink, until we in the filmmaking community have surrounded ourselves. Once wrapped up, nobody could move. Our theory is a great success, but nobody wants to see the films we make.

Seeing only one move ahead in a chess game of criticism can hardly qualify someone as a critic. Real critics are able to foretell at least two or three moves. We defeated Chiang Kaishek by not caring for the gain or loss of just one town or city, but in film criticism, we have been fighting for every inch of land. Films which are innovative receive harsher criticism. I worry about this.

At the Retrospective of British Film, held in 1984, one noteworthy movie was *Lawrence of Arabia* [1962, from a widely read 1935 memoir by T. E. Lawrence]. Set before World War I, the film tells the story of the Turks, who wanted to invade the Sinai pennisula and take control of the Suez Canal and were therefore in conflict with Great Britain, while the British imperialists felt it necessary to protect the "independence" of the Arabs. In this situation, Lawrence became a hero. On the surface, what he did seemed against the interests of the British Empire; when he asked the headquarters of the British army in Egypt for cannons, he was told, "One more cannon makes one more country." But in fact, his contribution to the British Empire was far beyond a few cannons. The effect of such a film outside Britain is also far more valuable than a few cannons. This is really a great masterpiece. Britain was once called "the country where the sun never sets." It is because of this that Lawrence's words and behavior, which seem harmful, do not overshadow the movie's contribution to Great Britain.

There is always an issue of insight in literature, art and film. When they are used for certain social benefits, they require that the society they serve be open-minded and farsighted. Emphasis must be placed on the overall picture, rather than on the trivial. In film criticism, it is detrimental to make judgments based on a few isolated words and phrases taken out of context. As soon as a filmmaker realizes he is politically responsible for every word, scene and action, he can never go on with his creation. Without creation, how can we expect to influence society and the world through our films?

Since 1980, we have adopted the policy of going abroad ourselves and inviting others here, with good results. In this, we should neither have too high an opinion of ourselves nor underestimate our own capabilities. It is quite necessary for our criticism to broaden the perspective of our film circles. However, we must by all means avoid taking foreign things as the most valuable; we have to be able to talk without mentioning the acknowledged leaders, André Bazin and Seigfried Kracauer. On the other hand, although in recent years our directors and cinematographers have made outstanding achievements, we should warn them not to put their own feet into other people's boots.

Colonialism was the global policy of the British Empire, but the British Empire rightly understood that the range of cannons was far shorter than that of humanism. Gunboats could blow open the gates of an underdeveloped country, but could never open the doors of people's hearts. The key to the human heart is humanism. If Lawrence had not risked his own life to save the Arabian soldier dying in the desert, how could he prove himself, a foreign devil, to be more lovable and more respectable than an Arabian sheikh? In the same way, the filmmakers stuck to humanism in order to show how people in the colonies were brought to submit to the British "humanities." This was a place where even classical British economics and sociology were powerless, but British film, the most popular art form, which does not necessarily need language to express itself, brought its power into full play.

Therefore I hold that professional criticism requires that the critic not only have the ability to foresee several moves ahead as if in a chess match, but also to judge a filmic work in its totality instead of in terms of a word, character or action. Furthermore, an artist must be evaluated historically and systematically. What he does not represent in this movie may be found in his next. What he does not describe today may be something he has already described in the past. This is also true of actors and actresses. An actor's failure or sudden fall from his previous level may perhaps be from frustration in his search for new methods, not being satisfied with his past performances.

That the wings of our criticism are short, in my opinion, is due to its ideological basis: vulgar sociology pandering to political demands. Are there times when a critic cannot even believe his own criticism? I am afraid there are such moments; to push others into the water is to protect oneself from falling in. But experience shows that this is unreliable. Once all principles are destroyed, a method suitable for punishing A today will be used to punish B tomorrow. We should stop vulgar sociology and political opportunism. If we did remove "vulgar" from the former and discard "opportunism" in the latter, could our film community be content with its present situation? No!

EQUIVOCAL REALISM TAKES THE ROAD OF LEAST RESISTANCE: FILM FAILS TO CONVEY WORDS AND WORDS FAIL TO CONVEY IDEAS

China now is a major nation in politics and sports, but not in film, where we still have many gaps. We have lost ten years or more of time, and film is a comparable art, unlike traditional Chinese painting. We can go right on painting

Chinese herbaceous peonies, tree peonies, high mountains and flowing waters for another thirty years. Foreigners cannot, after all, paint them.

On the flight from Osaka back to Shanghai, the following idea crossed my mind. Since Chinese culture is different from European and American cultures, but is in many ways similar to Japanese culture, why has only Japanese film won international fame? In my opinion, either the Japanese are more courageous, or they have less misgivings in their attitude toward reality. Take *Half-Breed*, *Homesick* and *The Story of the Yo Mountain*, for example. *Half-Breed* is, of course, a story of humiliation, but not the humiliation of ceding territory or paying indemnities. Worse, it is about American soldiers who slept with Japanese women, leading to the birth of a group of hybrids who know only their mothers. Could China ever make a movie about such a dirty debt? The second, *Homesick*, is set in the early period of Japanese capitalism. Some Japanese girls are sent to Southeast Asia to make money through prostitution. The money they earn is to accumulate capital; however, they are discriminated against. Many of them die overseas and lie in coffins with their heads pointed toward Japan. Could the Chinese make such a film? I'm afraid not. *The Story of Yo Mountain* is set in a tribal society of Japan. Because of the extreme backwardness of the tribe's economy, a baby may be born only when an old person dies; otherwise the tribe could not survive. Therefore, when people reach a certain age, their children carry them up Yo Mountain, where they are left to die from the cold and starvation and become food for hawks and vultures. Today Japan has entered into the age of electronics. Where, then, is their sense of the times, in an historical picture in which everything is described in such a nakedly primitive way? It is here that the disparity between the two nations lies.

A nation which has the guts to profane itself is more courageous than a nation which always claims that "I was far richer than you in the past." Profanation should not mean sloppiness. On the contrary, it should reveal how a nation once desperately in want of food and clothing, and later humiliated by others, has stepped into the age of electronics and become an economic giant.

This is the kind of thinking I want to see. This is why our criticism cannot be unified into a general sociology. As I said earlier, some sociological criticism itself is not satisfactory. Have we not seen enough feudal rubbish with a socialist label on it? Besides, there is also dogmatism, the pedantic habit of closed-mindedness, and the metaphysical style in which people indulge in too much loud and empty talk to see reality. How much effort have we ever made to resist them? I'm afraid our cinematology is still in its infancy, but to construct is better than not to construct at all. At our present stage of development in criticism, this is all that we have to console ourselves.

WE ARE NOT PLAYING A LEISURELY TUNE

I have been talking about innovation in filmmakers' attitudes toward life, as well as their ideas about cinema. Which is more worthy now? I think the social concept. Ding Yinnan's *Backlit* (1982) received good reviews, but his *They Are in the Special Economic Zone* (1984) was seen in an unfavorable light. This was partly due to the script, which provided a poor basis for the film because, at the time, the policy of constructing special economic zones had not been determined. Therefore, it evaded the crucial problem in the special economic zones. Dodging crucial problems while still talking about something exposed how far our social values lag behind the values needed in these zones. As we know, if the gears of social values cannot move, other gears will spin without really moving, spin vainly for the benefit of a few gear experts. In my opinion, we had better not let the gears spin in vain. We are, on the one hand, short of human and financial resources, while on the other, we have arduous tasks before us. We had better improve ourselves in practice. We need experimental works, but the experiments themselves ought to be given a definite and explicit purpose.

As for popular film, its purpose is already established: to enable as many people as possible to enjoy our movies. Now, however, a small number of young comrades seems to have other thoughts. Keen on letting the gears spin in vain so as to prove themselves gifted artists, they claim, at the same time, that they are right in making "popular films of dependable quality." Such ideas lead to a perverted notion of cinema. Is this another misconception caused by our study of film ontology over these past two years? If so, it is my responsibility to say that the reason to study of film ontology is to strengthen the capacity of film, in the same way our agronomists study wheat pollen in order to increase its reproductive capacity.

Theoretically, to divide realism into the objective and the spiritual can be very confusing. There is no such thing as objective realism. All arts are a combination of objective and subjective elements. In the past, we neglected the subjective elements; therefore, it is necessary now to emphasize the subjective function of the artist. However, this is different from spiritual realism. The spirit is varied and diverse. You insist on your realism; I insist on mine. What is the standard criterion?

TWO RHETORICAL PROBLEMS

Before concluding, I would like to say something about rhetoric. The first rhetorical problem I would like to address is whether we can substitute "the contemporary concept of film" for the so-called "new cinematic concept." This is not merely a problem of semantics. Although "new cinematic concept" does have connotations with which filmmakers agree—we agree that our understanding of film itself must be developed and deepened so films can better represent life and exert a stronger influence on our people—what we do not agree with is the "new concept" proponents' tendency to make film, a most popular art, a product for salons or a tangram of ideas. What is more important is that China has a population of billions, among whom the influence of traditional aesthetics is still very strong. We cannot adopt coercive measures in this case and stick only to the new.

In terms of the awakening of film consciousness, my theory of divorce aims at elevating and developing film and preventing it from becoming a half-breed of cinema and drama. But I do not oppose dramatic films. For instance, *Thunderstorm* (a well-known play by Cao Yu) should be made into a film, since people want to see it. It is not true that there are only new concepts abroad. *Guess Who's Coming to Dinner* (1967) is a film full of dramatization, yet is it not good? We must respect the habits and interests of the masses in their appreciation of art. This is a principle of democracy independent of human will.

Here I would like to correct the misconception that the contemporary concept of film opposes use of dramatization. Life is filled with dramatic twists and turns—how can one oppose that? Have we not had enough dramatic events in our lives over the past thirty years, some of which were not at all second to the events in Shakespeare's tragedies? If no one writes about them now, somebody will in the future. If Chinese do not, foreigners will. I can only conclude that anyone who opposes dramatization must not have the least knowledge of life, and that what that person says is nonsense.

The second rhetorical problem comes from the term "commercial film." I don't agree that all films that make audiences crowd into the cinema are commercial. Once put into distribution as commodities, all films are a part of commerce. If films with high box-office value are always to be labeled commercial, it will affect the popularly loved works we have always promoted, and some comrades making popular films will feel hesitant. Zhang Huaxun's *The Will of Warriors* (Wu Lin Zhi, 1983) was greatly appreciated; however, even before its release, Zhang determined that he would never make this kind of movie again. He seemed to have a premonition that if he continued to make action movies of such high quality, he would be regarded as the meanest in film circles. It's also because we are subject to such opinions that Huo Yuanjia (1983–84) could conquer Guangzhou in one strike, take Shanghai in a second move, and capture Beijing in the third attack. While the camel, *One and Eight* (1984), went through the eye of a needle, *Huo Yuanjia* was barging around and sweeping away all obstacles. Who says there's no drama in our lives?

Can we replace "commercial film" with "popular film," or give it another name, as they do abroad, where some books are called "best sellers?" Whatever we call it, I want to convey this message: Even those comrades who are enthusiastic about the modern concept of film do agree that films should win over a larger audience.

CONCLUSION

Film theory and practice since the early 1980s have been steaming hot, if not boiling. Today is the first time we've gathered to discuss cinematology. Whether we do this well is very important, but I think that we must always keep one simple fact in mind: making a film is exhausting work. What we see in half an hour is the result of many hours of production. To respect our filmmakers is to respect labor. To do research is, of course, also work, and it can be very hard, but without filmmakers, our research would be out of the question. At present, the relationship between filmmakers and critics goes very well. I hope all of us value this, and remember not to indulge in exaggerations and irrelevant talk, or regard ourselves as educators on film practice and criticism.

Futhermore, there is an issue of methodology. When several of us visited Hong Kong earlier this year, there was a discussion of Chinese film from the 1920s and 1930s which lasted more than ten days. My personal impression from this discussion was that our own work was quite good in terms of meticulous and serious scholarship, but that in terms of methodology we were somewhat inflexible. We tend to approach film from a more or less singular point of view. We cannot approach the same object from all sides, and our vocabulary is comparatively monotonous.

This indicates that we are still deeply restricted by traditional thinking. I do not think there is anything wrong with tradition. There is certainly nothing wrong with our revolutionary tradition and realist tradition. But if within the framework of our tradition we cannot innovate, develop and generate unique insights in the face of change, the tradition itself will wither away. Every age has its own aesthetic concepts. This is not contrary to tradition. If a tree cannot sprout new branches every year, it cannot prove where its vitality lies. Of course, there are many problems to be solved behind such a simple fact, but once theory is afraid to face problems, it, too, will wither away. Theory needs courage. This is not a matter of who is bravest, but a matter of what attitude we should have toward truth. We should neither be swollen with arrogance nor intimidated into silence. If we are too cautious, our theory will forever be a false and impractical play of words.

Filmmaking in recent years has proven that China has plenty of talented and gifted people. We should never underestimate ourselves, but we have lost a lot of time, the most valuable time, and time never turns back. I hope our first annual meeting will establish a good working style. We need a more scientific spirit, and we need to be more practical and realistic, and more farsighted, so that our theory does not suffer when compared with our film, and our film proves worthy of its era.

But let me put an end to my sermonizing. Thank you all.

NOTES

1. *Cinematic Aesthetics: 1982*, Zhong Dianfei, ed. (Beijing: Culture Association Publishers, 1983).

2. Lao She, review of *The Story of an Orphan Rescuing His Grandfather by Mingxing Studio, Shen Bao*, Dec. 26, 1923.

2

The Modern Consciousness of the Filmmaker

Wang Zhongming
Translated by Fu Binbin

1

The modern consciousness of a filmmaker is an issue of great importance; however, in China, it has yet to attract significant attention. Through examination of the recent feature *Backlit* (1982),[1] this chapter is intended to open a discussion of the matter.

Xia Yinyin in *Backlit*, a young woman, boldly declares to Liao Xingming, a young man, her standards for a husband: someone enthusiastic in all he undertakes, who at the same time knows how to dance disco. To young people in contemporary China, the end of the years of upheaval and turbulence meant the awakening of a new consciousness of the times. Freed from the shackles of the past, they looked forward to a healthy and cheerful life. Xia Yinyin's claim reflects this progressive trend, but it is puzzling why, in the end, the filmmakers were not courageous enough to equip Liao Xingming with disco skills. On the contrary, disco dancing, as in other films, is attached to the decadent, good-for-nothing son of the idle rich. Why?

Liao Xingming is brave, acute in thinking, eager for progress and poignant in manner. The film describes exhaustively and convincingly how he actualizes his views on material, foreigners, humanity and the world through his arduous exploration in his undertaking and his diligence in writing books and establishing theories. He embodies the uprightness of a generation of progressive youth and suggests the inevitable flowering of reform. What perplexes us further, however, is that Liao Xingming's ideas and understandings are not pursued to the end of the film. This is particularly clear in a sequence in which Liao tramps the streets, feeling bad after he has learned that Liao Xiaoqin, his younger sister, has given in to her boyfriend's wicked ideas and sold her body and soul.

As the scene opens, Liao Xingming walks toward the camera, which pans to follow him. Inside the large show windows of a store are displayed various electronic appliances made by Sony. In front of the window are crowds of people. Through the glass we can see them standing around, watching and talking with animated gestures. Various electronic products glow, as the camera tracks horizontally. There are also many people jammed in front of the show windows of the National Electronic Company of Japan.

These shots are obviously intended to externalize Liao Xingming's inner world. Liao, who is a fine thinker, realizes something from the Sonys and Nationals. Can it be that Xiaoqin's misbehavior has some connection with these products? Should we attribute Liao Xiaoqin's degenerate act to the Sonys and Nationals and the like? If we do, would it be justifiable to close the doors of the country to international intercourse once again? If we did, would that mean the Chinese workers would be forever poor and underdeveloped? In the final analysis, materialism, no matter which country it comes from, is created by the working class. The reason Liao Xiaoqin goes astray lies in her uncivilized attitude toward materialism, which leads her to reap without sowing and to ignore work and creativity. The description in the film seems to reveal a bias against foreign cultures and materialist civilization. A foreigner is either a devil or a taipan!

We must admit that the creators of *Backlit* were enthusiastic about new ideas and keen on expressing them. Yet if this is true, why do old thoughts find expression at the same time? I think this contradiction warrants careful consideration. In a time of reform, in which the old is being replaced by the new, people are animated by extraordinary and complicated social phenomena. On the one hand, all old ideas, without exception, seem to be pounded by new concepts and eliminated; on the other, practically speaking, people can hardly avoid being shackled to the old ideas, to which they are accustomed. But the pace of the reform is accelerating. Whoever hesitates will fall behind. This is the heart of the mistake in *Backlit*. The filmmakers intended to depict a new generation of the reform era and to eulogize the new metropolis, the new world and new customs, backlit by the bright sun; however, here and there in the specific manifestations of the film, a few gloomy will-o'-the-wisps and shades of death still glisten. This probably reveals the creators' subconscious. If this is true, then it all the more illustrates how important, yet how difficult, a task it is for us to abolish old concepts and stale thoughts. But *Backlit* achieved remarkable success in its pursuit of modern cinematic concepts. Its cinematography, for instance, won it fame in the Third Golden Rooster Awards. This, again, provides us with evidence that modernization of ideas has not attracted the same attention in our filmmaking as has modernization of cinematic concepts. However, to bring about modernization of ideological concepts should be considered a difficult yet urgent task for every filmmaker who vigorously seeks progress.

The world today is experiencing a radical economic transformation. According to scholars of industrially developed countries of the West, a new trend has emerged since the 1950s, the transformation from a national to a global economy, and from an industrial to an informational society. They believe breakthroughs in technology by the turn of the century will bring a huge advance in productivity and create a new informational society. For this reason, John Naisbitt, an American futurist, calls our time "an inbetween time . . . a time full of changes and doubts."[2] *Megatrends*, published in 1982, is known as one of the masterpieces published in the United States since the 1950s, a book that "is able to grasp precisely the impulse of the development of the times."[3]

To evaluate the Western scholars' research into contemporary society and the future is not a task of cinematic aesthetics, but in the rapidly changing society, those who study film can and should have diverse information. Taking the entire human world into consideration, the development of social productivity, with its unprecedented speed and strength, is crushing the old modes of production, ways of life and thinking, as well as social traditions. New waves of the world-wide revolution in technology are coming and will irresistibly change the face of our time. This change must be given full attention in examining the intrinsic relations between film, art and actuality in cinematic aesthetics. The concept of beauty is not an absolute, but changes with the times. In the early days of the industrial civilization, the rumbling of motors was probably quite pleasant to the ear, but now who wants to compose a song to praise it? Forests of chimneys were indispensable in a city scene of the past, but today people take them as a symbol of pollution, while fear and hate have replaced the earlier feeling of profound veneration. Thus we can see that ideas vary with the changes in a given time, with the differences between specific societies, and with different production modes.

In this great transformational period, contemporary China cannot help but change, mostly through international influences. Special changes must also inevitably take place due to the limitations of the situation in our country. The technological revolution, which now is on the rise worldwide, constitutes a new challenge to the economic progress of our country, yet it is also a chance for us to absorb certain technological achievements and create new productive forces, which we should do as quickly as possible. Thus, within a certain period of time, agricultural, industrial and informational modes belonging to different stages of history will, in fact, exist simultaneously in our country. The entire society will be a special display of extreme diversification, revealed as contradictions and changes in thinking become more complicated, and then fantastically multifarious.

Only by grasping exactly the general trends of human progress and changes of the times and by soberly and penetratingly observing, analyzing and repre-

senting life can we convey in filmmaking the rich yet fresh flavor of the construction of modernization, and in this way contribute to social progress.
Otherwise, we can hardly avoid repeating the mistake made in *Backlit*, in which
the filmmakers consciously or subconsciously allowed what is backward to in-
trude into the screen space and waste film, because little attention is paid to the
boundless world outside the studio.

2

Failure on the part of the filmmakers to keep up with the exciting life of the
times in terms of ideological concepts is evident in many other films. "They
are blindly ignorant of the new trend of thought which aims at a reformation of
the entire society, and become erroneous, narrow-minded and one-sided; thus
the thoughts in their works lower in quality."

In *Girl Students' Dormitory*, the camera focuses on contemporary college
students, a world where there should be bright prospects for learning about our
age and revealing the innermost thoughts. College students are fortunate enough
to live in an age of tremendous social reform. They are the most sensitive toward,
and least conservative about, the various new values, the credibility of law, time
and space, and aesthetics, concepts which have emerged continuously in the
New Era; more often than not, students hold the most favorable attitude toward
them. *Girl Students' Dormitory* does not successfully feature this. On the contrary, what is selected and revealed exposes to a certain extent the filmmaker's
bone-headedness and narrow-mindedness, as well as lack of interest in the modern consciousness.

An analysis of the book-buying scene alone will be sufficient to illustrate the
problem. A college boy forces his way out of the tight crowd in front of a book
stall, holding a large pile of new books in his arms with his chin pressing on
top of it. The camera turns behind him to show us the holes in his sweater. The
film does not hesitate to use an extreme close-up to highlight this irony. But this
is not only mediocre; it is not as touching as a similar depiction in *At Middle
Age*, and it is also problematic in terms of ideological significance, if given
further consideration. With the development of industry and the increasing abundance in material life, who still holds that the prosperity of the nation and the
wealth of the people are natural enemies of the socialist system? Conforming to
the trend of social reform, today's college students naturally vote down the so-
called "glory of poverty." Just as they are enthusiastic in their pursuit of truth
and knowledge, they are also particular about their clothing. This is normal
consumerism, not waste. The changing values in the domain of material consumption manifest vividly the progress initiated by social reform. In the movie,
however, enthusiasm is thrown into the contrast between new books and a ragged
shirt, as a limited expression of the general notion of "spiritually rich, materially
poor." This is not only incompatible with the present trend, but also of little
necessity in artistic expression. In my opinion, even if there are indeed college

students who are "spiritually rich but materially poor," it is not necessary to highlight them in such a positive way. As time passes, it becomes possible for us to strive justly for a simultaneous abundance in both spirit and material. There is no reason to sing out against social progress and the advancement of our times. To pinpoint and put an end to everything which is outdated and specious requires that a filmmaker be courageous and insightful. The pity is that courage and insight in art seem rare, at least for the moment!

We should analyze two other films: *A Colorful Bridge* and *Life Is Beautiful*. Since both are concerned with marriage brokers, both heroines, Huang Yan and Ding Yaxin, are labeled with the same name of classic elegance: Hongniang, that of a maidservant in the classic Ming dynasty novel *Story of the Western Chamber*.[4] Although the two films, especially *Life Is Beautiful*, attempt to make sense by combining the fact that young people were adversely affected during the decade of upheaval with the warmth society provides them after the reestablishment of order, the effort is more or less blind. Life is beautiful, but "Hongniang" is not. Hongniang belongs to the days of the *Story of the Western Chamber* hundreds of years ago, when the feudal ethic was a towering oppressive force. With regard to her own time, Hongniang represented a positive attitude toward life and a courageous spirit of revolt. The progressive meaning and revolutionary nature of this character are genuine only in a feudal society. In a socialist country, to marry freely and find happiness in love is almost a natural human right. A character may have many reasons to desire assistance from Hongniang while giving up this "right," but essentially it is not progress.

It is of course true that not all people will keep up with the times. There might be different ideas about love and marriage among people. At the same time, the marriage broker is probably more important in one time than in another, and "Hongniang" still has her popular side, for social and historical reasons. For instance, in a film such a character may be employed to reveal the internal inadequacies in social communication through a marriage broker, so as to inspire one to contribute to the flourishing and progress of society. It can also be treated as an ordinary circumstance, or be used to reflect other social phenomena. But if we depict "Hongniang" with greatest care and take her as a perfect figure for our society and times, I think that would be retrogressive in terms of aesthetics, and could not bring us fresh social and ideological content. After their release, these films received only an indifferent response, which indicates that they are in counter to the direction of our times.

3

The modernization of ideology is at bottom of an issue of the inclination of the mind. In an agricultural society, people lean toward the past; everything is done according to past experiences. When the society becomes industrial, people lean toward reality, since industrialization greatly accelerates social processes, and many problems cannot be solved by relying solely on past experiences. Upon entering an informational society, where a myriad of changes occur in the twin-kling of an eye, one's thinking must be biased toward the future, because plans that are worked out according to reality fall behind as soon as they are put into practice. This characteristic of social evolution combines with the ideals of socialist film art to require that our filmmaking be filled with the spiritual forces of progress. To emphasize the modernization of the mind is actually to stress that a filmmaker should always be in accord with the development of the times and the society, and *that* should represent and eulogize the rapid current of human progress.

However, in the films of 1983, we are surprised to find that, in several films which concern the lives of educated youths who go to work in the countryside, most of the protagonists end their stories in a retrogression. They return to the cities and encounter cares and frustrations, and they nostalgically recall past experiences. It dawns upon them that their lives are not supposed to be positioned in the cities of the present, but in the countryside of the past. We find this in Chen Xinan, in *Our Fields*, and Sheng Zhitong, in *A Journey to the Tian Mountain*. Their retrogressive attitude has been praised as "an exciting maturity" and "a confident sense of stability and a vigorous spirit for progress." Appar-ently, they naturally represent the so-called "thinking generation." But it is in these characters that we can see the outdated thinking of our filmmakers and their disturbed and bewildered state of mind after having been shocked by the winds of reform. In the characters' observations and criticism of modern society, especially of metropolitan life, we find an immature and nonprogressive pas-siveness which does not exist in reality.

At the end of the 1970s, the educated youths [who had been sent to the countryside during the Cultural Revolution] swarmed back to the cities, signaling the irresistible outburst of an emotional social crisis. Historically, however, this was obviously a negation of the years of upheaval and significant in that the whole society was turning from chaos into calm. Back in the cities, these young people could not help showing their happiness and excitement, but they soon found out that they lost in the cities the importance and admiration they had easily found in the countryside. As our country confronted diverse difficulties during this period of adjustment and reform, they, too, were met with new problems, such as the difficulty of finding employment. Many began to shift the curses they had directed at the countryside onto the cities, for they found their lives as depressed as they had been before. Examples can be found in *Our Fields*, in which Qu Lin is constantly aggrieved, and in *The Riverbanks in the South*, where Ah Wei casts fierce and malicious eyes on anyone approaching him. Chen Xinan and Yi Jie, unlike Qu Lin and Ah Wei, may not be straightforward in expressing their resentment, but their final retrogression is based on resentment just as much.

To be fair, Chen Xinan, Yi Jie and their like understand the historical function of modern cities from a narrow point of view. The urban society in our country, which has been ridden with turmoil and upheaval, was initially insufficient;

furthermore, the cities have always had their dark, uncivilized side. Even so, we have no cause to devalue or obliterate their development. The city serves, after all, as a concentration of progressive, productive forces. Nurtured in the first place by modern foreign societies through the open-door policy, it asserts a great influence upon the modernization of agriculture. The level of its urban society primarily decides to what degree a society or a nation is civilized. Since the years of upheaval, urban construction in our country has been developing at unprecedented speed. Facing the challenge of the technological revolution world-wide, our cities will undoubtedly quicken their steps. Therefore, every urban citizen, including the educated youths, is burdened not only with the task of construction, but also the task of reeducation, and this is conditioned by one's love and positive attitude toward urban society. That some young people were unable to readapt in the first days after their return, and thus held biased and unjust attitudes toward modern urban society, is an ideological matter which has little to do with "maturity." The biases, which came directly from their griev-ances, complaints and resentment, in turn lead to nothing but a preference for rural life and ultimately result in a retrogression. The cycle implies that these filmmakers, as well as their beloved characters, fall short of a deep and accurate understanding of both urban and rural life. To ridicule modern urban society while highlighting the reception the rural society gave the educated youths is inherently retrogressive.

After viewing *A Journey to the Tian Mountains*, we cannot forget how Zheng Zhitong, the protagonist, takes on the airs of a sober-minded sage and returns far into the mountains. As a member of the Communist Party, of course, his conduct deserves little criticism, but why are his comrades, who remain in the city, described so unsympathetically and listed as the kind of people he despises most? The brilliantly lit metropolis in the film, where tall buildings stand like a forest and the air is fragrant with flowers, is simply outlined as a paradise for the mediocre and addle-brained. How much evidence and artistic force is there in such a description? When we attempt to describe the educated youth movement which rose suddenly out of the fanatic patriotism of those years, we must fully understand its tragic nature. One can hardly find another generation which suf-fered such vast destruction and experienced such severe disillusionment and spiritual crisis as this one did in its youth. The tragedy reflected serious problems and remains uncured. The cinematic description of Zheng Zhitong produces a character who is artificial, lost in his obsession with what is called the beauty of primitive simplicity in the depths of wilderness, and reluctant to part with the "unsophisticated customs and sincere sentiments" in his life in the countryside. This, in fact, is an attempt by the filmmaker to play down or even deny the tragic nature of the movement of "going to work in the countryside and mountain areas."

It is also because of the retrogression in ideology that the final return of Chen Xinan to the Great Northern Wasteland in *Our Fields* appears unconvincing. On the one hand, life in the Great Northern Wasteland is greatly exaggerated, and thus becomes too wonderful, too interesting and too attractive. Those who died there, like Qiyue, are holy and pure, and those who remain, like Xiao Didi, are lovely and likable, while the bleak landscape and drab society are not fully depicted. On the other hand, a sense of disappointment and loss is imposed on the young people around Chen Xinan who have returned from the countryside, in order for them to be bored and unhappy and to lose their hope for the future. Ningyu, for example, is eager for happiness but unable to achieve it, while Qu Lin hopes for a leisurely life and is dissatisfied with work. Through his elevation and repression, Chen Xinan is equipped with a "sober" head and so surpasses all others, liberates himself from vulgarity and makes his "wise" decision. Since he does not intend to associate himself with the Qu Lins and Ningyus, who he considers weak, mediocre and even vulgar, it is natural for him to return to the Great Northern Waste and embrace the field to which he is sentimentally attached. Ultimately, retrogression turns out to be his bright road.

The final return of Yi Jie and Muzhen to the rubber plantation on Hainan Island in *The Riverbanks in the South* follows the same route. Consciously or subconsciously neglecting the majority of educated youths, who are now participating actively and vigorously in all walks of urban life, the filmmakers arbitarily construct an imaginary world. This world, with its "I remain sober while others get drunk," only indicates that these filmmakers have failed to follow strictly the creative method of realism in their understanding of life; therefore, their characters cannot but obscure the historical tragedy of the Educated Youth Movement.

To start with reality and reflect with vividness the bitter and harsh life of the urban youth in the countryside, and the spiritual and physical wounds it brought them, and to depict their sense of loss and ignorance after they returned to the cities, does not prevent one from portraying progressive young people who make unremitting efforts to improve themselves. This does not mean that cinematic description of the retrogression should be blindly rejected; we have to admit that one might return to the countryside from the city for many reasons, including idealistic visions. To abandon urban life does not necessarily mean retrogression or backwardness. The key point here is that we cannot simply use the countryside to deny urban life and use the past to negate the present.

More importantly, we cannot obscure the tragic quality of the Educated Youth Movement. Our emphasis on the tragic nature of the Educated Youth Movement is meant to indicate that only by firmly understanding it can we expose in depth its complex background and historical origins and help people, especially the large numbers of these young people, to get back as much as possible of what they lost, after they paid such a high price to walk more steadily toward their future lives.

The aforementioned films display nonessential yet superficially beautiful things, celebrate ancient landscapes and attractive pictures of life, and soothe lost souls and nostalgic minds with unreal memories. Can such descriptions provide any perspicacity in our excavation of new ideas? Obviously not. Now, in the 1980s, when economic and cultural exchanges are increasingly frequent and intimate, blind propaganda, which encourages retrogression, is tremendously harmful to the entire nation and to the younger generation in its persistent march to advance in the world.

To satirize the present while praising the past, and to mock urban life while beautifying the patriarchal society of the peasant economy in the countryside, is not the dialectics of life, nor is it the thread of vision contemporary film art ought to adopt. In reality, developments in the production of goods, an increasingly compact relationship between town and country has been established, and it is more and more obvious that the two are inclined to walk in sync. To return to the countryside will, in the end, turn out to be merely an illusion. It would be better to face the raging waves of reform and become involved in it, so as to wash off as quickly as possible stale concepts like "Emphasize agriculture, despise business," and "Value morality and loathe profit," hidden in the depths of the mind and stubbornly causing mischief. In the surging current of life, where does our hope lie? Where does the hope of our youth lie? It lies in Liao Xing-ming's diligence in *Backlit*, in Qin Nan's struggle against Old World prejudices in *Under the Bridge*, and Quhua's significant feat of "renovating the Great Wall" in *The Road*, . . . but never in purely illusory and fragile retrogression.

4

Not only is backwardness in ideology common in those "artificial, vulgar, and superficial" movies already mentioned, but it also exists in some first-rate films. This suggests that the problem is so serious that it needs special attention. But what is also worth noting is that many filmmakers have been aware of the modernization of their ideology and achieved remarkable success. They are inclined to bring a modern, scientific consciousness into their spiritual world when describing the fiery life of the construction of modernization.

In 1983, we were glad to see the birth of the screen image of Luo Xingang in *Blood Is Always Hot*. In terms of the social psychology and thinking of moviegoers, the film successfully conveyed the filmmakers' progressive thoughts and reform spirit, guiding their audience into a world of spiritual emancipation. This is what determines whether or not a film will have the vitality to conquer its audience through its reflections on the Reform Era.

The attractiveness and the social influence of the image of Luo Xingang demonstrates a new psychological need and a new feature of thinking: people are no longer satisfied with their present situation and long to broaden their field of vision and open up to wider and deeper unknown territories. We are happy to see in the character of Luo Xingang a filmmaker's true position and historical mission. What is hot in Luo's blood is undoubtedly also the quintessence of the makers of this film: their precision and sense of mission in the pulsing of social rhythms, their activism in renovating and equipping themselves with a modern consciousness, and their hatred of stale customs and outdated principles.

To raise the quality of filmmaking, it is important to fully affirm every effort the filmmakers of *Blood Is Always Hot* made in modernizing ideological concepts. This is not only because many films remain shallow and narrow-minded and remote from reality in their depiction of a reformer's life, but also because a good representation of a reformer requires that a filmmaker first reform his own mind and modernize his thinking. Although neither *Country Couple* nor *Under the Bridge* presents a bold description of the winds and clouds of reform, we can still perceive in them the fierce shaking reform has brought to the entire society and the whole era. It is only through a reformer's eyes that we can sense the unusual tragic quality of Tao Chun's pet phrase, "I'll go along with you." The fading of Qin Nan's formerly plaintive stare after she has resolutely taken her illegitimate son back from the countryside could be considered the withering away of an outdated notion and the awakening of a new idea. Human society is constantly changing, not only in a period of dynamic reform. A period of dynamic reform is a culmination or turning point in the gradual changes of society, and the gradual change carries within itself the seeds of sudden change. Filmic works concerning the reform should not dwell solely on sudden changes, but also pay attention to their relationship with gradual changes, especially the evolution of ideology in both periods. These works should reveal the desire and dynamics of change, as well as the illusory and dangerous nature of maintaining the status quo.

The modernization of ideology is a complex issue. Within the field of film, people generally have given more attention to the modernization of cinematic concepts. They become absorbed in new technologies and means of expression and ways of digging out expressive potentialities in the development of film art. They study the relationship between traditional and modern film concepts and modernize their ideas about such cinematic elements as shots, acting, sound and lighting. But considering the present situation in filmmaking and the rapid progress of the times, particular attention must be given to modernization of the mind. Even the most advanced cinematic idea can hardly compensate for mental backwardness. Whether or not a film can convey the progressive and moving spirit of the times is always the most crucial issue in art.

NOTES

1. From the script of *Backlit*, Zhujiang Film Studio, 1984.
2. John Naisbitt, *Megatrends: Ten New Directions for Transforming Our Lives* (New York, Warner Books, 1982).
3. Ibid.
4. In *The Story of the Western Chamber*, Hongniang helps the male and female leads fall in love with each other and get married at the end of the story. Her name has been used as the synonym for a woman go-between. For an English translation of Plekhanov's writings see: G.V. Plekhanov, *Art and Society*. N.Y. Critics Group: 1937.

Part II

The Issue of Culture

The Xie Jin model, the Fifth Generation, and the entertainment film are generally considered the three major directions Chinese film took in the 1980s. The melodramatic and sentimental Xie Jin model dominated the earlier years; the Fifth Generation dominated the middle period; and the entertainment film dominated the later period.

By the mid–1980s, the Xie Jin model had been criticized by radical critics.[1] According to them, while Xie Jin criticized the ideology of the Communist Party, he confirmed Confucianism, or traditional Chinese culture, and followed the Hollywood style, seen as a conservative approach to film aesthetics and culture. These critics believed Confucianism and communism to be the major causes of the problems in contemporary China. They even suggested that the Confucian tradition was the more fundamental cause, from which the Communist Party inherited its paternalism and concept of a hierarchy. Consequently, the key to modernization was to get rid of Confucianism and reconstruct the culture. Accordingly, radical Chinese intellectuals during the mid and later 1980s intensely criticized traditional culture. Scholars in Taiwan and overseas differed with those of the mainland over the relationship between communism and Confucianism, holding that the ideology of the Communist Party totally conflicted with traditional Chinese culture. Lack of space, unfortunately, prevents us from covering this subject here.

At the same time that the Xie Jin model came under criticism, films from the Fifth Generation, like *Yellow Earth* (1984) and *On the Hunting Ground* (1985), were strongly supported by the radical critics, even though they were not widely accepted by the general public and the authorities, who supported the Xie Jin model. This critical support, which was not just for the radical aesthetics of these films, but primarily for their critical reexamination and reevaluation of traditional culture from an ideological viewpoint, inspired the discussion of cultural issues and was closely related to the films of the Fifth Generation.

This new stance of critical reexamination of traditional culture in Chinese filmmaking, as in the work of the Fifth Generation and the criticism which supported it, can be seen as a new direction in the development of Chinese culture after Western influences reentered China in the 1980s. These influences gave intellectuals a new dimension in thinking. They were no longer positioned entirely within Chinese culture, evaluating which was better, communism or Confucianism, but stood between Chinese culture and the West as they sought new directions. In the mid and later 1980s, the response by the radical intellectuals on the mainland was critical of the traditional culture, including both communism and Confucianism, usually with an indirect and implicit welcoming of Western democracy and humanism. This can be seen both in the films of the period, works by the Fifth Generation filmmakers, and in the film studies, which celebrated these films and at the same time opposed the Xie Jin model.

The discussion of Chinese culture in film circles can be seen as part of the discussion of traditional culture within the overall society. The Fifth Generation has never received the wholehearted support that the Xie Jin model has had. However, the chapters in this section, a part of the studies about the Fifth Generation, not only justified the contributions made at its beginning, when its films were widely rejected by audience, critics and the authorities, but also inspired the movement and helped it establish an identity of its own. Two other pieces of important research on this topic, "What Does *Yellow Earth* Bring to Us?" by Li Tuo, and "On *Yellow Earth*," by Zheng Dongtian,[2] have been excluded for the sake of brevity.

NOTES

1. See George S. Semsel, Xia Hong and Hou Jianping, eds. *Chinese Film Theory: A Guide to the New Era* (New York: Praeger, 1990), Chapter 5.

2. Li Tuo, "What Does *Yellow Earth* Bring to Us," *Contemporary Cinema*, 1985, vol. 3. Zheng Dongtian, "On *Yellow Earth*," *Contemporary Cinema*, 1985, vol. 3.

3

After *Yellow Earth*

Ni Zhen

Translated by Fu Binbin

Taking the history of an ancient nation as its object of representation, *Yellow Earth* itself has taken a place in history. Simply speaking, after *Yellow Earth* appeared in 1984, no one, no matter with what attitude, could look upon Chinese film as in the past, before *Yellow Earth* was made. Praised or criticized, the film left an indelible imprint, a proof of spiritual extension. The waist-drum dance, filled with national vitality, and the ritual of the rain prayer, loaded with ancient tradition, transmitted a shock, a warning and a distant yet clearly heard clap of thunder to Western film circles, which had constantly evaluated and judged in terms of European cultural criteria. An Oriental culture had produced a film, authentic by all international standards, that was aimed directly at them. Therefore they referred to it as "a film likely to be regarded as a proclamation of hope and change, in which the leading roles are not only characters, but the yellow earth itself from which the Chinese people arose." They saw, indeed, "a Chinese story."

However, this very film, which won major awards at numerous international festivals, when first released at home attracted only a small audience. A cinema in Beijing even had to apologize and refund tickets and replace the film with another program. *Yellow Earth* failed to arouse enthusiasm until, in April 1985, it received acclaim at the Ninth Hong Kong International Film Festival and the comments and praise from international film critics reached home. In summer 1985, when an attempt was made in Shanghai to devote two or three movie houses exclusively to experimental narratives, *Yellow Earth* ran to capacity audiences for a week and had a nationwide impact.

The sense of strangeness and alienation that *Yellow Earth* produces comes from its makers' macroscopic contemplation of history and the symbolism of its images. An exploration into the evolution of the nation's history and psychic structure from the viewpoint of cultural anthropology and folklore, *Yellow Earth* does not fall into the ordinary category of films that dig into subject matter in terms of sociology or politics. Therefore it can hardly be evaluated in terms of the special functions and direct propaganda specific to them. On the surface, the film does have a narrative framework—Cuiqiao's marriage and misfortune; the arrival of Gu Qing; Cuiqiao's refusal, through Gu's enlightenment, to accept the ancient fate of women; and her attempted escape to seek a brighter future. But as everyone can perceive, in actuality the film merely uses the story as an entrance, while the emphasis is on diachronic reflections into the nation's history, especially that of the peasants, and into the traces of China's spiritual culture over thousands of years. The descriptions of the land and of the peasants who have lived on it for centuries is unfolded with historical wholeness. The revelation of this immense body of humanity, of its conservatism, ignorance and back-wardness, and of its strength and potential rejuvenation, surpasses events in any specific time and place.

The depiction of the peasants is in no way a duplication of the life of the 1980s, anymore than it is an accurate description of the time in which the story takes place, since the film, through symbolism, aims to surpass the real look of its subject matter in order to trace back the remote cultural history of the nation. This retrospection is actualized in three highly symbolic sequences: the bride-greeting parade, the waist-drum performance and the rain prayer. Alien to the story and comparatively independent of the structure, these sequences provide the spectator with a clear understanding of the intended abstraction by breaking through the limitations of time and space.

In light of the causal relations of the characters, as revealed in the surface story, the film, with its optimistic ideology, achieves a positive social effect. Gu Qing, a member of the art troupe of the Eighth Route Army who is on his way to collect folk songs, stops in a mountain village far from Yanan, then the Chinese Communist Party headquarters. His arrival brings to the villagers the communists' call for change. Cuiqiao, with her family, experiences a spiritual shock, a change her forefathers never had, and is motivated to choose her own path in life. But why are some people, unaccustomed to multi-faceted revelations of life and history, inclined to measure the film in terms of propaganda given through linear causes and effects? Perhaps it has to do with the feeling of strangeness produced by the filmic language, and with the fact that people differ greatly in their understanding of artistic works as spiritual products. This is where the film reflects, in a sense, the past and present psyche and the national culture.

Based on life in North Shaanxi at the beginning of the Anti-Japanese War (1937–1945), *Yellow Earth* looks back in time by transcending reality via sym-bolism. In fact, no matter how many personal elements or emotional factors are poured into its film language, if its general form remains in the domain of perceptions, a film cannot convey rational artistic information to its aesthetic subject. Symbolism leads to abstraction, which makes a specific frame, or an object within a frame, change or even lose its original attributes, raises the aesthetic subject to the rational level, and makes one think in broader terms.

It cannot be said that symbols and metaphors have not been used, at least partially, in our previous filmmaking. Landscapes have been used to separate sections of the plot, and symbolism has been inserted into some sequences. However, a totally symbolic structure can hardly be found before *Yellow Earth*. Consequently, our audience, without such aesthetic experiences, was not prepared for this film. As a result, the artistic information conveyed by its symbolically composed, surrealistic shots and sequences could not be entirely grasped. This is where the issue of the relationship between experimentation and adaptability, which I will discuss later, arises.

The narrative pattern of *Yellow Earth* is a language system of shots in which image is more significant than plot in regard to meaning. Compelled to meet the needs of a symbolic structure, the plot framework is flattened and simplified to such a degree that its original attributes are altered. Thus, the film as a whole is elaborated through image, and subsequently conveys ideological content and artistic information in terms of shots and by revealing specific objects within the frame. For instance, the shots of fetching water, ploughing, tending sheep, weaving, playing drums and praying for rain, and of the yellow soil, the Yellow River, hillsides and moonlit nights, convey meaning directly. This requires that the viewer have a proper understanding of film culture; that is, to appreciate the film, a spectator must open his eyes and ears and use his imagination, rather than simply be passively satisfied with plot development and dialogue. The composition of *Yellow Earth* is highly realistic and true to life; however, its use of shots, a combination of montage and long take, especially the merger of montage with free-style configurations in its three symbolic sequences, provides the film with a chance to take root in reality and at the same time lets it transcend reality and achieve a surrealistic effect.

I have roughly sketched the characteristics of *Yellow Earth*, but the emphasis of this chapter is on the state of Chinese film after the film's appearance. What can be said, then, about our films, especially our experimental narratives, now that more than a year has passed since *Yellow Earth* was released?

DIVERSIFICATION IN CHINESE FILM

Yellow Earth was made in the summer of 1984, a time when the group experiments, dominated by middle-aged directors from 1979 to 1983, had reached a comparatively stable stage. The first wave of Chinese new film, which lasted four years, had subsided, and filmmakers such as Wu Yigong, Hu Bingliu, Huang Jianzhong, Zhang Nuanxin and Teng Wenji were experiencing an interval of meditation, reorganization and renewal before launching a second breakthrough. During this interval, *Yellow Earth* appeared. This film, together with *One and Eight*, *On the Hunting Ground*, and *Shedding Blood in the Dark Valley* (1984) and others which emerged at almost the same time, signaled the coming of new, multi-dimensional films. This trend toward diversification was first revealed by the growing separation between the older, middle-aged and younger directors in terms of their philosophical outlook. This philosophical difference is of great significance in the development of our film, since it is the essential prerequisite for diversity in overt style.

Another aspect of this trend is that the directors of the younger generation have refused to accept the homogeneity of the group style, and have vigorously and willingly begun to seek individual styles. Young directors, such as Chen Kaige, Tian Zhuangzhuang, Wu Ziniu, Zhang Junzhao and Zhang Ziming, who later proved their value, showed great diversity in their maiden works. This is extremely noteworthy in film art. The directors of the 1950s and 1960s hardly compare with them, since the older directors' styles were so alike. Even the middle-aged directors of the early 1980s were remote from these newcomers.

For years we have advocated "Let one hundred flowers blossom," and even intentionally planned the proportion of different genres and themes intended to bring diversity to production. However, since our filmmakers lacked individuality in both genius and experimentation, their use of genre and theme was often similar. The trend toward diversity of form in Chinese film, so vividly revealed by the young filmmakers, came about because art, and especially literature, in our country had reached a magnificent period of subjective consciousness, and because these young artists, as well as those who have followed them, received their education and initiated their experimentation in a time of subjective thinking and creativity. The trend, then, is not the result of advocacy and encouragement, but an outcome of the times.

EXPERIMENTAL NARRATIVES: ADAPTABILITY AND POTENTIAL

It is impossible for me to elaborate here on the success or failure of the symbolic approach in *Yellow Earth*, but its use tells us that it is quite possible to use symbolic, imagistic and metaphoric devices to excavate national history, portray group characters (as in the drum dance and rain prayer scenes), and widen the space for poetic Chinese film. There are still many pieces of virgin land yet to be cultivated, and many "new continents" for us to discover. For Chen Kaige, a poetic young experimentalist, *Yellow Earth* is only the beginning paragraph of a long piece of writing, and Tian Zhuangzhuang's gradual explorations of the free souls of the Inner Mongolian prairie, the Tibetan grasslands and elsewhere seem to slowly reveal the upper part of a long scroll of folkloric imagery.

But as we look at and approve this adventurous spirit, dedicated to history and the plain and simple people on the land, we must point out that experimental film must be flexible. This is something more or less ignored in *Yellow Earth*, *On the Hunting Ground* and the like. The ability to adapt represents the artistic vitality of the experimental narrative; this ability serves as an essential mechanism for its survival and a self-regulating device for its development. Our experimental film, of a socialist nature, is inevitably conditioned by both the political system and the psychology of mass art. Thus adaptability is not only necessary, but also possible.

The subsequent release, in 1985, of *Black Cannon Incident* and *Swan Song* should be considered as a quest for suitability in experimentation and for harmony between alienation and comprehensibility in the conveyance of artistic information. These two films are a response not only to the first experiments of the young film directors, but also to the worldwide trend toward modernism among socialist filmmakers. Thus, in the two films, the unity between realist means and symbolist devices, plot and image, realistic and representational image, true-to-life and stylized color becomes more natural, much closer to the audience, and stronger in terms of perceptibility and readability. No one would deny the filmmakers' obvious inclination to experiment; yet most audiences can derive enough meaning from the audiovisual information to remain intense and excited while viewing the films.

The matter of adaptability, of course, has two sides. Young artists making experimental narratives should be aware of their suitability for the audience, and not to go too far beyond the present level of film culture in regard to film form, a matter undoubtedly of immediate importance. However, it is urgent that the level of our audience be elevated, for the level of understanding of film by our overall population is incompatible with the times and inappropriate in a modern nation. Though the nations's aesthetic requirements of film can be classified in terms of various groups, education and social strata, these requirements must be continuously improved and elevated. Furthermore, film, as a universal language of expression, is taken as an important mark when evaluating the cultural quality and construction of a nation. We cannot confuse ourselves with capitalist countries in terms of ideology, but there does exist a comparable artistic standard and production quality with regard to film culture. Thus, besides ordinary filmmaking, we must also admit the need for explorative movies. The need for such films to continue to adjust, stress essential adaptability and readability, and strengthen their relations with common films and the ordinary audience, an issue that requires further research, has already captured great attention.

TREASURING AND PROTECTING THE GOLDEN AGE OF CREATIVITY OF THE YOUNG FILM EXPLORERS

For any kind of cultural activity, the ages between 25 or 26 and 38 or 39 are the most vigorous, imaginative and creative. The great figures of human culture who either began to vigorously pioneer a great cause or already displayed their talents and genius during this age span are too numerous to mention. This is especially true of film art. As demonstrated in film history, film is not only a young art, but also "an art of the young." In our own film history, for example, the filmmakers of the older generation, such as Cai Chusheng and Wu Yonggang in the 1930s, started early and were at life's full flowering when their best works, in their case *Fisherman's Song* (1934) and *Street Goddess* (1934), were made. In the early 1950s, many young directors from the Liberated Area who had had military experience, like Cheng Yin, Shui Hua, Su Li, Wu Zhaoti, Lin Nong and Wang Yan, made their maiden works around the age of 30. This now middle-aged generation is an exception because of the disastrous decade of the Cultural Revolution which seriously disrupted their careers. Now we have the young generation of the early 1980s, which made *Yellow Earth* and *Black Cannon Incident*, and which will continue to develop.

In the overall history of world cinema, however, too many film pioneers have produced spectacular maiden works but suffered later on the frustrating road of artistic creation. As everyone knows, D.W. Griffith was down and out after the failure of *Intolerance* (1916); Sergei Eisenstein, who gave us the wonderful *Battleship Potemkin* (1925), never had plain sailing; and Orson Welles, who at age 26 made *Citizen Kane* (1940), could hardly realize his later ambitions. For Eisenstein, Welles and others, their tragedy lies in the fact that their lives were always full of artistic illusions, and their restless characters, blind to convention, were often crushed in the hard face of social reality, the audience and the commercial nature of cinema. But it is their zealous, restless and vigorous creativity that not only brightened film history, but also has been extraordinarily alive in the hearts of the younger generations of explorers.

We know this too well in our own film history. Consider Wu Yonggang and Cheng Yin. The former, whose first work, *Street Goddess*, is a treasure of the silent film, could never fully display his artistic talent after he made *Big Waves Washing Away Sand* (1966). Only in his later years did he tell Wu Yigong, "When we made *Night Rain on Ba Mountain* (1980), we preserved 'our own' style!" What an earnest and meaningful statement! And Cheng Yin, a director of epics, initiated a new style with *Iron Soldiers* (1950) and *Fighting North and South* (1974) when he was only in his early thirties. What followed, however, was nothing but frustration. Only with *Xi'an Incident* (1982) did he draw a satisfactory end to his career.

From now until the beginning the next century will be an important period, when the Fifth Generation directors, those known and those yet to emerge, will temper themselves and reach maturity, a time in which they will be in their golden age and create their best films. By the beginning of the twenty-first century, most will only be in their early forties and will, together with the currently middle-aged directors, raise our film to new heights. The issue before us is how to treasure and protect their golden period. We must learn from the instances of Wu Yonggang and Cheng Yin (and there are, of course, many other examples) and learn to protect and treasure the creative time of the young film artists. This does not mean merely to guarantee them a chance to make films—which, of course, is not easy to do—but more importantly to cherish and protect their individual creativity, and treat the issue of success or failure in artistic experimentation carefully. Whether it is successful or not, we must assume the necessity of experimentation, for it is because of experimentation, because of the attempt to reach the heights of nonconformity and the unusual, that "weightlessness" can be achieved. If one moves only on the level of normality, one cannot sense the unusual, nor experience an astonishing pleasure one has never had before.

A strange and magical tree grown out of our land, *Yellow Earth*, if rooted deeply and wide, will flourish in the future. We must see to it that there can more such cultural trees, full of creative vitality, grown out of our deep, firm land, whose thick green shade will satisfy our eyes.

4

The Debate Over *Horse Thief*

Xia Hong

Translated by Wang Xiaowen

Participants:

Xia Hong: Editorial Department, *Film Art*

Yang Ni: Editorial Department, *Film Art*

Ma Ning: Foreign Section, China Film Corporation

Tian Zhuangzhuang: Director, *Horse Thief*

Zhang Rui: Scriptwriter, *Horse Thief*

Kong Du: Beijing Film Institute

Qian Jing: Literature Section, China Social Science Institute

Liu Shusheng: China Art Institute

The release of the controversial film *Horse Thief* generated a heated discussion in a symposium hosted by *Film Art* in Beijing in 1986. The publication of this debate here is intended to open the subject to further discussion.

Xia Hong: After the release of *On the Hunting Ground* last year, Tian Zhuangzhuang has brought us another stranger, *Horse Thief* (1987), set in Tibet.

In our country, this film is considered to be experimental, yet in contrast
to the praise or criticism such films usually receive, there has been little
reaction, even within film circles. That's no surprise, for a number of people
have said that *Horse Thief* presents a difficult riddle, not only to its audience,
but to theorists and critics as well. To some degree, it alienates its audience,
for it deviates far from traditional aesthetics and thinking. Yet whether or
not you like it, you must admit that the film is rich in creativity and very
special in form. It constitutes a new film phenomenon and is thus worthy

of study and evaluation. The significance and value of this film in relation to Chinese cinema and aesthetics should be analyzed.

Ma Ning thinks: Tian Zhuangzhuang explores the relationship between humankind and religion, especially the impact religion has, but his exploration is not very deep, remaining on a superficial level, expressing only a few symbolic signs and rituals.

Tian Zhuangzhuang does not totally agree, but admits there is a question of the difficulty of communication between two different areas. . . .

Ma Ning: Earlier, the director spoke of the relationship of humanity and religion. To me, besides being the expression of a system of thought and an imaginary social order, religion, including Buddhism and Christianity, is also a part of society. Religion has its own social stages, which I am not sure the director considered in this film.

Tian Zhuangzhuang: Actually, I didn't want to analyze religion, but to show that religion is one aspect of ideology, a kind of social force. As a matter of fact, I was ambivalent toward the subject while making this film. When you see the Tibetans worshipping in the temple, you see the place which bears the history, culture and music of the nation. I didn't want to do anything to harm the Tibetan religion, but thought the relationship between humanity and religion should be dignified. Furthermore, the religion in the film is more symbolic than real. I didn't concretely document the relationship between Tibetans and their religion. I simply wanted to make this particular film there.

Zhang Rui: Ma Ning's thinking may divert us from our original emphasis. When you mention that religion is an index of society with its own stages, you are talking about religion from a political point of view. However, religion plays a very important role in Tibet. It permeates every corner. If you want to document Tibetan life, you must present the mental impact of religion. If we approach religion from another angle, such as the viewpoint of culture and history, religion is a form of culture. In the same way, Christianity, the result of thousands of years of Hebrew culture, a kind of sediment of history, is also a philosophy, no matter whether materialistic or idealistic. The Tibetan religion also includes customs, which are an extension of the culture and an expression of Tibetan ways of thinking. The assertion that religion originates in fear stems from a cultural point of view. We approached the Tibetan religion from both a cultural and historical point of view. (A noted documentarion) Joris Ivens was correct to state that religion is a major theme. It doesn't matter whether you are a filmmaker or a critic; you can approach religion from different points of view, but first of all, you must respect Tibetan culture and its traditions.

Ma Ning: The reason I mentioned the relationship between humanity and religion is because since the Renaissance, Western philosophy has emphasized hu-

man values. It was not until the twentieth century that some questioned
Descarte's "quality of human being," arguing that there was no such innate
quality. Psychoanalysis claims that newborn babies have only animal qualities, that only after going through the mirror phase, the language habit,
the Oedipus Complex, and subsequently the symbolic world do they become
subjective beings. In other words, society establishes human subjectivity.
What it means to be human is determined by society, and within it, ideology
plays a vital role. Some Westerners, like Althusser, divide the superstructure
into two parts: (1) the state apparatus, including the government, the military
and the legal system, which must exist to defend social order and economic
relations, and (2) the ideological apparatus, including families, various
institutions, churches and other cultural organizations. What ideology expresses is the imaginary relationship of a human with the external social
life. In capitalist countries, the ideological apparatus makes the capitalist
social order seem natural and perfectly justified, through imperceptible
influences over thought. One cannot change that, but only try to find a place
for oneself.

Back to Zhuangzhuang's film. Zhuangzhuang explores the relationship
between humanity and religion, especially the impact of religion. He makes
excellent use of superimpositions. The shots of the temple and the Holy
Scripture show the imperceptible influence religion has on life and thought.
Religion is inevitably linked to the entire social structure, so it would be
improper to speak only of the religious system of thought, especially in
Tibet, where religion influences the entire society.

Tian Zhuangzhuang: You are right. The major cultural activity in Tibet is
religious, and that's different from the cultural priorities here and or in
other countries. We have been criticized for overemphasizing religion, especially in the shots of the temple, perhaps because we didn't sufficiently
describe the inner relationship between religion and our characters. Another
reason may be the alienation the audience feels about the strange things
that happen in Tibet.

Ma Ning: An important aspect of contemporary theory is the study of the
influence of ideology on people and society. Some people consider film,
like institutions and families, as an ideological apparatus. The major characteristic of the Hollywood style is its creation on the screen, through every
means possible, of the illusion of reality, including social reality. It's good
that our young directors resist the Hollywood style, but to restrict themselves
to one specific style wouldn't be wise. For example, though Zhuangzhuang's
film does not follow the Hollywood model, when he explores the relationship
between humanity and religion, he doesn't go far enough, but only superficially shows signs and rituals while ignoring their social function. Certainly
it's impossible to treat everything in a single film, yet Zhuangzhuang did
make an attempt. NorBu, for example, is exiled because he steals the gifts
the governors are sending to the temple. But in general, Zhuangzhuang's

exploration is not very deep. Even if the rituals had been presented in documentary style, only superficial social phenomena could have been recorded.

Tian Zhuangzhuang: I disagree. Consider the ghost dance, for example. Ordinary people would see it simply as a ritual, but actually it is a complete and complicated religious story. Only if you understand this story can you understand why NorBu goes to see it. Consider the scene of "seeing off the river ghost." In the past this was done by the poorest men in Tibet. Even our actors hesitated to do it. You just can't feel the intensity of it, but only see the ritual. All native Tibetans understand its meaning, but our people cannot understand it at all. This is a question of communications between two different places, which simply cannot be stated in a couple of sentences.

Kong Du: In general, I understand the religious circumstances as a cultural phenomenon. Let me ask a question. Can these scenes and rituals accurately represent the cultural history of Tibet? Are these rituals a combination of those of Sichuan Tibet, Gansu Tibet and Qinghai Tibet, or are they only those of specific places you visited? These questions are related to your personal understanding of your main character. If you consider this character to be abstract, then it would be proper to show us a combination of the rituals of the entire region. As far as I can tell, the character must be abstract. Yet if you want to give us a concrete character, especially to represent his state of mind under specific circumstances, then we have a question worthy of study. What would Tibetans think after seeing the film? Would they think some things inappropriate, or some scenes unrealistic? Would they doubt that the rituals shown in the film actually depict the impact they have on them? I don't see anything in the film that addresses this, but maybe it's because I'm not familiar with customs there. Nonetheless, the audience should think about it.

Tian Zhuangzhuang: Usually when we talk about Tibet, we think of the Putala Palace and the style and cultural atmosphere it represents. However, I thought, while I was working on the film, that as long as something was Tibetan, it would do. Every county in Tibet is different, including the customs. In the film, the costumes, headpieces, habits and customs were all designed in accordance with NorBu's actions, including his psychological and emotional constitution. We used everything that coincided with his character and created artistic effects. We didn't design them in terms of a specific region. Because the character is not concrete, the costumes, makeup and props were not necessarily restricted to a specific region.

Ma Ning: I think NorBu is concrete, a Tibetan who lives with wife and children and survives by stealing horses. A character in an artistic work is not necessarily identical with a specific person in a specific region, and it's fine to have little differences in details. The question is whether you wanted to express the relationship between humanity and religion. The rituals and characters in your film come apart for lack of a detailed description of the character. Rituals closely relate to the economics of a community and become essential conditions for a nation; thus they formulate a specific life-style for a specific region. *Horse Thief* should focus on this point, to refer to the relationship between humanity and religion. Because you apparently wanted to present pure ritual and ignored representation of the economic basis of the specific community, your film appears to be merely a quest for novelty and an accumulation of folk customs.

Xia Hong: Besides, human beings exist within social relationships. It is impossible for art to explore the relationship between humanity and religion abstractly. Nowadays people like to talk about anthropology. The major methodology of anthropology is to study the relationship between humans and their rituals, customs and social life from a structural point of view. The reason Tibet has the rituals of "seeing off the river ghost" and "sunning the Buddha" is that they are necessary to the life-style of the society. It is gratifying that Zhuangzhuang has attempted this anthropological study of Tibet, for it shows his exceptional insight and explorative spirit. But as regards *Horse Thief*, I think the director only explored form.

Xia Hong: I think there are two points of view in the film: Tian Zhuangzhuang's and NorBu's. The major characteristic of the form is the frequent intersection of these points of view, yet I feel that the transfer is not smooth, at least not organic. It seems to lack a chain of essential inner linkages. For example, the opening scene of the "celestial burial" and the later scene of "sunning the Buddha" are impressionistic rather than related to the character's action and fate. I found hardly any relationship between them, especially on my first viewing. Of course, I don't require the director to show clearly the causes and effects of the rituals and the character. However, I think the director could have given an overview of his film and revealed the inner relationship between rituals and character, whether referring to plot, state of mind or emotional line, if he had a microscopic control and a detached view of the whole film. Without that, parts of the plot appear loose and less organic and fail to create a tight and logical narrative structure. That's why you're accused of hunting for novelty and collecting customs. Of course you can argue that you did introduce the background of the protagonist, since religion permeates every corner of Tibet and every holiday is religious. However, in terms of the effect on the screen, the design of the scenes, especially your use of large amounts of subjective sound and visuals, like panning the camera, are expressions of your subjective feelings and narrative. What do you think about that?

Tian Zhuangzhuang: I understand what you mean. In the early days, Zheng Dongtian also discussed that with me, but I think it would be too easy to connect the rituals directly to the behavior and state of mind of the character.

Ma Ning: Actually, what was just said is not a question of understanding customs. We are trying to find the connection between character, custom and rituals. In many masterpieces, the subjective viewpoint is that of the characters. In *Horse Thief*, you used many subjective shots; however, this subjectivity derived not from the character, but from you as director. That's why the audience finds it hard to penetrate deeply into the character's heart.

Zhang Rui: You mean subjectivity should be represented by the characters?

Ma Ning: The subjective world is the author's world, not NorBu's. If the audience could get inside the world of NorBu, it would identify with the film. Modern film may not emphasize plot, yet it is necessary to have actions, and their causes and effects. That's what makes a film.

Tian Zhuangzhuang: I'm talking about distancing; you're talking about identification. We have different points of view. Are they harmonious? If you understand the sound as subjective, why can't the character be objective?

Kong Du: I think this film begins with a lack of identification and ends with identification. I agree that it contains two points of view and I think they blend well. The director sees the events totally as an outsider. When he tells the story, he sometimes borrows NorBu's point of view, forming the intersection of the two viewpoints. I think the film is built around these two points of view. The character's state of mind is permeated with religion, so the dramatic component of the film is weak, but its historical and cultural elements are strong. Since religion is a very important part of Tibetan culture, the state of mind of NorBu is not only his, but has a general significance which the director is seeking. Because of this search, the film has a detached feeling. The reason we cannot frequently be caught up in the character's state of mind is that it's too general. If we look at his narrative from this point of view, it's somewhat complete. Since he pays less attention to the dramatic element, the plot we expect to be there disappears. What remains is the character and his relationship with religion. That's also the reason for the character's relative indifference for his wife and children, and even that is controlled by something general—the power of gods and religion. Once Tian Zhuangzhuang chose his own way to represent the theme of the Tibetan nation, his film had to look like what we now see. The original ending had NorBu crawling to the Celestial Burial Ground, but Zhuangzhuang didn't agree with this, so the film ends with blood, knives and the Celestial Burial Ground. The home to which the character may return is his conversion to religion. Whether or not he finally achieves this is left up to the audience. This is a narrative question and a wise intentional omission, yet it is definitely a barrier to audience understanding.

Tian Zhuangzhuang: I think the audience should understand this. The film is both a personal and a national story. *Horse Thief* is different from *On the Hunting Ground*. The latter represented killing and harmony among people through the Mongolian spirit and the laws passed down through the history, as well as through my own will. *Horse Thief* is more personal. Our nation has seen enough of sorrows, spirit and dignity, as well as backwardness on the screen.

Liu Shusheng says: There is a current saying that a film that cannot be understood is not necessarily bad, and that the one that can be understood, or partly understood, may be good. Xia Hong resists this idea.

Xia Hong: Some films cannot be understood immediately, and sometimes not for a long time and only on certain levels; others can be understood only with effort. That's why some films which should be understood fail, while others are not intended to be understood. When we first see *Horse Thief*, we sense that the intermingling of the two viewpoints is not organic and harmonious and have difficulty accepting the film. There are two reasons for this. First, the aesthetic experience and receptivity of the viewer is determined by his/her social and economic background, job, education, interests and hobbies, and personality. If one doesn't have a basic grasp of Tibetan history and culture, one will have a hard time understanding the film, and the distance between the director and the viewer will be great. When I asked Zhang Rui if he would like the film if he hadn't written the script, he replied positively, saying he's interested in and loves Tibetan culture. His position is significant. To me the second question is even more important, which is whether or not the director considered his audience when making the film. To be frank, my understanding of your film depends upon your explanation, your understanding of your thoughts and intentions. If we must rely entirely upon what is given on the screen, we will have a hard time understanding it, yet most of your audience can communicate with you only through the film. No matter what you wanted to show, about laws and regulations through the way people behave on the hunting ground, or about humanity and religion through the fate of a horse thief, you should first have allowed your audience to understand and accept your film. It would be another matter if the audience disagreed with your point of view.

Tian Zhuangzhuang: Did you find that the narrative is unclear, or that you didn't feel as you should have when you saw the film, or it is not harmonious with your own aesthetics?

Xia Hong: As I said earlier, I didn't respond as I thought I should have, but I think the source of the problem is your narrative.

Tian Zhuangzhuang: I think we're addressing the same issue. If we are concerned with intention, both Zhang Rui and I wanted to express our own feelings and mood; that's why we chose this theme. As for our attitude toward this story, it isn't a matter of whether we told it clearly or not. The story is only one part of the film, and not the most important. It has an equal position with other elements. I didn't set out to give the biography of a horse thief. If I had, I'd have gone about it another way, beginning with horse theft during the grandfather's generation. Since you realize that the film expresses the relationship between humanity and religion, between life and death, you do understand it. What you would like is to understand more of the details and to clarify each specific point. That's normal.

The major question in the film is still that of national and regional culture. Everyone has his own territorial identity. I've maintained contact with our ethnic minorities for some years now. The scene of "seeing off the river ghost" is only mentioned once in the novel, yet I immediately understood its importance, whereas others might not have paid it much attention. That's why I believe everyone's territorial identity is different. Yang Ni was excited by the superimpositions, Ma Ning with the ghost dancing, Xia Hong with the sound. Tibetans have a strong national identity and a powerful sense of religion. It was impossible for us to state clearly all of Tibetan history, not even for the natives. For example, only a few lamas knew the custom of "seeing off the river ghost," which predates Liberation.

When Zhang Rui and I discussed the structure of the film, we wanted every scene of customs to be linked to the main character, so they were carefully selected and worked out. Tibetans customs are plentiful, with dozens of holidays, each with its specific significance. I thought then and even now that it might be necessary to subtitle the five holidays in the film, for each is quite complicated. These customs are the major obstacles the Chinese audience confronts. They would pose no problem for most native Tibetans.

Liu Shusheng says: In the past, we paid too much attention to audience understanding, indulging them in laziness. The release of *Horse Thief* hammers always at traditional viewing habits. Tian Zhuangzhuang responds by saying: I'm not saying that whenever I want to make a film, I think it proper to make it in the same way as this. I want to go a different route from others. . . .

Liu Shusheng: There is something to Zhuangzhuang's statements. Some films are hard to understand if you don't have a particular knowledge. In the past we gave too much attention to making sure the audience understood a film, which made the medium the most easily read art. This has advantages for a large audience, but it leads to viewer laziness. Obviously it's much easier for ordinary people to understand a film than a painting in a museum, let alone modern art. Music, dance and literature are also more difficult for their audience than is film. *Horse Thief* and earlier films, like *Sister* (1983) and *Yellow Earth*, hammer away at traditional viewing habits.

It is insufficient to analyze *Horse Thief* in the normal way. First of all, the critic should have a background in Tibetan culture and its customs; otherwise he/she might raise stupid issues which would be asking too much of a comparatively short film. A number of recent films demand thought and repeated readings in the same way we study literature, music and painting. Sometimes they force us to do a little research in order to understand them.

Xia Hong: Let me raise a question. Obviously we all feel that the second viewing of a film differs greatly from the first. We have more understanding of it. We all talked with Zhuangzhuang about *Horse Thief* before the second screening. If we saw it a third time, we would find something new, or be closer to the director's intentions. But this is impossible for the ordinary film audience. They have little chance to speak with the director; they're not willing to pay to see the film twice; and they won't spend days doing research, as did Shusheng. Since every director hopes the viewers will understand both the film and the director, obviously *Horse Thief* has problems meeting this goal. I wonder what Zhuangzhuang thinks about this.

Qian Jing: That's an interesting question. But Zhuangzhuang doesn't care if the audience understands it immediately or not, and he doesn't let the audience take a normal look, either. He offers us a new aesthetic in which some can understand most parts, some less. That's only a matter of quantity. Some may never understand *Horse Thief* at all; other may say it's not even a film.

Tian Zhuangzhuang: I understand your reservations about the narrative, but I'm used to telling a story in my own way. I'm very stubborn about that. Maybe this is a shortcoming, but at the same time, it's a plus. I didn't take everyone into consideration when making the film. It's impossible to do that. It's hard to judge whether or not an audience will understand. As our film culture develops, though, I think audiences will gradually come to accept my work.

Qian Jing says: Both of Tian Zhuangzhuang's recent films share a common characteristic, which is the difficulty of reading them. But once this new genre exists, it creates new demands on the audience. Audiences create films, but films also create audiences.

Qian Jing: Both of Tian's films share a common characteristic, which is the difficulty of reading them. I was startled when I first saw *On the Hunting Ground*; this time, even though I had prepared, I was also surprised when I saw *Horse Thief*. I don't believe anyone would boast that he understood it on first viewing. It's difficult.

Actually the concept of difficulty is not immutable. The reason we cannot understand is because we cannot easily assimilate the information on the screen. This information is useless to the audience, but organic to the film. Such films may be mastered by an audience willing to prove its ability. Viewers can consider the problem as a process of reading.

Xia Hong: I agree that a good work of art is not necessarily easy to read, but this is only one side of the matter. The other is that a good work is not necessarily difficult to read, while a dull work may be very difficult. We cannot judge the quality of a work by whether it is difficult to read, any more than we can judge a film by its box office returns. I mentioned earlier that the reason Zhuangzhuang chose this unusual form to tell the story is because other forms were inappropriate. It's the critic's job to study a work carefully and judge it on its merits. Today what we are debating is exactly this point, that is, how *Horse Thief* accomplishes the director's intention.

I have another matter to present. I have seen *On the Hunting Ground* and *Horse Thief* twice, and each time I felt differently. At the second viewing I responded on the deeper level of cinematic elements, on the logic that was difficult to discern the first time, and found the junctures I failed to find the first time. Because of this, I now think the narrative logic is complete, yet I seldom find on a second viewing a deeper level of meaning than appeared in the first. That may be my personal feeling and what dissatisfies me about the film. I believe that if the director of a film brings his audience, consciously or subconsciously, to an understanding of a film, that is, to a film's grammatical and semantic elements, he is most likely to make his audience ignore, consciously or subconsciously, its connotations, that is, the film's metaphorical level, which is the more important level. This is certainly not intended. Should a director reduce or avoid the possibility of ignorance when he designs and structures a film? Any artist has the right to choose a theme he likes and control the form to express it. We don't argue this; on the contrary, we look forward with excitement to each promising artist's unique work, Zhuangzhuang's among them, undoubtedly.

Qian Jing: This new film genre, once established in China, will raise a new requirement for the audience. It is not only that the audience creates the film; the film also creates the audience! The new films offer us new aesthetic experiences, which demand an adjustment and familiarization. The audience has to be restructured aesthetically, which isn't at all a bad thing. Our art and film theory puts too much stress on established models and prefers the stability of fixed art forms. This puts one at a disadvantage when confronting something new. Certainly we can criticize and nit-pick over the details in films like *Horse Thief*, but first we must be able to read the films and understand them. That's a precondition of evaluation.

Our film aesthetics group often discusses why China did not begin to make films in the Western style after Bazin and Kracauer were introduced. This is an important question. Zhuangzhuang said that he is on the fringes of film circles and that so are his films. But his films are not made step by step according to the recipe of a foreign theorist. They are an expression of Chinese aesthetics, whether he is aware of it or not. This cultural awareness has its own function.

Many people misunderstand the directors of Zhuangzhuang's generation. They wonder why these filmmakers go to the border regions and deserts, or torture themselves in the snow-capped mountains like explorers, why they are interested in minorities. I think the reason is that this generation doesn't want to restate what's been said before, but at the same time, these young filmmakers cannot deny their aesthetic ideals, their responsibilities as artists. These things appear in their works in purely theoretical forms and are permeated in their life experiences. And the consciousness that is directed against falsity, decoration and sentimentality not only exists deep in the filmmakers' hearts, but also is revealed in the unique, dispassionate style of their works. They are straightforward in confronting reality. Their films are tough. The masculinity of their films is a strong contrast to the gentle and delicate films of other generations. Zhuangzhuang has a broad and promising future, but the most exciting thing is to capture those raw, simple and wild life-styles and characters. That's why he focuses his camera on Ya Sigulem, an ordinary and undecorated herdsman, and on NorBu, a lower-class peasant fallen to stealing horses. Although the films depict different events and have different characteristics, they are both tough. The appearance of this type of "tough film" is not an isolated phenomenon. From a broader perspective, it indicates a cultural aspect of the collective consciousness. These films bring a breath of fresh air to the screen. Their appearance leads our cinema out of its traditional pattern and forward into the future.

Xia Hong: Our debate seems to be heating up. While we all agree with one another in the long run, we seem to disagree over finer matters. The director of the film cannot convince the critics on a number of issues, while conversely, the critics cannot convince the director. Unfortunately, time limitations force us to leave our debate unfinished. After the meeting, each of us will go our own way. We hope we will have the opportunity to get together again, to continue our communication. We hope this debate has given each of us new insights and information, and that it will help promote further study and research.

5

Historical Roots and Modern Consciousness: A New View of Chinese Film

Chen Xihe
Translated by Fu Binbin

A CLOSE-UP AND A LONG SHOT

This close-up appears in the film *Life*: Song Qiaozhen covered with a scarlet wedding veil stained with sparkling tears. This close-up, which has touched countless audiences, heightens the tragic atmosphere of the wedding scene and tempts emotional identification with the dramatis personae. As a result, the audience, deeply experiencing Qiaozhen's tragic lot, strongly condemns Gao Jialin for his immorality. True sympathy may be successfully stirred, but the shot also causes many to misread a social tragedy as a personal one.

By contrast, in *Yellow Earth* the tragedy of Cuiqiao's wedding is rendered through the opposite device: a long shot reveals a bridal parade zig-zagging through the barren hillsides, beating drums and blowing trumpets, and all thirteen shots of the scene duplicate precisely the scene that opens the film. The long shot and the repetition distances the audience, avoiding the cheap devices of emotional provocation and perceptual stimulation, allowing the viewers to stand back and contemplate Cuiqiao's fate in a broader historical context. This apparent superficiality conveys a stronger and deeper anxiety. It makes us realize that this is not a personal tragedy, but the fate of Chinese women for hundreds of thousands of years. Therefore, our solicitude for the personal fate of Cuiqiao is elevated to a reflection upon history and culture. Such reflection, on the values and norms of traditional Chinese culture, has produced an extraordinary train of thought in contemporary filmmaking.

Country Couple and *A Woman from a Good Family* (1985) approach the familial structure and ethical code of ancient China and their tragic collapse in modern society. *At the Beach* (1985) reveals the contradictions between a traditional agrarian and a newly born industrial society. *On the Hunting Ground* relates how Genghis Khan's *zhasa* (legal system) has been rejuvenated in modern times. *Yellow Earth* represents the ancient culture and way of life, nurtured by the yellow earth, going from stagnancy to eruption, a theme also found in the comparison between the Han and Dai cultures in *Sacrificed Youth* (1985) and in the description of the frustrations of the old and new generations of farmers (Gao Jialin and Song Qiaozhen) in *Life*.

In *Yellow Earth*, the long shot is raised from the technical level to aesthetic heights. The use of such shots suggests, first of all, that these films take the general culture of our nation as their objective. Although most of the stories are set in modern times, the formation of life they represent is deeply rooted in our nation's thousands of years of history. The films are endowed with a deep sense of history. Further, they are not political or moral interpretations of life, designed for quick success and instant profit, but deeper and broader reflections on the nation from a modern perspective. These two points embody the basic traits of this train of thought.

CLASS AND CULTURAL LOGIC

For years we have been accustomed in our films to approaching problems from the viewpoint of class consciousness and politics, and our literature and art have represented life in the same way. However, life itself contains not only political connotations, but also cultural connotations, which are a more solidified and persistent factor in our lives. Today especially, when the exploiting classes as a political power have already been eliminated, it is impossible to grasp completely the complex and profound meanings of life from the point of view of class. That women submit to men and peasants pray to Heaven for rain are not products of class alone. To marry one's daughter to a man she does not love and let her be violently humiliated is not an act stemming from the logic of class, but from a cultural logic. Thus, we go beyond the smoking gun of political and class struggles and discover that what we face is a conflict with an ancient culture.

Of course, once things are related to culture, it becomes impossible to simply decide their nature in terms of class and politics, because under the same flag are both good guys and bad guys, sincerity and hypocrisy, the beautiful and the ugly. In the benighted conservatism of Hanhan's father in *Yellow Earth*, one can also find honesty, kindheartedness, tolerance and power. In *At the Beach*, Old Manli's obstinate and superstitious character contains his unusual human nature, and when, facing the sea, he kneels, we are moved by the primitive, simple pursuit of perfection bursting from his soul. Both, however, out of "paternal love," push their daughters to the brink of destruction. In *Country Couple* and *A Woman from a Good Family*, female meekness comes at the cost of apathy and the blood of the soul, and in *Yellow Earth*, the prayer for rain is a mixture of the traditional idea of God's will and the struggle against fate. The rich and complicated connotations of the national culture cannot be approached using only the simple scalpel of class analysis, but need to be understood in a more careful and fuller way, and to be displayed in a multi-faceted, multi-leveled, multi-vocal manner. This forces artists to explore new devices of expression and new relations between the screen and the audience.

A TWO-WAY RELATIONSHIP AND TRANSPARENCY

A traditional movie establishes a one-way communication between screen and audience, representing precisely what it intends to relate. Consequently, it usually employs routine compositions and cinematography, fluent editing, consistent narration, clear causality and a definite (or comparatively definite) conclusion.

A modern film, on the contrary, strives to construct a two-way relationship between screen and audience. The audience, while viewing the film, is inspired to actively participate in the creation of meaning, and the director seldom frankly and directly reveals information to the audience, as exemplified in the analysis of Cuiqiao's wedding. Another example is the water-fetching scene, which exceeds conventional length. Besides indicating clearly that fetching water is a daily routine, the scene also makes one feel the stagnant rhythm of life. This also happens when Cuiqiao's and Hanhan's father and Gu Qing sit face-to-face on the *kang* [sleeping platform] for a long time. The long, static shot and silent frame puts one on edge and generates eagerness for change. Thus, unlike the close-up in *Life*, the entire significance of which can be quickly understood at first glance, other meanings wait to be realized by the active reading of the audience.

To move the audience to ponder all that takes place on the screen, modern films have developed a series of non-traditional devices: inconsistent storytelling, jump cuts, irregular compositions, abnormal durations of time, repetitions, counterpoint, open structures, open editing and so on. Through such techniques, a space for thinking is established between screen and audience, and it is only through this thinking that the significance of the film can be understood. In this sense, modern films are opaque, while traditional films are easy to see through. If one knows a few established cinematic strategies, one easily acquires the meaning of a conventional film. The opacity of modern movies should not be considered a game of techniques or obscurity, however. In fact, one could hardly imagine how to convey the entire significance of *Yellow Earth*, *Country Couple* and similar films in any other way.

REFLECTION—THE CULTURAL SPIRIT OF THE NEW ERA

The emergence of this direction in filmmaking, considered in terms of individual works, seems fortuitous; however, it also has its inevitable social and historical background. In the first place, it forms a counterattack against the theory of a simple relationship between art and politics, especially the metaphysical aesthetics of the Gang of Four.

For years, works of art more often than not applied a simple method of political and class determinism in their depictions of life and human conduct. An arranged marriage was the product of the landlord class, and feudal superstitions were products of the exploiting classes. We tried to categorize all things as proletarian or bourgeois, socialist or capitalist, worker or exploiter, revolutionary or counterrevolutionary, turning the richness of life and society into a few unvarying formulas. Such practices are undoubtedly necessary in the political struggles of one class against another, for they help us see clearly the immediate causes of certain phenomena. But artworks of this type, taken to the extreme, become simple stories of good guys and bad guys, overly simplified answers to life which fail to inspire people to think of its complexities. The Gang of Four oversimplified most traditional culture as "feudal" and "capitalist" and told us to discard it, and called backwardness, superstition and poverty "proletarian" and told us to inherit them.

The complicated practices of the Cultural Revolution brought this flat, one-dimensional notion to total collapse, because people could not find an answer to life in such works, nor in the way of thinking they provided, and so people were led to feel that the works were hypocritical. Afterwards, people began to reflect anew upon good and evil, the beautiful and the ugly, the true and the false, progress and reaction. Thus, the transparent and pure concepts of life of the 1950s and 1960s became historical remnants of the past. On the basis of reflective thinking, a complex, solid and multi-faceted concept of life was born.

One might feel frustrated and pity the loss of innocence in the national consciousness, but just as one's childhood understanding of the world was constantly filled with beautiful, subjective visions, the old concept of life was also not an accurate portrayal of the world. Life needs to be more richly and deeply understood, and the entire national consciousness must mature through reflective thinking. Reflective thinking in cinema rests in the maturation of the national consciousness and, paradoxically, pushes the national consciousness toward maturity.

POLITICS, ECONOMICS AND CULTURE

The entire society has shifted focus from the political attempt to bring order out of chaos to the historical march toward modernization. In concert with this change, the reflective consciousness in the realm of cinema also altered its concentration on social and political reality (witness *Troubled Laughter* (1979); *A Corner Forsaken By Love*; *The Legend of Tianyun Mountain*; *At Middle Age* etc.), and began to extend its scope to every aspect of national culture. Because the modernization of China has staked a new claim, not only in economics and politics, but also in cultural ideology, it has attracted wide attention in the world of culture.

China, as we all know, is a country with an ancient civilization. Its history not only endows her with a rich heritage, but also leaves her a heavy burden. Modern Chinese culture, in particular, has taken a tortuous, unique path of development, turning from a feudal society into a semi-colonial and semi-feudal society before entering directly into socialism. This cultural tradition, which arose in the environment of an agrarian civilization, was never totally sublimated and reformed. To counter the historical inertia and indolence, the country musters every bit of her strength to take a single step on the road to modernization. Therefore, in order to realize modernization technologically, economically and sociologically, this tradition must be revitalized into a new form of reality. For the modern Chinese, pondering the cultural values and standards of tradition and the historical choices they confront has naturally become an important task. All of this leads to a new perspective, that of cultural anthropology, or the science of national culture.

THE SEARCH FOR NEW IDEALS

Certainly all our films are identical insofar as they represent the past, present and future of the cultural values and norms of our national tradition and the cultural replacement of the old with the new in any given period of time; however, they are also distinctly different. The differences are not only embodied in the dimensions of life and the depth of history they concern, but are also revealed in the emotional orientation they show toward the great turn of history.

From the two scenes analyzed at the beginning of this article, we can see clearly the difference in emotional orientation. In *Life*, Qiaozhen, the peasant woman, conforming to traditional norms, is so beautiful, pure and idealized that the audience, busy shedding empathetic tears, has almost no time to notice the cruel limitations which separate her from the direction of the times, while Gao Jialin is observed with a reflective eye. Consequently the two characters are not posited on the same aesthetic level: Gao Jialin is a realist, while Qiaozhen is, in actuality, an idealist, into whom the author pours all his sympathies.

In contrast, *Yellow Earth*, a sober contemplation of traditional culture, reveals its beauty yet does not conceal its ugliness with superficial sympathy, an attitude that has been criticized as a display of backwardness, as strange and indifferent. In fact, to let people see this backwardness clearly is to stimulate change. While the film maintains a passionate attitude toward traditional culture, it is, at the same time, realistic in representation and does not confuse the audience with romantic visions. It shows desperate desire and death-defying courage in pursuit of the new cultural spirit. The filmmakers' passion can be felt most strongly in the sequences in which Cuiqiao attempts to cross the Yellow River at night, and Hanhan rushes over and over toward Gu Qing against the sea of people praying for rain.

When in *A Woman from a Good Family* Xingxian bids farewell to the old family, a long take depicts the scene in which she kowtows to her mother-in-law and her little husband, still a child. As the camera draws away, we find the heroine posed above a tract of thatched roofs; this shot expresses, undoubtedly, a positive attitude toward her action. Later, when the little husband catches up with her in the forest and says goodbye, again we have a display of sentiment and pain.

Although *At the Beach* exposes the brutal and dark side of traditional culture through its narration of Little Sister's humiliation, shots of the mode of life in the traditional culture are beautifully composed with a warm and lyrical touch, while the petrochemical plant, which symbolizes industrial civilization and gives Little Sister freedom to love and choice of life, is shot in a cliché style. The cold tone of the dinner party in the plant's dormitory forms a distinctive contrast to the warm colors of the feast in the fishing village. Thus, in visual terms, the author's positive presentation of the agrarian civilization unfolds negatively through the storyline, while the industrial civilization, visually negated, is ambiguously represented in narration, making it difficult for one to grasp the director's intentions.

All these films show the need to transform the traditional culture into a modern one, but a number of them also reveal a touch of nostalgia for its passing. Perhaps these filmmakers do not intend to wax sentimental over the gradual demise of traditional culture, but just feel the loss of a kind of beauty, a perfect beauty beyond reality and history. Of course, beauty represents a certain value, but the progress of history and culture has its value, too. Furthermore, progress manifests itself as a kind of beauty, a continuous drive toward perfection. This, compared to abstract beauty, is more specific and more realistic.

Wang Meng once argued that "Aesthetic psychology is more often than not the outcome of historical accumulations, and sometimes likes to look backward." It therefore constitutes "a nostalgic mentality." This may well warn us not to identify with the past when returning to history, but to try to do away with the traditional nets that constantly bind us, so that, like Hanhan, we can rush without hesitation toward the new cultural spirit and seek a new balance in life and a new perfection.

6

The Cultural Film: A Noticeable Change

Li Suyuan
Translated by Fu Binbin

To explore the ancient Chinese way of life and state of mind and analyze the national psyche and character, imbued with and forged by traditional Chinese culture, from a historical and cultural viewpoint has become an artistic endeavor. This is revealed in recent films, especially those of young and middle-aged directors. With keen insight and judgment, these directors have extended their perceptions into the depths of social life. Some have ventured onto yellow plateaus to trace the historical footprints of the Chinese nation; others have wandered the wild and isolated mountains, listening for sounds and fury from the depths of the heart; still others have indulged in profound meditation, cherishing the memory of past simplicity and savagery or, excited by contemporary life, shouted their longing for cultural improvement and humanitarianism.

Confident, though at times restless, they express with a unique language their understanding and recognition of the world and the future. Their films, permeated with a profound philosophy of life and brightened by sparks of oriental humanism, demonstrate a strong cultural introspection. Labeled "cultural film," these movies distinguish themselves from conventional cinema in terms of viewpoint, objective and means of artistic contemplation. They have taken themselves out of the common run with their indomitable yet distinctive characteristics, unusual aesthetics and creative spirit, and have become the most spectacular side of the multi-form structure of contemporary Chinese film.

An unusual phenomenon, the rise of the cultural film cannot simply be explained by the influence of a fanatical search for cultural roots on film practice. It has more profound social and historical origins. Undoubtedly, the embodiment of cultural introspection on the screen is a spiritual product of the increasing and deepening social reform and, at the same time, of a development in Chinese film motivated by social reality. As can be seen in reality, reform not only changes one's life, but causes a tremendous shock in the depths of one's heart. The serious inconsistencies of feudal ideas and values with the present development of a market economy and political democratization make it difficult for the course of reform to take further steps. The contradictions and conflicts between backward, conservative cultural/psychological accumulations and material modernization have captured the attention of many filmmakers. In their anxiety, they have introspectively examined the traditional cultural/psychological structure. They clearly understand that both the hopes and hardships in the ongoing reform lie in elevating the cultural quality of the whole nation, rejuvenating the psychological constitution of the entire society and modernizing its social concepts. Unless the shackles of tradition are shaken off and historical burdens discarded, the will to vitalize and promote our country will become little more than nice-sounding but idle talk. Pounded and bent by strong anxiety and a clear sense of social responsibility, some filmmakers have turned their lenses to the broader historical and cultural background. Focusing on a people surrounded by a national culture, these filmmakers scrutinize from a higher level the traditional culture and social mentality, unfold the development of traditional psychic structure and analyze the national soul and spirit in terms of modern consciousness and thought. This consequently gives them a seemingly detached, but actually closer, perspective from which to contemplate changing reality.

Films like *Country Couple* can be considered the earliest attempts at this. Their emergence indicates that the development of Chinese film in the New Era, after experiencing political clarification and economic reform, has turned to a cultural introspection which casts its light first on peasants, women and intellectuals, the social groups in which the traditional culture has its deepest roots and the national character finds its most obstinate origins. Subsequently, first-rate films like *Yellow Earth*, *In the Wild Mountains* (1986), *Life*, *Black Cannon Incident*, *Old Well* (1987), and *Red Sorghum* (1989) appeared. Their introspective eye centers around the human psyche in a specific cultural atmosphere. In both historical reflection and realistic contemplation, they are like multi-colored paintings, drawn to reveal the psychological history of the Chinese nation. With the unfolding of these scrolls, we can reflect historically and culturally on social reform and derive inspiration and creative power from it. It can be said that the manifestation of cultural introspection on screen, the birth of the cultural film, represents the penetration of modern social concepts into filmmaking and a new awakening of Chinese film.

The appearance of the cultural film has attracted widespread attention and has, in effect, raised a crucial theoretical question: What is the relationship between innovation in film and social awareness? This is a matter of utmost importance in elevating the ideological and artistic quality of the entire film industry, including that of the cultural film itself. It could be argued that innovation in filmmaking depends essentially on experimentation and the renewal of social consciousness and ideas. Any reflection or exploration into the deep structure of the national culture must unquestionably be related to a modern consciousness.

This requires one to investigate and analyze in terms of synchronic and diachronic methods, making reference to both the historical evolution of our nation's cultural psychology and the development of world culture. That is, one should illuminate history with modern thoughts and view oneself with a global eye. The making of cultural films shows a strong awareness of subjectivity, which, sparked by modern ideas, forms a penetrating ideological power. The ancient Chinese civilization developed a brilliant culture which nurtured many fine qualities in its people; however, backward and conservative trash, which accumulated over the years as a result of feudalism, have been preserved in its tradition and psychic structure.

To explore the complex constitution of the national soul, its origins and modern manifestations, is a feature of the cultural film. In depth and from a cultural level, the works depict the national state of mind, both past and present, and carefully analyze its subtle and painful changes during the current period of social transformation.

On the screen we can witness the survival and miseries of humanity, the distortions and resistance of human nature, the progress and stagnation of society, the history and present reality of our nation. Moreover, we can perceive clearly the eruption and power of life that has accumulated over a long time, and flows vigorously on like an underground fire. *Red Sorghum*, then, is an unrestrained eruption of this power, and in Wanquan, Hehe, Zhao Shuxin, Gao Jialin [the main characters in *Old Well*, *In the Wild Mountains*, *Black Cannon Incident*, and *Life*, respectively] and others, this power takes on other forms. Either in the form of meditation or wisdom, in these characters it turns into an inner heat. In the past it was this power that guaranteed the survival and continuity of the Chinese nation, and this power that makes it possible today for China to catch up with more developed countries. The celebration of human life and power is, as a matter of fact, an affirmation of humankind, of human nature and values, reflecting the deep influence of modern humanism on film in contemporary China. One of the most important discoveries of the cultural film is that it opens a new world to our minds.

Since a number of distinctive cultural films won international awards, both in the East and the West, *Old Well* and *Red Sorghum* especially, how to march Chinese film out into the world has become a popular topic. The success of these films proves again that only when it contains the essence of its culture and links with the common future and destiny of humankind can a film receive international recognition. This should inspire us to seek the most effective route to the international film world.

Many filmmakers, when using their cameras to portray the Chinese nation, are filled with an ambivalence of love and hatred that provides their films a strong emotional force. In particular, their revelation of the backwardnesses and deep-rooted inferiorities in our culture makes their audience tremble. For this, they have been criticized. But how can one explore a nation's soul without unearthing its dark side? Our traditional culture, a complex of democratic nectar and feudalist filth, is the spiritual prop on which the Chinese people rely for survival, but it is also a psychic burden under which they can hardly take another step.

When confronting the actual practice of social reform, people more often than not are sensitive to the resistance they encounter, inheriting the anxiety peculiar to the Chinese intellectual since Lu Xun. With a humanistic spirit and a will to change society, they attempt to discover the buds of a new spirit in the soil of the backward and benighted culture. In other words, they make an effort to rid themselves of old bondages in the hope of finding a new civilization.

Almost all the cultural films, however, are less profound and captivating when depicting the new cultural psychology than in illustrating the old state of mind. In part this is because life itself has not provided artistic creation with enough raw materials. At the same time, this reveals that our filmmakers still lack profound insights and deep meditation. We expect them to make new discoveries and create new works.

The cultural film is characterized not only by its unique contemplation of social life, but also by its unusual means of artistic expression. Its creators, a group of courageous and pioneering filmmakers, are good at using other films for reference and at making their own discoveries. Since they are different from each other in character and aesthetic orientation, they do not confine themselves within one pattern, and thus are free to create. As a result, their films are much more pronounced and distinctive in individual interests and artistic originality. We cannot describe the artistic features of the cultural film with a single color. However different from conventional movies, cultural films display, on the whole, the common aesthetic pursuits of this special group. Generally, they emphasize subjective independence, stress inner feelings, and seek profound philosophical thoughts, which constitute a way of cinematic thinking characterized by the personalization and emotionalization of social life. In their preference for subjective experience and emotional expression, they usually clarify their understandings and impressions of life via originally configured frames and describe on the screen the perceptual world captured in their mind's eye.

Expression of subjective feelings and perceptions generates on different levels rich symbols and metaphors, which reinforce the emotional plane and form a unique system of imagery. This indicates that with the deepening of their understanding of the essence of film, many young and middle-aged directors, already dissatisfied with objective imitations of the external world, seek to express their subjective ideas through close representation of reality. Both true-to-life scenes and highly meaningful frames can be found in their works. In an effort to integrate representation with expression, realistic description with pure imagination and concrete images with symbols, they have created a system of images full of life and philosophical significance.

As a matter of course, those who make cultural films are different in style, since they choose different subject matter and have different personal interests. Some pay particular attention to realistic depiction; others prefer symbolic expression; while still others concentrate on rational clarification or adeptly convey feelings and emotions. Regardless, a basic tendency in the cultural film is emphasis on subjectivity and the ego. The priority of plot is obviously weakened to a certain degree, while expressive elements are enhanced to form a comparatively complete system of images; thus the method of depicting character and personality through plot is considered relatively old and stale and is replaced by techniques of analysis and anatomy which gradually reveal the inner life of a character. Objective representation of details combines harmoniously with the personal expression of the filmmaker to create a clear individual consciousness and sense of the subjective in a realistic depiction of life, subconsciously ushering the audience into the realm of introspection and meditation.

The cultural film, in terms of aesthetics and artistic techniques, is not a mere mimesis of modern films in the West, but a deepening development of realism. Its emergence demonstrates that Chinese film in the New Era has surpassed its documentary-like phase and is taking steps toward aesthetic ideals on a higher level. Meanwhile, it should be noted that even a successful creation is never perfect. As an exploration of film art, the cultural film can hardly avoid losing sight of one thing while attending to another, owing to lack of experience and skills.

Very often one can find both merit and defects in a single film. Some of these films are casually made or overbalanced by philosophical notions; others are devoid of interest or obscure. Even *Red Sorghum*, in which philosophical notions are closely integrated with enjoyable elements, has imperfections in its general framework and artistic treatment, leading to inconsistencies in style. The way to harmoniously combine the narrative and the expressive, merge plot and imagery, and fuse profound philosophical terms into the natural flow of emotions, awaits further exploration and practice. We are pleased that these films experiments continue to deepen. Currently in the ascendant, the cultural film will assuredly raise the tide of innovation in Chinese film to a new level.

Part III

Yingxi

In the later part of the 1980s, Chinese film theory, in its critique of traditional culture, developed in two directions. One was the discussion of filmmaking, the pro–Fifth Generation position; the other was a reevaluation of traditional Chinese film theory.

Traditional theory considered the primary function of film as a form of social education. This concept was intensively attacked by modern theorists at the end of the 1970s and into the early 1980s. The attack focused on the definition of film form. Modern Chinese theory declared that film should "divorce" itself from drama and modernize film language. By the mid–1980s, the issue of film as drama was raised again; however, the perspective of the discussion was no longer on the aesthetic, but on the methodology of theory itself. Rather than center on matters of film form, theorists began to address the philosophical and cultural foundations of theory. In other words, the focus was on the theoretical construction of traditional film theory, on Yingxi.

Yingxi is a word group containing a noun and its modifier. The key word, *xi*, means drama, or play, while *ying* means image on the screen. This basic definition suggests that though drama is the essence of film, image is the means of presentation; the term can be loosely translated as "Shadowplay." The early Chinese filmmakers called film Yingxi and emphasized the dramatized story and action, but did not give much attention to the characteristics of shots, editing, camera movement, time and space, and so on, which were taken as merely the means for recording story and action. In addition, these filmmakers emphasized the educational function of film, which came with the traditional, dramatized principles and combined with them. This concept and model of film continued on down to the political melodramas made under Communist Party rule during the Cultural Revolution.

In this discussion, young scholars argued that traditional film theory was synthetic rather than analytical, and that it defined film in terms of story/narrative, rather than as image/photography. This methodology was directly related to one of the major characteristics of traditional methodologies in China, which is sythesis rather than analysis. In contrast, Western theories were analytical. They also argued that traditional Chinese film theory took an ethical and moral, rather than a physical and cognitional, approach to the studies of the nature of film and therefore defined film as a tool for moral and political education. This position directly related to the traditional culture. On the other hand, Western theories dealt with film from a scientific and cognitional position. Finally, they argued that traditional Chinese theory was a practical theory, a guide to filmmaking, not an explanation of film, and that this approach closely reflected Chinese habits of reasoning.

The above opinions first appeared in Chen Xihe's paper, "Shadowplay: Chinese Film Aesthetics and Their Philosophical and Cultural Fundamentals," which first appeared in 1986 and is included in *Chinese Film Theory: The New Era*. Later that year, Zhong Dafeng traced the origin of Yingxi theory, and in 1987, Dai Jinhua analyzed Xia Yan's theory of scriptwriting, one of the most influential theories in China, taking it as the modern constitution of Yingxi theory and its methodology.[1] The discussion of Yingxi, on the one hand, defined the national identity of Chinese film theory. Before this, most people in film circles believed China had no serious theory. On the other hand, it criticized this identity.

NOTE

1. Xia Yan. *Problems of Screenwriting*. Beijing: Chinese Film Press, 1959.

7

An Historical Survey of Yingxi Theory

Zhong Dafeng

Translated by Fu Binbin

Yingxi (Shadowplay) is a term the Chinese people commonly used to refer to motion pictures during the first 30 years of this century, when film was introduced into China, took root, and laid its foundation in terms of art, production and other aspects. As they explored the new medium, filmmakers of the first generation gradually evolved a system of film concepts and a filmic means of expression. Yingxi theory is a preliminary interpretation and summation of these concepts and techniques. Although this theory, never appeared as rigorously structured, carefully developed in scholarly monographs, as have Western theories, it could be found in diverse film criticism, in remarks about filmmaking experiences and in writings about film techniques. This article traces the emergence and development of Yingxi theory, in the hope of establishing a clear understanding of traditional Chinese film theory and the basic way film is understood.

THE ESTABLISHMENT OF AN ARTISTIC CONCEPT

The importation of motion pictures into China began with screenings of foreign films, and the first opinions of the Chinese about cinema were reflected in their impressions of them. In the two earliest articles, published in 1897 and 1898, people marveled at the capacity of a film "to bring things thousands of *li* afar close at hand without magically shrinking the earth, and to display successive shapes and figures in no way different from the wonders of modern or ancient times which divulge the utmost secrets of Creation."[1] If this idea can be grudgingly considered a kind of film concept, it can hardly be taken as a concept of art, but at best a concept of "game."

After stepping into the twentieth century, the Chinese began to make their own films, at first, shooting documentaries of traditional operas and newsreels, and later gradually turning to feature films. People came to realize that films could not only represent moving images, but also be used to make a performance and tell a story. What is more, one could express personal ideas through performances and stories. This was a great leap in the understanding of cinema. Thus people changed to some extent their recognition of Yingxi. It was no longer merely a game of moving shadows. The *xi* (play) in the term *Yingxi* already contained the meaning of "drama." This development took place around 1920, and can be considered the real beginning of Chinese film theory.

The earliest film magazine in China, *Yingxi*, came out in 1920. In his introduction to the second volume (November 1921), Zhou Jianyun stated in the first sentence that "Yingxi is a play without utterance, a play which has images but no sounds, a play recorded by photographic skill." Similar statements were made by many film people at that time. The close relationship of filmmaking in this first stage to "civilized plays" (*wen ming xi*) is not only the direct reason for this opinion, but also a reflection of this theory on film practice.

Films were still considered a vulgar form of entertainment in the early 1920s. In the Chinese *Play Magazine* (1922), articles about Yingxi were still listed in the "Appendix of Games." Film workers in the early days made great efforts to elevate the level of their creation, and also to elevate the social status of cinema, via the construction of film theory, in the hope of making motion pictures an art form. In accordance with traditional concepts of art, they drew an analogy between motion pictures and commonly acknowledged traditional arts such as drama and literature, demonstrating that film possesses similar functions of artistic expression. They also introduced theories of drama and literature into the study of filmmaking. Thus the theory of Yingxi gradually took shape. Hou Yao's *On the Writing of Yingxi Scripts* is a comparatively systematic and representative interpretation of this theory.[2] The theory reflected the views of the majority of filmmakers toward cinema at that time and determined the basic features of Chinese filmmaking of the first period, a situation which did not change until waves of montage theory reached China in the mid–1930s.

THE BASIC FEATURES OF YINGXI THEORY AND ITS DUAL STRUCTURE

What kind of theory, then, is Yingxi theory? Its basic position could be summarized by Hou Yao's statement, "Yingxi is a kind of drama, possessing all the values a drama has."[3] The concept of photoplay did appear in Western film theories of the early days. It can be found, for instance, in the work of Hugo Munsterberg and Freeburger. This concept, on the surface, seems analogous to Yingxi. However, in actuality, Chinese film theory and Western film theory, originated from different cultural traditions and thinking, and differed from the very beginning in their understanding and grasp of cinema in terms of method and viewpoint. Therefore, they developed in totally different directions.

The film theories of the West followed a microscopic analysis of cinematic means of expression, aimed at locating the differences between a photoplay and a stage play in terms of form, while Chinese theory, starting from an overall grasp of the expressive functions of art, aimed first at finding the points shared by the shadowplay and drama in terms of narrative function, and the similarities between them in expressive form.

"To convey the principles of morality through literature and art" is one of the key points in traditional Chinese thinking. This understanding of art in terms of function places emphasis on practical rationalism. More often than not, the advocates of Yingxi theory drew an analogy with drama and literature, demonstrating that they have the dual function of educating through entertainment and fostering aesthetic appreciation. Thus Yingxi theory inherited the theory of function and purpose of traditional aesthetics.

Demonstrating that film is a kind of art, Lu Mengshu held that motion pictures, like drama, could also "enlighten human life" and "be used for entertainment." Furthermore, this kind of entertainment "aroused a viewer's appreciation."[4] In his introduction to *On the Writing of Yingxi Scripts*, Hou Yao first explained the four functions of drama, to represent, criticize, modify, and beautify life. He then pointed out that cinema, benefiting from its technical advantages of cinematography and sound recording, is more "true to life" and more "economical" and "bears a nature of universality and eternity" at the same time as it is an excellent instrument for education. Through his analysis of the functions of cinematic expression, Hou Yao concluded that "Yingxi is a form of drama . . . that possesses all that a drama has. It not only has the four functions of representing, criticizing, modifying and beautifying life, but it is also much more influential than other forms of drama."[5] This analogy was used to compare not only with drama, but with literature. As Hou later noted, "Literary works must have four essential elements: emotion, thought, imagination and form. All these conditions are suited to cinema. Cinema is literature and cinema is living literature."[6] Whether cinema was considered literature or drama, its significance was the same in Yingxi theory.

From the very beginning, the theoretical methodology which started with function and purpose determined that Yingxi theory would fail to emphasize film's ability to objectively record. To some extent emphasis was placed on the ability of film to represent the subjectivity of a filmmaker. Furthermore, what was represented was not abstract philosophical ideas and emotions, but attitudes toward life and modes of behavior which had a concrete social and historical content.

Since Yingxi theory understood cinema by proceeding from the specific functions of content expression instead of the concrete elements, such as images and shots, that construct film, cinema was primarily considered a form of narrative art. Hou Yao frankly proposed a screenplay-centralism, by stating that "the screenplay is the soul of a movie."[7] People evaluating the merits and demerits of a film, more often than not used the success of its narrative as their basic standard. In the first stage of filmmaking, fully completed scripts were seldom used. Most filmmakers relied mainly on brief scene schedules or story synopses, which indicates that they took the making of a good story as their central task. As for the method of screenwriting, "there is no need to care whether it's beautifully written or not, a script will work so long as it's not a mess, and everything is solidly clarified in proper order."[8]

Someone at the time summarized three main problems of domestic movies: "(1) The story is flatly unfolded in a dull way, lacking the magic of twists and turns; (2) captions and shots are tediously long and not economical; (3) the gist of the movie is obvious, leaving no room for imagination."[9] Whether this was accurate or not is a moot question; however, all three points were raised from the point of view of narration, from which came most theoretical elaboration at that time.

Hou Yao thought that "crisis, conflict and obstacle are the three essential elements that should be included in the material of Yingxi,"[10] Li Huailin also noted that "the method of structuring a motion picture serves as an expressive instrument to convey to the audience the emotions, thoughts, imagination and experiences from the depths of the author's heart."[11] All these propositions mirrored the basic way people understood cinema at the time. With dramatic narration as its standard, this method was the core of Yingxi theory and formed an ontology of Chinese film that was totally different from Western film theories.

That we consider narration as the core of Yingxi theory does not mean that we ignore the theoretical exploration into the special features of film art and the specifics of filmic expression within it. At that time, film people already recognized that "film is a scientific invention, and the screenplay is a synthetic art generating from the combination of both art and science. In all forms of art, it is the most difficult and complicated and the last to take shape."[12] They noted that the "play of moving shadows has an original nature independent from a stage play. The value of a moving shadowplay depends entirely on whether its capacity is cleverly used in terms of screenwriting and cinematography."[13] In the overall framework of Yingxi theory, however, the theoretical research concerning cinematic features and the specifics of filmic expression exist only as formal and technical factors attached to the ontology of narration. "Although Yingxi is independently popular, it is on every account a sort of drama in terms of artistic expression. The form of drama can vary, but the art of drama is the same."[14] If we understand this, it is not difficult to understand why, in the early phase of Chinese film, essays on film theory often sharply criticized the dramatization of motion pictures on the one hand, and on the other, applied many propositions of dramatic theory to the interpretation of filmic phenomena.

Fewer parts of Yingxi theory concern film techniques than concern film ontology, but the parts about theory are obviously more complex. On the one hand, no discussion about film techniques can exist without referring to the technological processes and technical conditions of filmmaking. People are thus compelled to treat the specifics of the medium seriously, to try their best to understand its advantages and limitations and to explore its potential for art. On the other hand, as a newborn art, film is devoid of a long-established tradition in both theoretical research and production practices. Concerning film practice, Chinese film of the early days basically inherited the entire creative experience of the civilized play (*wen ming xi*). Influenced by this, theoretical research of the first period also turned its focus on the theory of drama. This, in turn, gave Yingxi theory a heavy dose of dramatic theory.

As discussed previously, people had realized the ability of film to record images as soon as motion pictures were first introduced into China. But after Yingxi theory took shape, few people mentioned this anymore. This is an instance of theoretical catering to the traditional concept of art. Yingxi theory seldom emphasized the quest for realism. Only in the domain of acting were such requirements as "naturalness" and "realism" often heard. Since film, different from a stage play, often uses close-ups, "it's not suitable for affected artificiality in acting. Even the most subtle unnaturalness might risk going too far to be real, be it a move in facial features, a smile or a knitting of the brows."[15] In contrast, Yingxi theory paid more attention to another basic feature of film, the freedom to structure time and space. Someone said that "the first special feature of Yingxi lies in its structure."[16] Hou Yao even made a specific suggestion that "the appearance of a scene should start with a grin-in or fade-in. A long shot may be used at the very beginning to display the whole scene to the spectator, then mid-shots and close-ups may be applied to indicate important actions or things in the movie, or it can be also done by using close-ups and mid-shots first, followed by a long shot."[17] This was obviously influenced by the editing methods of Hollywood. In the creative practice of Yingxi, the exploration into shot structure was also the most obvious use of film's special means of expression. In spite of this, Yingxi theory only made a start in this direction. The term "shot" in Yingxi theory had not yet taken final shape as a basic structural factor in filmic narration. Such terms as "act" or "sequence" (or "scene") were generally employed in the understanding of the cinematic structure of time and space, though the potential of shots as independent narrative units was not fully understood. In Xu Zhuo Dai's *The Knowledge of Yingxi*, although the term "shot" was used, it was used only in the optical sense of "lens."[18] When considering the "shot" as a concept of art, the dramatic terms of the stage play were generally inherited. For example, a far shot was called a French stage, and a mid-shot was called an American stage. Furthermore, some uses of shots were roughly labeled in his book as the application of "scenes," while film directors and art designers were called stage directors and stage designers. On the technical side of Yingxi theory, what was stressed most was directing and acting. That is, attentions were paid mainly to acting skills and the rehearsing techniques of a film director. Someone at the time proposed that "the most important ingredients of a motion picture are the 'screenplay,' 'director' and 'acting,' while 'cinematography' and 'directing' manuals are supplementary elements to assist a movie to success. Therefore, whether a film is good or poor in quality depends entirely on these three major points.''[19] This statement, in fact, represents the hierarchical status of every productive section in the overall framework of the technical aspect of Yingxi theory.

In brief, within such a dual-structured theoretical framework, on the surface Yingxi theory was a system of techniques with a strong dramatic color. It approached, to a different extent, each and every element, from narration to structure, not without some insights into certain specific traits of film art. However, its basic way of understanding things followed the theoretical tradition of the stage drama.

Under the guise of dramatization, the deep structure of the theoretical framework of Yingxi was pregnant with an ontology of filmic narration, starting from the point of view of function and purpose. The formation of this structural core was of course due partly to the influence of drama on film theory and practice, but its reasons were far more complicated and profound. The structural core, viewed vertically, inherited the traditional thinking pattern and spirit of practical rationalism that in China has lasted for thousands of years, understanding the world in a perceptional and wholesome way, and was horizontally influenced by the Hollywood narratives that were flooding the Chinese market at the time. It also could not overcome its given social and historical circumstances. Compared with the dramatic shell of technical methodology, the structural core of narrative ontology was more deeply rooted and far more influential. After Yingxi, as a creative phenomenon, had died a natural death, its structural core retained its influence on thinking about Chinese film.

THE SUBLIMATION OF YINGXI THEORY

Yingxi as a dominant phenomenon of filmmaking gradually withered away after the rise of the Chinese left-wing film movement in the early and mid 1930s. The main reason for this is that a new batch of literary and art workers had joined the ranks of filmmaking and brought with them a new idea, a new culture and structure of knowledge, and were able to "see the world with their own eyes." However, since filmmaking in China had first developed under unusual historical conditions, most of the early creators had turned from the declining stage of civilized plays to the film screen. They were not much prepared in terms of knowledge to accept film culture, but made films only "out of a little bit of interest and curiosity." Some of them had not even seen any movies. "Because it is shooting shadowplays, it is quite natural for one to associate it with the old-fashioned plays China already had.''[20] Thus Yingxi was formed with a strongly dramatic character. Though it is not true that these early filmmakers had never learned from foreign films, in their practice of Yingxi their study was "to make use of Western learning to serve the Chinese." They studied and selectively imitated film techniques and acquired technological skills under the prerequisite of a dramatic conception of motion pictures.

With the rise of the left-wing film movement, in Chinese film theory and practice, montage theory succeeded Yingxi theory. As early as the end of 1928, Hong Shen translated *The Sound Film*, a manifesto by Eisenstein, V. I. Pudovkin and G. Alexandrov (the Chinese translation was published about six months after the original article).[21] The article, though it contains much brilliant exposition of montage theory, failed to attract widespread attention from film people, since Yingxi films were then in their golden age.

By the 1930s, the situation had greatly changed. It became increasingly clear that Yingxi films could no longer adapt to the rapid development of the times. Filmmakers of the new generation began purposefully to turn their eyes to the world, trying to assimilate the latest experiences of film art abroad so as to enrich their own creation. Film ideas of every hue were introduced at this time: the pure films of the avant-garde, expressionist films, the kino-eye, Eisenstein, Pudovkin, and so on. Among them, Pudovkin's theory was the most systematically introduced and had the greatest influence upon the theory and practice of Chinese film. Xia Yan, Zheng Boqi, Chen Liting and others translated *On Film Directing*, *On the Film Script* and *On Film Acting* as well as a number of articles.[22] Meanwhile, a number of writings on the techniques of the Hollywood narrative were also introduced. Shen Xiling, for instance, translated *A Study of Filmic Continuity*, written by a Japanese scholar about American techniques of film editing. These translations became the major sources from which new film workers learned cinematic techniques.

Confronted with these new theories, Yingxi theory, which copied indiscriminately from drama, proved definitely inferior and was gradually discarded. A system of film techniques which combined the theory of Pudovkin with the Hollywood experience and was characterized by narrative montage began to take shape, and replaced step by step the dramatized techniques of Yingxi theory. Hong Shen's *A Dictionary of Cinematic Terms*, *Twenty-Eight Questions on Scriptwriting*, Sun Yu's *On Film Directing* and other writings were the first results of this. They not only expounded narrative techniques in general terms, but also began to pay attention to such issues as whether objective facts can be visualized, and they discussed the proper use of shots and frame composition.

This theoretical work, however, was not a total negation of Yingxi theory; instead, it was a selective sublimation. It pared away the skin of the old theory, but re-formed the structural core and handed it down. Chinese film theory of the 1930s did not give up the concern for function and purpose found in Yingxi theory, but endowed the abstract proposition of film for life and social cultivation with a more specific content of the times and classes, attempting to make film a weapon in the propagation of revolutionary thoughts. Under this theoretical premise, the kernel position of the narrative ontology in Chinese film theory did not waver in the slightest. What merely happened was that the specific concept of time and space in cinematic narration was somewhat broadened and evolved. People no longer adhered rigidly to the conventional acts and scenes of the stage, but used a number of concentrated sequences to unfold the narration, trying to present life with a broader and richer time and space. At the same time, although theoretical approaches addressed the differences between film and other forms of art and the media, and film techniques increased in quantity and became more specific in content, in the overall framework of Chinese film theory, technique remained subordinate to narration.

With this in mind, it is not difficult to understand why Chinese filmmakers, when confronting so many foreign theories, did not accept Eisenstein, but chose Pudovkin and the Hollywood model as their primary subjects. The theories they chose to study were most suitable for dramatic film, which unfolds its narration along a rigid, solid chain of the plot. Films of this type had been the mainstream of Chinese film for a long time. The complete system of film theory which was gradually formed and perfected in the selective process of the sublimation of Yingxi theory in the 1930s had specific social and political functions. It took dramatization as its core, and was characterized by narrative montage.

This theoretical mode and the cinematic concepts it represented deeply influenced Chinese filmmaking and became the basis of its traditional aesthetics. In the several decades thereafter, its specific content underwent great changes and developments, but the theoretical framework remained untouched and became a superstable structure, with a great ability to merge with others and a powerful mechanism of self-adjustment. Its influence is still easily seen in today's film theory, criticism and practice. Although this theory lacks the exquisite and subtle analysis of some film theories abroad, it embodies a cultural background and a point of view different from that of the West. This method of grasping things embodies, in a sense, more factors of the dialectical way of thinking. An important task of today's film theory is to unearth the essence of traditional Chinese theory and combine it with modern scientific ways of thinking in order to understand more precisely the laws of film art. In this regard, both egotism and nihilism are not desirable.

NOTES

1. Quoted in Cheng Jihua and Li Shaobai, eds, *History of the Development of Chinese Film*, Beijing: Chinese Film Press, 1963, vol. 1., p. 9 (footnote).

2. Hou Yao, *On the Writing of Yingxi Scripts.* (Nanjing: Taidong Press, 1926).

3. Ibid

4. Lu Mengshu, "A New Evaluation of Film in Literature and Art," *Chinese Film*, no. 11 (February 1928).

5. See Hou Yao, *On the Writing of Yingxi Scripts*, pp. 1–8.

6. Hou Yao, "The Position of Film in Literature," *Pure As Jade and Clean As Ice*, special issue of *Ming Xing Biweekly*, July 1926.

7. Hou Yao, *On the Writing of Yingxi Scripts*, preface.

8. Xu Zhoudai, *The Knowledge of Yingxi* (1924), pp. 55–56.

9. Tian Lang, "Comment on *A Lady from Shanghai*" *Young Master Feng*, special issue of *Ming Xing Biweekly*, September 1925.

10. Hou Yao, *On the Writing of Yingxi Scripts*, vol. 13.

11. Li Huailin, "How Can One Become a Screenwriter?" *Chinese Film*, no. 11.

12. Sun Shiyi, "The Position of Filmplays in Art," *Friendship of Moral Justice*, a special issue of *Shenzhou Magazine*.

13. Xu Zhuodai, *The Knowledge of Yingxi*, p. 2.

14. Xu Zhuodai, "Yingxi is Drama," *Three Years Later*, a special issue of *Ming Xing Biweekly*, December 1926.

15. Zhen Zhenqiou, "Can't an Actor of Modern Drama Play a Role in the Shadow-play?" *Young Master Feng*, special issue of *Ming Xing Biweekly*, September 1925.

16. Wei Nan, "The Specialities of Yingxi," *Screen Star*, no. 15, December 1927.

17. Hou Yao, *On the Writing of Yingxi Scripts*, p. 50.

18. Xu Zhuo Dai, *The Knowledge of Yingxi*.

19. Zhu Xu. "Comments on *The God of Peace*," *Screen Star*, no. 4.

20. Zhang Shichuan, "Since I Became a Film Director," *Ming Xing Biweekly*, vol. 1, no. 3 (May 1925).

21. Eisenstein, Pudovkin and Alexandrov; "The Sound Film"; *Close Up*, London, October 1928.

22. The Chinese published sections of Pudovkin's writings available in English translation as: V. I. Pudovkin, *Film Technique and Film Acting*. Ivor Montagu, translation; New York, Grove Press, 1960.

8

On Reading Xia Yan's *Problems of Screenwriting*

Dai Jinhua

Translated by Fu Binbin

New China has yielded a singular relationship between art and history. The tortuous route of literature and art in New China has always coincided with the bumpy yet glorious history of the Republic. (We won't discuss, for the moment, the achievements or mistakes, the rights or wrongs of this synchronism). Related to this is the tendency of art in New China to contain a high degree of social, ideological and political content, with emphasis upon its basic content and functions, its typicality.

Also the art of New China presents an intimate combination of theory and practice rarely found in the history of literature and art. Theory, the summation of practice, at the same time directly influences and instructs it. The creation of art is conscientiously directed by theory, and good works, in turn, confirm and substantiate theory. Thus a system of practical aesthetics and theory, unique to our country and based on realism, has gradually taken shape. The system, with regard to culture, embodies a certain openness due to its distinctive ideological content, while in regard to theory itself, it forms a closed circle of self-sufficiency and establishes a structural analogy between the artistic text and its cultural content.

Xia Yan's *Problems of Screenwriting*[1] (1959) could easily find its own position in this theoretical framework. The book, a harmonious part of the score of the art theory of New China, was at the same time an unquestionably fresh tune. It is a free-styled, practical guide to screenwriting techniques, a textbook for screenwriting majors at the Beijing Film Institute, rather than an abstract monograph. Therefore, the book explores form and formal aesthetics within a theoretical framework, wherein the decisive power of content over form is strongly emphasized. It could be considered, in a sense, an effort to seek balance in the unbalanced.

Determined by its given cultural context and social basis, art and art theory in New China, especially in the 17-year period following Liberation, has not been, and could not possibly be, an aesthetic castle in the sky; nor is it a modern labyrinth constructed through extremely abstract forms of media. Its distinctive practical and political nature makes it look more like a pyramid based in the soil of culture, a stable triangular structure. It asks not to reflect on social phenomena via artforms, but to distill social life through given forms of art, those the masses love to see and hear. In the popular domain of film, the classical mode of the given artforms is a dramatically structured film of the Yingxi tradition. Xia Yan's book is an interpretation and perfection of this art form during that time. This was the only work on screenwriting in Chinese film history for a long time; this impoverished situation continued until the 1980s, when *Eight Lectures on Screenwriting* and *Basics of Screenwriting* were published. Xia Yan's book summarizes the collaborative efforts made in films of the 1950s; it exerted a deep influence upon a whole generation of filmmakers. The book determined, to a certain extent, the narrative pattern, plot construction and technique of films in the 1960s and, for the most part, in the 1970s, and continues to be influential. Its golden age came at the end of the 1950s and in the early years of the 1960s.

To reread this book today will help those of us who are as old as the book to understand many important phenomena in the cultural history of New China, to appreciate the cardinal position and major contributions of Xia Yan to its literary and art history, and to recognize an important narrative pattern in Chinese film history, that of the dramatic film as characterized by Yingxi theory, from an historical position that time has tolerantly bestowed to newcomers.

THE FRAMEWORK OF PRACTICAL ART THEORY INITIATED AT THE CROSSROADS OF TODAY AND TOMORROW

Engaged in film for half a century, Xia Yan began his career in a time of blood-stained terror, shouldering the leadership of the left-wing cultural and film movements in areas governed by the Kuomindang. It was a hurricane-like period which required everyone to make a crucial decision between the rival propositions of the times. The ivory tower of pure art fell apart under the pressure of the darkness and spiritual depression of the times. Art, because of its innate functions, could no longer be the creation and pursuit of pure beauty, but was related to politics, with the struggles of the times and the changing destiny of the nation. As a result, "the Chinese proletariat in literature emerged at the crossroad where the present meets the future, and grew up in calamity and oppression. . . . Young people of social intelligence and wisdom realized their mission as pioneers, so they called for battle far earlier than everyone else."[2] Led by the Chinese Communist Party, revolutionary and progressive writers and artists in the Kuomindang-ruled area declared to the whole of China and the entire world; "Our art cannot be but dedicated to the blood-stained struggle of 'victory or death.' "[3]

The chapters being written in the blood of the left-wing cultural movement were greater than those written in ink.

"To the broad masses of the people, revolutionary culture is a powerful weapon for revolution. Revolutionary culture is an ideological preparation for revolution before revolution, and is, in the course of revolution, a necessary front line in revolutionary thought."[4] Art should serve proletarian politics, the broad masses of the people, and the workers, peasants and soldiers. This was not only an artistic thought, but also a social reality in that great era, a programmatic instruction and, at the same time, a demand of the times and a need of the struggle. To obey this instruction and to meet its requirements is the tradition of "obedient literature" in the left-wing cultural movement. The reality of the struggle, and the guiding principles of art in literary and art circles during the revolutionary war years, became the historical origins of the bulk of the practical art theory of our country after the founding of the Republic, and also became the core of Xia's aesthetic theory.

A CONVERGENCE OF COLLABORATIVE EFFORTS

The art of New China is not merely the legacy and continuity of the left-wing cultural movement, nor simply the accumulation of aesthetic principles of the left-wing cultural movement and the spirit of "the speech on literature and art at Yan'an" in the Liberated Areas. The formation of the framework of practical theory in New China is indebted to left-wing writers and artists in the Kuomindang-ruled regions and the literary and art workers in the Liberated Areas. It is the collaborative result of the two troops and the two generations. This is also true of Xia's book, in terms of its theoretical background, which has a unique relationship of art with ideas and previous achievements.

Due to the deep influence of Soviet literature and art upon the May Fourth Movement, as well as the given international political situation of the early 1950s, art theory and creation in New China was greatly impacted by the creative principles of Soviet realism, the gist of which is that "artists are required to realistically, historically and specifically depict reality in the development of revolution. At the same time, the authenticity of artistic depiction and the specificity of history must be combined with the task of reforming and educating working people in ideological thoughts with a socialist spirit."[5] As in every stage of the development of literature and art in New China, these principles were mirrored in the theoretical system of Xia's work.

When the left-wing film movement was at the height of prosperity, dramatic films also reached their golden age. "The structure of the dramatic film," wrote Xia, "possessed a supreme dominant position in the film world of China and abroad. Although the Italian neorealist film was rising vigorously in the 1950s, it was only in its realistic subject matter, its social significance of themes and their affinity to the people, as well as its cinematic forms and devices, that it exerted an influence on the filmmakers of New China. This trend did not strike a destructive blow to the formal system and method of codification of the dramatic film in China.'' Xia's book, a complete text on screenwriting techniques combined with features of the Soviet montage school, summarizes, perfects and develops the genre of dramatic movies.

In order to meet the demands of practical theory, and because of his deep foundation in the culture and in art, Xia permeated his work on screenwriting with the Yingxi tradition peculiar to Chinese film, working it into the genre which combines the dramatic film with Soviet montage. This was a merger of the narrative patterns of ancient Chinese operas and novels and civilized drama, adapted to the nation's situation after the May Fourth Movement. The organic fusion of these things forms the unique theoretical body of the book which is Xia's contribution to film theory in New China. A generalization of the broad and rich phenomena of film art, it also embodies a convergence of collaborative efforts made by two generations of artists.

The framework of this practical theory was manifested in the book through the following:

1. Purpose. As the first requirement of thematic art, purpose was related to an understanding of the functions of film. Within the framework of practical theory, the answer was clear: ''Film is the most popular and the most powerful weapon of propaganda.'' In other words, film should ''reform and educate people in ideological terms with socialist spirit.'' To achieve this, a filmic work must be distinctive in the ideological content of its theme. In the formal system, each and every code must provide a rigid structure for its conveyance. At the same time, as a work concentrating solely on screenwriting devices, its emphasis on rigid purposefulness also meets the given need of dramatic film structure. The core of the dramatic film is a rigid and solid chain of plot. As Xia emphasized: ''Any piece of the plot, or any action, dialogue, set or prop, must have a definite purpose. Every push or pull of the camera, cross-cut or close-up must be even more distinctive.'' Purposefulness requires not only a distinctive theme, but also a precise structure.

2. Typicality. Typification is a special proposition of realist art. In our realism-based theoretical system, it is also the essential core. Typification serves as the primary way to load and carry the theme, mainly by abstracting, generalizing and reconstructing reality. In the theoretical framework of the book, purposefulness and typicality are closely interrelated. Artistic expression of rigid purpose constructs a typical environment so as to portray ''typical characters in typical environments,'' which directly embody the thematic ideas. Xia defined a typical environment as ''a synthesis of time, place and social background,'' the gist of which lay in ''the political atmosphere and the pulse of the times.'' Xia demands of screenwriters that ''every typical environment and typical time has its typical scene; you must understand it.'' This demand contains the specific law of practical theory concerning artistic conduct and processing, which is that it must reflect life. It requires that the microcosm of art not only partially duplicate and represent life, but also reconstruct life according to given themes or frameworks.

3. Affinity to the people. This, in the system of practical theory, is crucial, for it embodies and inevitably extends the given understanding of the features and functions of art.

To have a close affinity to the people is the only way to actualize the purpose of art as a revolutionary weapon and propaganda instrument. With regard to the specific form of cinema, an affinity to the people is not only an extension of the features of the art, but also an understanding of its nature. "Characteristic of film is its popularity. . . . Film is the most popular art, and the language of film literature is a direct instrument for propaganda and the education of hundreds of millions." Therefore, Xia Yan insisted that "when taking up a pen to write a screenplay, the first thing to bear in mind is that your writing is intended for hundreds of thousands of working people, which requires popularization of film art, and that cinematic language and structural devices must be simple, explicit and easy to understand."

The claim that requires art, especially film art, to develop a high affinity to the people establishes in itself a specific practical/theoretical criterion: The majority of the people must be able to understand it. Disputed for dozens of years, this proposition was recently argued further and modified in critical comments over a number of films. However, it has been an authoritative criterion up to now. In Xia's discussion, the criterion serves also as one of the principles for making films. "Whether or not the majority of the people can fully and smoothly understand is supposed to be the right principle. . . . The films we shoot ought to be understood by the Chinese, by working people." This is a practical theoretical coordinate, with time/politics on a longitudinal axis and people/nation on the latitudinal, while typicality is an important constant. It requires that form serve content, and that aesthetics give maximum service to cognitive and educational functions.

A DIRECTED PURSUIT OF FILM FORM: NATIONALIZATION

If the literature and art of the May Fourth Movement caused a "great break" between modern and classical traditional art in China, contemporary art in New China, then, with its distinctive modern ideology and new language structure, its themes and unique patterns, has created an obvious displacement. If it can be said that "Chinese literature and art in the Twentieth Century takes reform of the national soul as its general theme,"[6] then contemporary art has used a sub-theme, opposed to the critical and negative direction Lu Xun suggested. As a positive sub-theme, it "explores the 'backbone of the Chinese' and calls for the rise of a generation of new people, or portrays ideal heroes the whole society could follow."[7] This also is one of the connotations of typicality in the framework of practical theory.

The crucial claim for theme determines at the same time the specific formal system and language structure of contemporary Chinese art. It is not that a new form or language produces a "displacement" from traditional arts, so that it conveys a reflective consciousness and is self-referential; the truth is that the routine method of codification, emphasized so as to gain as many spectators as possible, manifests directly the demands of New China's art for purposefulness and popularity. This, in Xia's book, becomes a directed pursuit of film form: the nationalization of film art. It can be said that contemporary art in New China again breaks the intense, dynamic balance between tradition and innovation.

Different from the May Fourth Movement, it is biased this time toward tradition, the rediscovery of national arts. The intention is to bring the art forms introduced after the May Fourth Movement into line with their endless flow, to "make the past serve the present and foreign things serve China" and to excavate and use the arts the broad masses "love to see and hear" so as to "achieve education and propaganda."

Xia expresses this directive in simple language: "No matter what we are going to do, we must first consider whether 600 million Chinese can understand and appreciate it. Our service is meant for the 600 million who want us to make our films in the national forms and national styles of China. This is perfectly justified, and it's our duty and responsibility to satisfy them." In practical theory "this is not a technical question, but a political question, a question of who film serves."

This proposition of the times, in Xia's book, is primarily presented as follows:

1. Purpose and form. In order to "achieve education and propaganda," Xia demands that the form used in film "in the first place be understood and appreciated by the masses," that is to say, it should conform to national tastes and psychology. The most direct way to do this is to use the accomplished conventional forms of art; that is, forms characterized by distinctive national styles, so as to eliminate "the sense of alienation" new languages of art inevitably bring with them. The routine codification of these national forms is supposed to make them easy to understand, so that the film audience can easily and willingly accept their themes and so that the realistic art of socialism will form a perfectly harmonious relationship with most viewers.

   Xia suggests that screenwriters derive nourishment directly from traditional operas and novels, as well as classical theories, and continue to develop the tradition of the dramatic film and the "shadowplay film" of the 1930s and 1940s.

2. Identification and coercion. Xia's argument on the formal techniques of screenwriting is based on the theory of identification, which requires that art be used to move the audience, to affect its viewers and to make them change their facial expressions. He points out, "When a tragic scene comes, the entire audience heaves a deep sigh and weeping can be heard. To so move them is good. On the contrary, if the audience is disquieted and cannot concentrate at a certain point in the development of the story, the scene was not very well handled." What is required is to allow the audience to "indulge in the play," to identify with the film rather than be quiet spectators, alienated from it. Since cinema is a one-way communication, Xia emphasizes that film should use montage to achieve identification, to forcibly guide the audience. To do this successfully, Xia makes a specific requirement for dramatic film: "What's important is to interlock one ring tightly with another, without a letup or break, so that every link, every piece of the plot, is in accord with the mind and emotions of the audience."

3. Narrative and composition. In order to realize identification, Xia makes specific demands on the elements of narration. He stresses "the weight of the theme thought" and "the plots and actions that reflect it." He suggests that the construction of the chain of the plot be tight, clear and fluent, and that "one ring be tightly interlocked with another" so as to endow the actions of characters and events with the rich dimension of time. This specifically embodies the affinity of art with the people and

the nationalization of art forms.

Xia points out that the leading role "is the character who can most convey the theme," that "the most important point is that the leading role must be vividly and distinctively depicted." The first appearance of a character must have three essentials: "First, a brief introduction, second, characterization, and third, entry into the play. The brief introduction ought to be natural and explicit. . . . Upon entering the scene, the actor must be distinctive in character. . . . Only a distinctive character can attract the audience's attention. . . . To enter into the play is to immediately raise questions," that is, to construct dramatic suspense.

A screenwriter should immediately involve the audience in the climactic situation specific to the drama, and the chain of the plot should spontaneously unfold a process of dramatic crisis. This is precisely what a dramatic movie requires. As for a Chinese dramatic film, however, Xia not only requires that a character enter into the action and involve himself at once in the dramatic crisis, but also insists that a character "strike a pose" in his action and "brief his origin and background" through his own action or dialogue. In view of the specific appreciative habits of our nation, Xia emphasizes that what's important is to make a clear introduction. He even makes the specific suggestion that important scenes "be shot with close-ups, and the actor be clearly articulate in pronunciation."

Within the formal system of film, the most important aspect of composition is montage. It is interesting that although the theory and practice of the Soviet socialist film is widely quoted in Xia's book, he does not follow the classic definition of montage, which serves as the flag and soul of the Soviet school of film. On the contrary, he chooses a definition by René Clair, who doesn't stress "collision" but "the logical development of plot" and "programming attention." Montage is defined as a fluent editing device. Xia points out that "montage is the method of connecting a film," the way of composing it; its key point is that it must "conform to the logic of life and the visual. . . . If it looks smooth, reasonable, rhythmic and comfortable, then it is brilliant." This is indeed one of the major characteristics of the Chinese dramatic film. It shows impartiality to both Soviet film and the film of the West, especially the Hollywood model, and represents the effort toward nationalization of film form.

By taking the established conventional forms and routine codes of ancient Chinese operas and novels for reference, Xia emphasizes continuity and fluency of plot, argues for the normal order and the completeness of the chain of the plot, and requires that "the plot be specifically explained and carried from the beginning through to the end in an orderly way. . . . The arteries and veins of the plot ought to be clear and unobstructed, and the threads of thought be tightly knit." Thus a film can more directly affect the feelings of the audience, understand and move it more powerfully, and induce it to indulge in the play, identify with the film and accept its theme.

4. Structure and choice. Xia Yan prescribes that the Chinese dramatic film maintain a certain structure in the construction of this orderly chain. He pursues the classical structural model of traditional Chinese art: introduction, development, change and conclusion. "The first part is the beginning, where possible conflicts are foreshadowed through characters and events; the second develops and accumulates them; the third part is the struggle and its transformation; and the fourth is the ending, where the conflicts are solved." Again Xia Yan stresses the power of choice and the purpose-

fulness of art, and argues again that the overall structure of the plot should be concise and fluent, and bear that feature of classical Chinese art which likens the beginning, middle and end of a good work as "the Phoenix's head, the pig's belly and the leopard's tail," respectively.

Such a structure presents another trait of the Chinese dramatic film, which in terms of content reveals a given openness, since it is synchronous with the times and shares an analogous structure with the culture. In terms of form, it suggests a closeness, due to its complete and orderly plot structure. An open world and a closed story is a complex structure, in which entertainment, that is, an art form loved by the masses, and serious political content come together. To achieve a perfect form of art by realizing education through entertainment is to use art as a tool and to make it serve the cause of the Chinese Communist Party to the largest extent.

Today, twenty years after its publication, we benefit tremendously when we read Xia's book. Its significance can never be merely that of a textbook or a thesis on screenwriting, for it marks an entire era in the film history of New China and serves as a key to our understanding of many of its artistic phenomena.

Time is passing, and the theory and practice of art are continuously changing and evolving. Discussions of the issues of nationalization are still intensifying, and the structures of film art have already shown their pursuit of multiformity, while the system of practical aesthetics continues to progress. This book of Xia Yan's, however, as an important step on our road of progress, will constantly provide us with new inspiration and enlightenment.

NOTES

1. Xia Yan, *Problems of Screenwriting*, Beijing: China Film Press, 1959. Unless otherwise attributed, quotations in this chapter are from this work.

2. Lu Xun, "The Revolutionary Literature of the Chinese Proletariate and the Blood Shed by the Pioneers," in *Double-Hearted: A Collection of Essays*.

3. Theoretical program passed at the Inaugural Meeting of the Alliance of the Left-Wing Writers.

4. Mao Zedong, "On New Democratism," in *Selected Works of Mao Zedong*, vol. 2, p. 701.

5. "The Constitution of the Association of Writers of the Soviet Union," in *Literary and Art Issues of the Soviet Union*, pp. 12–13.

6. Huang Ziping, Chen Pingyuan and Qian Liqun, "On Chinese Literature of the Twentieth Century," *Literary Criticism*, no. 5, 1985.

7. Ibid.

Part IV

The Entertainment Film

Following the aesthetics of Confucius, Chinese film used to emphasize the function of film in moral and political education. After 1949, the Communist Party combined this traditional view with its own political principles and made Chinese film a propaganda instrument. Since the 1970s, some of the Party's political principles, as well as traditional Chinese culture, have received critical reexamination and reevaluation, first in Xie Jin's model and later in the works of the Fifth Generation. Meanwhile, with the economic reform and the modernization movement in the society, economic consideration of film gradually increased, while ideological consideration declined. Entertainment film, rather than ideological film, began to be an important trend. Entertainment film was important not only for its commercial potential, but also for its ideological and cultural significance. Like the Xie Jin model and the Fifth Generation, but from another direction, the entertainment film is opposed to the principles of traditional Chinese culture and also of those of the Communist Party.

The trend toward entertainment had earlier been seen as only a matter of commerce and had never been given serious ideological consideration. In 1987, however, a group of radical film critics tried to justify the entertainment film in ideological terms by declaring it in conflict with the traditional culture and with the Party's political principles. This initiated a debate in which they argued that traditional culture emphasized the submission of the individual to society and the repression of personal desires, whereas the entertainment film provided a release, not a repression, of personal desires. Therefore, the entertainment film gave a position to the individual that traditional culture had not. Of Dialogues I, II and III, presented in the following chapters, the commercial entertainment film is given a radical color in ideology in Dialogue I, while in Dialogues II and III, other filmmakers and scholars advocate entertainment films, from more moderate and traditional assumptions. Under the influence of these discussions, the entertainment film reached its peak and became an important trend in the later 1980s. The issue of the entertainment film became so popular that the slogan "The entertainment film should be the mainstream in China" became a basic theme of the 1988 Conference on the Entertainment Film and was even approved of by liberal authorities.

From beginning to end, of course, the discussion on the entertainment film was controversial. At the end of 1987, shortly after the discussion began, the opinions of radical film critics were strongly criticized by another group of critics, and after 1989, the entertainment film, as both a filmmaking trend and a theoretical position, was officially denounced. "The film should follow mainstream ideology" (*zhu xuan ying pian*) became the new official slogan.

9

The Entertainment Film: Dialogue I

Yao Xiaomong
Translated by Fu Binbin

Participants:

Chen Xihe: Research Fellow, China Film Art Research Center

Hao Dazheng: Research Fellow, China Film Art Research Center

Kong Du: Professor, Beijing Film Institute

Li Tuo: Critic, Beijing Writers' Association

Place:

The editorial offices of *Contemporary Cinema*

Time:

October 15, 1986

REVIEW OF AN OLD TOPIC

Chen Xihe: The entertainment film recently has come under endless discussion. Zhong Dianfei brought up once again the question of box office value; Shen Jiming published an article on audience psychology in *Contemporary Cinema*; Li Tuo and Chen Huangmei released their correspondence on melodrama. In addition, we have had Shao Mujun's exposition on commercial film and Zheng Dongtian's speech on commercialism at a recent conference of film directors. Although this issue has always been considered, I think it is necessary now to bring it to the forefront.

During 1985, two significant discussions arose, one about experimental narratives and the other about entertainment films. At the time, both debates attracted the attention of the media. Toward the end of the year, experimental narratives were criticized and suppressed, but at the 1986 selection conference for the Golden Rooster Awards, their reputation was restored, and at the very next meeting they were given some recognition. However, serious conclusions about entertainment films have yet to be made, in part because some have been crudely made, but also in part because many people still adhere to the traditional view that such films don't appeal to refined tastes.

In 1985, more entertainment films were produced than in the entire decade of the New Era—more, in fact, than since the founding of the Republic. Every studio attached great importance to commercial entertainment. This was no accident. Since the studios had close contact with distribution, and had direct audience feedback through financial reports, they sensed that audience demand for entertainment was on the rise. Consequently, they elevated the production of such films to a higher position. In contrast, theoretical circles ignored them. That's why it's necessary now to consider on a theoretical level the films designed as entertainment, to elucidate the rationality for and values of entertainment in theoretical terms. Although weighty and systematic writings on the subject are still not on the horizon, different opinions have already been articulated.

This flood of entertainment movies must have been brought about by the changes in the socioeconomic system, which led people to modify their thinking and to reconsider consumerism. First, the socioeconomic reforms made people aware that striving for commercial gain, economic efficiency and box-office value is not a disgrace; second, the economic reforms changed our conception of social life and stimulated our awareness of consumption. In the past, for example, food and clothing only satisfied hunger and kept us warm, but food is now a matter of taste and nutrition, and clothing a matter of fashion. Works of art no longer serve only as vehicles for moral principles and dogmatic teachings, but also bring pleasure and mental recreation. As long as modern life remains intense and fast-paced, people need change and relaxation. If there is a difference between "refinement" and "popularity" in art, then literature probably emphasizes refinement and motivates thought, whereas film leans more toward popularity, providing relaxation and entertainment, though, of course, films of refinement can also be made.

Li Tuo: Let me get a word in here. If we want to change Chinese film, we first must find a breakthrough point. Where is that point? It's supposedly different in different times. A few years ago, it was probably right to encourage experimental narratives. As middle-aged directors reached maturity and the Fifth Generation arose, the experimental narrative consolidated its position and achieved recognition. *Yellow Earth*, for example, had widespread support from audiences in Shanghai and elsewhere. This is in no way a matter of the preferences of only a few experts.

Chen Xihe: Social recognition of avant-garde films has a lot to do with what the critics say. This isn't the case with popular films.

Li Tuo: *Yellow Earth* and others have already found their own audiences, so the experimental narrative is no longer an issue. What worries me now is that we might take it too far. The other day, at a meeting of the Filmmakers' Association, when I said that twelve or so experimental filmmakers is enough, someone responded: "A dozen or so is not enough. We should have another dozen, or more!" It seems to me that since a single film now costs 60,000 yuan, and some even more, if we make ten experimental narratives a year, that adds up to 7 or 8 million. That's already a heavy load. What more do you want? Even in the major filmmaking nations, experimental filmmakers are a rare sight these days: two or three in Germany, three or four in France and no more . . .

Hao Dazheng: There's only Alain Resnais in France, and in Italy, only Federico Fellini and Michelangelo Antonioni. As for the other big countries, there are no "pure" directors at all.

Li Tuo: A dozen or so is more than enough for China. Whether or not their works show real skill is yet another story. Anyway, what they pursue is the avant-garde, the experimental, which is why our next step should be to give more attention to entertainment. Currently, some people deride us for having advocated the new concept of film and experimentation, but now we've come to the end of our tether and must return to the entertainment film.

This notion does have its interesting side. Personally, however, I believe if it hadn't been for those previous efforts, including changes of cinematic concepts, research into cinematic specialties on both practical and theoretical levels, as well as explorative filmmaking—if there hadn't been those attempts, today's discussion of entertainment films would be dangerous, because shooting entertainment films without a solid grasp of the cinematic elements and modern film language may produce nothing but nonsense. Now that we do have some experimental narratives and directors, it's possible to go back and work on entertainment films, especially in theoretical research. Furthermore, this problem is increasingly urgent and should be put on the production schedule. Anyone who continues to ignore it is a fool.

I quite agree with Chen Xihe. When we talked about entertainment films in the past, none of us, including myself, took cultural changes into account. Now we understand the issue of entertainment on a higher level, that is, as an issue of the consumer-and-entertainment culture that has emerged in contemporary China.

Chen Xihe: Pop music, pop songs, popular novels, disco . . .

Li Tuo: Right. The emergence of the entertainment culture is actually a negation of Chinese feudalist culture, a struggle of a new culture against the old.

Hao Dazheng: Let me be an alarmist. Consider this paradox: if we had allowed popular culture (pop novels, music, entertainment films) to continue its course after Liberation, through our socialist methods of creativity and the high ideological consciousness of our audience, China would now have a first-rate popular culture internationally. This, of course, couldn't happen. We can explain it this way: denial of popular culture was the price we had to pay in order to achieve a major turning point in our history. But in the end, we bungled an opportune moment. That's my first point.

My second is that popular culture came into existence before consumerism and will disappear much later. That is, a consumer society has a shorter lifespan. I'm afraid that's nothing we can control; maybe we can call it a "law." Refined or not, everyone likes entertainment films, and that includes me. I'm constantly taken as a guy obsessed with "empty theories" *(everyone laughs)*, but my interest in entertainment films is no less than my interest in refined movies, even greater. The feeling a gentleman had in the time of George Melies, when he lowered the brim of his hat before sneaking into a moviehouse, is still with us. You feel ashamed to admit you like entertainment films, and the maker of such films cannot help but feel unworthy of your company. You're both making psychological distortions, although from opposite sides of the matter. As for me, when I view an entertainment film, I'm governed by feelings separate from other viewing experiences. It's a different sensation, rather pleasant, to be honest. I wonder if there's more than one mechanism at work in the brain when we view a film. There must be. The trouble is that different mechanisms cannot be modified by human power. In this regard, people are still free.

Li Tuo: Why are entertainment films invariably profitable? Nobody can outdo Hollywood, not Antonioni, not Fellini. The last time I went to Europe, I found that although many intellectuals looked down on films made only for entertainment, ordinary people, including the intellectuals, went to them when they needed to be amused. Yet if you asked them what they liked to see most, they'd still insist on Fellini or Antonioni. If you mentioned Steven Spielberg, they'd frown and tell you he's in bad taste, but they go to his movies nonetheless. This is an unconscious self-repression.

Hao Dazheng: Self-repression? That's the "job" of the superego. The more refined you are, the more strongly it affects you.

Chen Xihe: Let me say a word about this. Why do we consider consumerism and pleasure self-indulgent? In feudal society, only a king or emperor had access to these things. It would be more humanistic if everyone had the same privileges.

Hao Dazheng: Want to know what films Jiang Qing and Wang Hongwen liked? That might prove interesting, psychological material worthy of study.

Chen Xihe: Mass production of entertainment films mirrors the present rise of consumerism, and this in itself is a reflection of changes in the overall socioeconomic and ideological structures. In other words, artistic entertainment films give expression to changes in social and ideological structures. In this sense, films made for entertainment can be considered a distorted reflection of changes in the political and economic structure of our society. I think in our analysis of the entertainment film as a genre, we can integrate Marxist sociology with Freudian psychoanalysis in our methodology, because the formation of the psyche reflects the formation of the economic and historical conditions of society. That's why it can be said that the emergence of entertainment films reflects a change in our economic and ideological structure. At the same time, it represents a change in artistic form itself. Unlike *Villagers* (1985–1986) and other films that directly depict the Reform, entertainment films could never have come into consequence without the present atmosphere, the present situation and concepts of reform.

Yao Xiaomeng: If I remember correctly, in his analysis of advanced capitalism, Althusser pointed out that changes in consumption bring a change in ideological structure. He wrote that changes in social life, brought forth by high consumption and a variety of other factors, turn humans into one-dimensional creatures who have lost their critical class-consciousness. Once people reach equality in their consuming habits, they "partially change their traditional view of social status and class." If so, then the appearance of entertainment films in China as a kind of consumer culture becomes even more significant. Because they entertain people from all social levels and classes, they're more democratic.

Obviously, entertainment films, namely popular films, must improve their art; that is, popular films need to explore themselves. I've always insisted that we can't stay at the same level and merely emphasize their commercial value. The basic problem is whether or not we can further explore their value as art. If the aesthetic value of entertainment films cannot improve, they'll remain mediocre no matter how many we make. People are currently changing their ideas of consumption. As I just said, it's a problem of values.

In classical economics, value means the value of labor, and the value of a movie depends on how much abstract labor is needed to make it. Modern Western economics stresses the theory of diminishing returns. To a thirsty man, the first cup of water has the highest value, and the second and third cups have increasingly less. Similarly, *Shaolin Temple* (1982), the first of its kind, had the highest value, whereas *Shaolin Kids* (1986), *Heroic Lads* (1985) and *Shaolin Disciples* (1983), decreased successively in value until many people became bored with martial arts films. This is why, as once again we discuss the entertainment film, we should pay more attention to artistry and experimentation. Even Hollywood entertainment and genre films are constantly changing and developing, to meet the ever-changing needs of a consumer society. The aesthetics and cinematic devices of experimental and art films can also be used for reference in the making of entertainments.

Hao Dazheng: Refined films represent what's deep, while popular movies display what's on the surface, but as long as it's film, it cannot help but provide direct audiovisual stimulation. A popular movie is supposed to display what's on the surface to the extreme, for that's its aim, whereas a refined film takes what's on the surface as a pretext, as a vehicle in the realization of its purpose. Popular movies provide the cultural foundation and financial support of refined films. Without a sufficient number, refined films couldn't survive.

Yao Xiaomeng: Popular films and refined films are interlinked.

Li Tuo: What you said is important, but the problem at hand is which should be given first priority. If I say eating is important, you might ask, "Isn't drinking?" Of course it is. What's most important is what you actually need most at the moment. You propose that popular films and refined films are interlinked. Of course they are, but this is not the time to emphasize that fact, for the more you do, the less of a chance you'll have to make entertainment movies in the future.

Chen Xihe: What's the major problem we want to solve in today's discussion? We want, first of all, to assert that it is perfectly justifiable to make a film to satisfy the need for entertainment. Clearly this relates to other considerations.

[At this moment, Kong Du enters. After being briefed on what has previously been discussed, he immediately begins to "play his part."]

Kong Du: Entertainment films are like handicrafts. Does every household hang the same stuff on the wall? You can never tell for sure what a family will choose. If you like a carefully decorated piece of cloisonné, fine, but if someone else likes rococo, what are you to do? You have to satisfy him, too. This is consumerism, a sort of cultural consumption. If someone likes something, he or she can simply go out and buy it. Handicrafts shouldn't all be the same color. Maybe you like abstract paintings, so you buy one and take it home feeling really good about it—but a lot of people don't enjoy modern stuff. They may still prefer overly elaborate, brightly colored illustrations. No matter what you like, you have to take their wishes into consideration. If we addressed the issue this way, it would become more understandable.

Hao Dazheng: Popular films have always been around, except for that one specific period when they were banned [the Cultural Revolution]. Now it's just a matter of restoration. They were held by the throat, but once the grip was loosened, we found they were still alive—that's all there is to it.

Chen Xihe: But conditions have changed. In fact, the issue of entertainment grew out of the atmosphere surrounding reform.

Hao Dazheng: It's really not a new problem, nor is it something brought forth by reform. There's no need to associate it so tightly with reform.

Li Tuo: Maybe this isn't the case for popular culture in the abstract, but the popular culture we're talking about now is different in nature from that.

Hao Dazheng: I disagree. You still need to make up a lesson you missed about what was made as early as the 1940s and 1950s. Movies based on Qiong Yao's bestsellers were already passé in Taiwan when they became the vogue here, a disparity of at least a dozen years. What's the difference?

Li Tuo: It's still different in nature. Let me give you an example. A popular culture such as Hollywood is completely different from the popular European culture of the eighteenth or nineteenth century. The popular songs that are now prevalent in China are likewise different from American pop songs.

Hao Dazheng: If you released song-and-dance and anti-westerns now, ordinary people in China wouldn't accept them. You need to start back at the very beginning. Zhang Xianliang insisted that capitalism was unsurpassable, a proposition well worth thinking about. It's useless to suppress it. Didn't we begin to discuss Western theories in the 1980s, starting with Bazin, who in the West belongs to the 1950s and 1960s? We may have caught up quickly; however, we've been in a great hurry, and we still lack a deep understanding of them. I suppose our entertainment films need to start from Hollywood in 1949. We have to start from where we left off, no doubt about it, and frankly, that means to return to Hollywood. The French did this in the 1950s, and it proved very positive, with few side effects.

Li Tuo: Shao Mujun correctly held that the term "commercial" is often rejected by the Chinese because their traditional mindset regards agriculture as superior to commerce. They're annoyed when you mention commerce.

Chen Xihe: I think we'd better call it the entertainment film, because we are speaking of it in connection with the psychology of aesthetics. As a concept of consumerism, "entertainment film" is also a good term. Of course, once it goes into social consumption, it has box-office value and therefore becomes a filmic product for commercial profit. But we're not discussing how a film can accumulate more capital. That's not our approach on this level. We've generally insisted that literature and art convey moral principles; now we're talking about their nature as entertainment. Both relate to the function of literature and art. That's why "entertainment film" is the better term.

IS THERE AN AESTHETIC FOR THE ENTERTAINMENT FILM?

Chen Xihe: In fact, recognition of the demand for and the value of entertainment films involves re-thinking human nature and our psychic structure. If we divide psychic structure into the rational and the perceptual, art, as an externalization of our intrinsic power, deals primarily with emotions and perception. But in Chinese tradition, only after being standardized by practical reality and our ethical code can we express our feelings and emotions. Confucius said, "Expression of emotions should be confined within rituals."

Yao Xiaomeng: In *Mao Shi Da Xu [Introduction to Poetry*, by Mao], probably.

Chen Xihe: Yes, that is, do not see anything that doesn't conform to ritual. According to that, most films, then, are not supposed to express the abstract. He also said, "Do not listen to abstractions, do not speak to them, and do not practice them." In other words, abstractions should be eliminated. Thus the Chinese ethical code directly influences creativity, for it sees the ultimate purpose of art as moral perfection. In the expression of human nature and feelings, only works that conform to ethics and rituals should exist. As a result, Confucian idealists of the Song and Ming Dynasties later proposed to "cherish heavenly principles and perish human desires." This is how they understood and normalized humanity. The result is that natural human feelings that ought to be acknowledged and expressed were repressed in feudal society as immoral and irrational.

Now, as we can see, these same feelings may be expressed, which is why Sigmund Freud's research into the subconscious is regarded as a rediscovery of humanity and an affirmation of our natural character and its legitimate existence. Therefore, what we should get from artistic expression, including entertainment films, is not only a moral and rational education, but also entertainment, pleasure. In this regard, it is a betrayal of the traditional culture. Although this new principle has yet to be encouraged theoretically, it has already been put into practice by *Popular Film* and *Popular TV*. The front covers of both magazines have long refused to obey the "moral doctrines," but have instead provided pleasure. If they didn't print photos of movie stars, they'd never sell. If we still refuse to affirm theoretically that people have such hopes and desires . . .

Li Tuo: There's another problem with visual pleasure, which is its psychology. Traditionally, the Chinese principle of pleasure emphasizes pleasure through moral perfection, while in the West, pleasure is achieved through knowledge. . . .

Yao Xiaomeng: In fact, this is where Western philosophy and Confucianism completely differ in their orientation of "goodness." In Confucian philosophy, "goodness" is accepted as a necessity of extrinsic disciplines; therefore, "once self-abnegation is realized and the ancient rites are restored, the whole world finds its way to humanity." In contrast, in Kantian philosophy, "goodness" represents a principle of self-discipline. Taking rationalistic self-judgment as his premise, Socrates held that seeking the real is the fundamental way to the ultimate good. What's interesting is that "goodness" based on ethics in Confucianism is sometimes taken as a pleasure from the acquisition of knowledge. For instance, an antithetical couplet in *Story of the Western Chamber* reads: "Learning comes from insights into human affairs / writing originates out of wisdom of the ways of the world."

Chen Xihe: Freud's "pleasure" of the subconscious has always been rejected in China. I'm afraid the truth is that the sort of unconstrained pleasure one really feels is bound to be irrational and amoral. It primarily follows the "pleasure principle."

Hao Dazheng: Amoral doesn't mean anti-moral. The thinking that there are two sides to every issue always muddles problems of this kind and wastes a lot of time.

Yao Xiaomeng: The "cherishing heavenly principles and perishing human desires" of the rationalists of the Song and Ming Dynasties could well be considered the culmination of traditional Chinese philosophy. It severely affected the culture. Yet interestingly enough, it is in the Song Dynasty that Zhou Bangyuan's matchless amorous Ci-poems [lyrics] and Hua Ben stories appeared. Later, in the Ming Dynasty, marketplace literature, including pornography, began to emerge in large quantity, forming a literary revolt against traditional philosophy. *The Three Yan and the Two Pai*, edited by Feng Menglong; the folk songs of the Ming Dynasty; as well as *Jin Ping Mei*, our first romantic novel, were among these works.

Here I'd like to give particular attention to the folk songs. Feng Menglong edited two collections, *Guazhier* and *Mountain Songs*. In quantity and quality, the folk songs of the Ming Dynasty have never been equaled, but they have never gotten the attention they deserve. Why? Because most are descriptions of bold, ardent love between men and women, things absolutely excluded from the "rituals." However, at least we can perceive in them that the larger population dug its own channel for catharsis in the repressive atmosphere of "cherishing heavenly principles and perishing human desires."

This is also true of film. That is, a film also operates on two planes. On one plane are the overt expressions of meanings as determined by the text; on the other are its effects upon the subconscious. For example, when we saw "model dramas" during the Cultural Revolution, on the one plane, we were getting the so-called revolutionary education, while on the other, many were asking: "Why isn't Fang Haizhen married?" Thus, while viewing *The Seaport* (1972), subconsciously audiences were also imagining Fang Haizhen's sex life.

Chen Xihe: That's true. Let me give another example. Karl Marx undertook serious scientific research, but he also read the novels of Alexander Dumas for entertainment. Considered in terms of human nature, even a great teacher of revolution responded to his subconscious.

Li Tuo: I suppose in our theoretical research we should consider the pleasure of the subconscious. Both of you are speaking in terms of psychocultural structures, and certainly you could study the collective unconscious in traditional culture. The core of Confucian culture lies in its pursuit of the ideal personality, its moral-centricity or moral determinism. Ancient sages such as Yao, Shun and Yu have been discussed repeatedly in the quest for the ideal. "The Divine land of China is filled with 600 million Shuns and Yaos." Everyone can be a Yao or a Shun. This has had a profound influence on art. Ancient poetry, for example, represents the pursuit of the ideal, be it in poems of mountains and waters, allegories, pastorals, or poems about the frontier. This pursuit, to be sure, had its advantages. Fan Zhongyan's "worry before everyone worries, be happy only after everyone is happy," for instance, certainly represents anxiety.

But the other side of the story is that it also had drawbacks for Chinese culture. It denied entertainment as one of the major purposes of culture, as well as satisfaction of various desires through forms of amusement. Art for entertainment was more often than not hindered or restricted by Confucian culture. Why did the Ci-poems of the Five Dynasties and Song Dynasty have a lower position than other poetry in the eyes of officials and the literati? Because they usually contained lots of "non-ritualistic" material—material related to feelings and emotions. Another example is in the pre-Confucian *Book of Songs*: "To a lady of gentleness and grace / a nobleman is wooing his court." Clearly these two lines are about love, but in ancient times, interpreters of poetry were good at giving irrelevant and strained interpretations. Confucius insisted, "Of the three hundred poems in *the Book of Songs*, in a word, there are no evil thoughts." But in his *Interpreting the Book of Songs*, Zhu Xi in the song dynasty admitted that there were indeed bawdy poems in the book.[1] Although he was honest, he was also critical and thought such poems should not to be tolerated. In short, literature and art became "civilizing" instruments and then forms of entertainment. In response, traditional popular culture diversified to include such entertainments as dragon lantern shows, land boat dances and the like.

Hao Dazheng: For more than two thousand years, Chinese culture choked in the suffocating air of Confucianism. Nevertheless, the undercurrent of popular culture continued to flow without compromise. The oral tradition found in local operas, Dagu in the North and Pingtan in the South, as well as folk songs in the forms of Huaer and Xintianyou, continued without interruption.

After Liberation, popular culture came under increasing attack, usually through the crude form of *laogai* (reform through labor). Yet even though the popular culture could be brought to a halt for a time, the population's demand for entertainment could not be "reformed" or abolished. It could only be suppressed, by warning, "No entertainment allowed. Violators will be fined." We should include this problem in our theoretical study.

Althusser proposed that a society needs stability. Yet within society there will inevitably be conflicts and contradictions. One cannot crudely blurt out all his thoughts. Social stability requires the repression of primitive desires through a number of devices so as to secure the normal operation of a society. Althusser divided repression into the basic repression required by any civilized society and the additional repression required in a given culture at a given social stage. After Liberation, we went so far beyond the additional repression a society needs that everything personal was suppressed. In governing the country, personal will prevailed over the laws of social development and produced a series of social upheavals. Cultural hunger was one result. As soon as the doors of the country were slightly ajar, every corner echoed with the song: "Having slept lethargically for a hundred years . . . " A hungry person is not choosy about his food. How pitiful and sad! Now there's not just the problem of reaffirming and restoring popular culture, but of establishing a rational social position for it. This is also a task our research should shoulder.

Chen Xihe: Although art as a whole is the expression of perception, it never is unalterable. The principle of realism in creativity stresses more often than not the rational side of perception, for it makes a logical contemplation of reality. However, an entertainment film is more likely to follow the irrationality of emotions. As is true of music, too, the rigid principle of realism cannot be applied to the entertainment film. In a martial arts film, the story line is secondary; what is important is the fighting. The organization of the fighting as a formal element conveys the tensions and repressions one feels in actuality. A martial arts film might be set in ancient times, but the aesthetic experience is entirely modern. Thus, in an entertainment film, the aesthetic experience and meaning conveyed through its form is quite important. This is entirely different from realistic films or experimental narratives.

One of the major explorations in films of the New Era, the examination of the human condition and the representation of the values, desires, and ultimately the fate of humanity, has been encouraged since 1976. But this is only one side of the matter. On the other side, entertainment films take their own forms as manifestations of humanity and construct an exchange, a dialogue for the basic demands of human nature. In the past we only accepted the rational plane, thinking that it alone had the right to exist, and refused to affirm the perceptual plane, that is, perceptions which violate logic and moral principles. If we now accept these perceptions through entertainment films, then what they have achieved, in a sense, is a more complete person. Thus entertainment films, experimental narratives and realistic films together compose a more complete structure of humanity.

Hao Dazheng: Hypocrites who posed as men of high morals but were privately dirty and licentious have always been a part of our society. Why? Because the more you repress, the more counteraction you get. If the right way is tightly blocked, one has to take the wrong one. That's even worse.

Yao Xiaomeng: We've said that the psychology of entertainment in film meets our need for catharsis of the irrational and the subconscious, and that the subconscious originates from the repression of consciousness. I guess cinematic entertainment, then, could be considered anti-repressive.

Repression may be approached from two sides: the physiological, or basic, repression Chen Xihe has already explained in humanistic terms, and social repression, the accumulated traditional or moral consciousness and the converse mentality initiated by sociopolitical factors. All are irrationalities hidden deeply in the subconscious. The theme of the infatuated wife with the dishonest husband, for instance, can be found everywhere: in *Life*, in *The Spring River Flows East* (1947-1948), in *Qin Xianglian* (1955), in Gao Ming's *The Story of the Pippa*, in *The Story of Yingying* of the Tang Dynasty, in the Tang legend *The Story of Li Wa*, as well as in "Mang," in *The Book of Songs*. This is the collective unconscious, a national and traditional sense of morality. We could argue that it wasn't Cai Chusheng who made *The Spring River Flows East*, but that the film made Cai Chusheng. *Gao Ming's The Story of the Pippa* was written at the end of the Yuan Dynasty, but early in the Song Dynasty, Lu You had already written "The Story of Cai Zhonglang was heard everywhere in the village." This is popular culture, and was the way women could achieve a catharsis from social repression in the feudal society, in which they were often initially seduced and subsequently deserted. This suggests that entertainment films as a form of popular culture also have the task of reflecting traditional culture.

Li Tuo: What you said is complicated and concerns the reform of Chinese culture. Does it mean, for example, that we should eradicate our belief in honest and upright officials? This is well worth discussing. We are trying to construct a spiritual socialist civilization, but how can we without breaking away from old concepts? Of course, the other side of the story is that in most cases movies made to entertain have to go along with traditional concepts and values. For example, ordinary people in China are particular about filial piety. If our entertainment films launched an all-out attack against filial piety, they would surely fail at the box office, while if we shot a film about a son's filial obedience to his parents, it would easily attract a large audience. Of course, it would have to be carefully made, like *Xi Ying Men* (1981).

What Chen Xihe just gave us are physiological and psychological considerations (let me use these tentative terms for the moment). He talked about our awareness of the irrational, which led us to discuss that, as well as various inner desires, psychological experiences and so on, and you immediately added one more point, the collective unconscious, which reminded me of an article by Bela Balazs in which he analyzed Hollywood films in terms of class. Hollywood films were consciously made to meet the illusions, dreams and feelings of the petty bourgeoisie. They depicted, for example, how a poor man became a millionaire, and so on and so forth. The article is well written and convincing, though of course it's a leftist analysis. The same is true of your point. Both try to relate popular movies to a given social consciousness, but actually, the social consciousness in entertainment movies is more often than not traditional, conservative rather than avant-garde. Popular films throughout the world tend to be traditional and conservative, as are American westerns.

Yao Xiaomeng: American westerns are different now.

Li Tuo: That's another story, which concerns changes in the social mentality and values in American society. For instance, *The Color Purple* (1985), *Indiana Jones and the Last Crusade* (1989), and *Raiders of the Lost Ark* (1981) are greatly different from traditional Hollywood films because they more or less reflect these changes. But no matter what you say, ordinary audiences tend to be conservative and traditional. It is the task of intellectuals to ponder new problems and ideas. That's why intellectuals have become the largest audience for experimental narratives. That's where the difference lies. Therefore, the difficulty of shooting an entertainment film lies in that we have to have a good sense of propriety, of how to go along with the conservative social mentality, yet not overly affect the ideological level of the film or go against the historical course of modern civilization. But, considering the actual situation, what is more important now is to give our people a better understanding of what an entertainment is. In my opinion, at this time, we must emphasize what Chen Xihe said. In fact, the moment you begin to talk about social consciousness, someone's going to respond immediately and stress yet one more time the importance of "education through entertainment."

NOTE

1. Zhu Xi, *Interpreting the Book of Songs*.

10

The Entertainment Film: Dialogue II

Shen Jiming
Translated by Wang Xiaowen

Participants:

Song Chong: President, Beijing Film Studio

Zheng Dongtian: Head of Directing, Beijing Film Institute

Rao Shuguang: Critic, China Film Art Research Center

Place:

The editorial offices of *Contemporary Cinema*

Time:

December 23, 1986

Shen Jiming: For a variety of reasons, the discussion of the entertainment film initiated last year (1985) brought little response. Now, both theoretical and filmmaking circles feel it necessary to raise the subject again. Whether you accept it or not, as many as 70 percent of each studio's productions are entertainments. These movies, now a major part of the landscape of Chinese film, have directly influenced the quality of Chinese film and its box-office values. Though some people think of them as nothing more than martial arts movies, entertainment films have a far broader horizon. Even many filmmakers are still greatly confused about the peculiarities and artistic principles of entertainment movies and have no clear creative understanding of them, because in the past we dared not discuss them openly for fear of being accused of ignoring politics. We also didn't have the guts to discuss them widely as an important subject for theoretical study.

Of the more than 140 films produced last year, only a dozen or so were experimental narratives. I agree that a dozen or so filmmakers working on such movies are enough for China. The majority should stick to entertainment. Some think it easy to make entertainment movies, that whoever wants to make them can do so handily, whether mentally and artistically prepared or not. The results of this supposition are not hard to imagine. Not too long ago, in hopes of correcting this impression through serious research, we invited several people from theoretical circles to discuss the entertainment film, centering on its functions and aesthetic values. Our next step was to invite filmmakers to join the discussion, and ultimately to draw conclusions in theoretical terms. If we continue to do this effectively, I believe it will benefit the development of Chinese film.

ENTERTAINMENT AS IDEA AND CONSCIOUSNESS

Song Chong: To begin with, China should establish an award for best achievement at the box office. Entertainment films have no status in this country, yet they sustain the entire film industry. Today every studio must consider three matters in working out its production plans. One-third of its entire production budget must go to films which will succeed at the box office, another third to those that will not lose money, and the final third must be for experimental works, predestined to lose money. That final third is sustained by the first, which indicates that entertainment films have a large audience. If a movie is appreciated by several million viewers, we shouldn't ignore it, but instead should examine its aesthetic values.

Rao Shuguang: Its aesthetic values are embodied in the size of its audience.

Song Chong: Any film appreciated by the larger population must have some merit, because it meets their need for aesthetics and entertainment. Several years ago, when *Romance in the Lushan Mountains* (1980) was voted an award, some said the award should not be granted. When I heard this, I was annoyed. *Popular Film* had received 2 million votes for it. Were those 2 million people idiots? Their votes indicated their recognition of its artistic attractiveness and ideological content. Even today, entertainment films are not accepted by some of our leaders and artists and a few other people. They are ignored by the government's film awards and left out in the cold by film experts. Only their audience appreciates them. *(Laughter)*

Today three different awards are given for film. The Government Award represents the government's concern for propaganda and education; the Golden Rooster Awards are for explorations, developments and aesthetic achievements in film; the One Hundred Flowers Awards, though related to a certain degree to entertainment films, still emphasize aesthetic and ideological content. These awards are insufficient. I think we should establish an award for best box office achievement, to promote entertainment films. We need to trust the judgment of our artists.

As a director of several entertainment films, I feel frustrated because I am ignored. After shooting *Drip-Drop Guanyin*, I thought it a failure and decided to try one more time, so I made *A Deal under the Gallows Tree*. But many people, including my friends, wrote that I was degenerating and should continue the direction I took in *Carefree Bachelors*. After I shot *Carefree Bachelors*, I was celebrated in the newspapers, received by the government, given a One Hundred Flowers Award and sent abroad. I felt a sudden rise in my scholastic status, too. After I had made several entertainment films, however, I was gradually forgotten by the artists. Thus I felt I was going downward and became determined to take up artistic and experimental films again. This thinking was forced on me by society. Yet if, when asked by audiences what films I had made, I said I had made *The Girl Who Sells Flatcakes* and *A Deal under the Gallows Tree*, they would tell me these films were really terrific. If we don't assert their economic and artistic status, entertainment films have little chance to develop. Both the government and filmmakers ought to adopt certain measures to encourage them.

Entertainment films pay off in terms of visual psychology, as the success of Hollywood clearly shows. When making *A Deal under the Gallows Tree*, I stated publicly that we were going to do an entertainment film, and that our ultimate purpose was to attract and amuse filmgoers and to earn a profit. Objectively, according to statistics of the China Film Corporation for the first half of 1986, *Juvenile Delinquents* won first place at the box office and *A Deal under the Gallows Tree* came in second. But *Juvenile Delinquents* had organized audiences, whereas audiences came to see *A Deal under the Gallows Tree* of their own accord. Thus we can see that I achieved my goal.

The major device I adopted was the Hollywood model, and I put forward four elements: (1) luxurious settings, (2) a fortuitous story, (3) beautiful stars and (4) fashionable costumes. *(Laughter)* And the locations: Shenzhen, Hong Kong, red lanterns and green wine, modern buildings. We chose Hong Kong in consideration of visual psychology. Our entire cast was good-looking, and the costumes, which were the latest from Japan and France, were why many came to see the film. In Freudian terms, you compensate for what you want but cannot have through visions, illusions and dreams. Film is dream. What you want and cannot get can be compensated for on the screen. *A Deal under the Gallows Tree* took advantage of its setting, in Hong Kong and on the mainland. The settings brought novel aesthetic interests to domestic audiences; many more went to see it for this. The aesthetics of the entertainment film must take this into account.

Currently, many high school and college students indulge themselves in Qiong Yao's bestsellers, to compensate for emotional vacancy. After the Cultural Revolution, people favored comedies, because during the years of chaos, they had been repressed, deprived of laughter and spiritually frustrated. To gain spiritual compensation, they were looking for laughter in literature and art.

Shen Jiming: The vice-manager of the Guangdong Film Distribution and Exhibition Company once spoke about the situation in that city. According to him, Guangdong has a generally higher living standard, and because of this, people no longer want to see thrillers. What they want are comedies. The most widely distributed films in 1986 were *Father and Son* (1986) and *A Matter of Life and Death* (1986). People go to the theater solely for recreation, which shows that recreational interests are related to material life. It's a need for consumption.

Song Chong: It's primarily a matter of the rhythms of life. After Guangdong put a market economy into practice, people busied themselves with making a living, and their lives became tense. Working all day long tired them out, and they longed for laughter and relaxation to give them a spiritual release. This is also the case in Hong Kong. In a leisurely society, people favor complicated stories because they have nothing else to do! They have enough time to enjoy them, even those traditional operas that can last dozens of days. Apparently it's somehow related to the rhythms and life-styles of a culture.

Film viewers are our gods and, at the same time, our enemies. When we proposed that filmgoers were our gods, we were criticized for following the vulgar policy of catering to the audience. At the same time, other critics insisted that the viewers were our enemies. In my opinion, while both propositions have a certain validity, generally speaking, both are biased. According to their reasoning, the kind of movie you want to make determines what attitude you should take toward the audience. If you want to make an entertainment film, to amuse filmgoers both mentally and physically, and if you want them to see your film, then they must be your gods. Entertainment films must take their viewers as gods. No good entertainment film could ever be made without first considering the audience. In contrast, if you want to make an experimental film, to break with tradition and customary visual psychology, then traditional viewing habits become an obstacle. In this sense, the audience is an enemy, and accordingly, your film can expect to have few viewers.

In short, considering the significance, purpose and objectives of film-making, of course there are different audiences. In terms of human nature, people are half gods, half devils, and that includes our audiences. On the one hand, they appreciate and support films; on the other, they're an indolent power, obstructing the development of the industry. If we yield to their vulgar tastes, film cannot develop. We must understand both points of view. It's easy for some to negate and oppose the theories of others in order to prove their own opinions correct. I'm not taking the middle road, but I do think that everything has a reason for its existence, and we ought to understand and explain it. We have to admit that entertainment films are made for amusement.

Rao Shuguang: The idea itself of education through entertainment reverses the order of ends and means. Entertainment is taken merely as a means bound to be surpassed, and education is the end. Actually, to force some film genres, say martial arts films, to achieve "education through entertainment" would be counter to aesthetics. For instance, the idea that one can be loyal to the emperor and save the country through boxing, prevalent in martial arts movies, is pernicious and ought not to be taken as education realized through entertainment. In fact, entertainment itself is an entity, and is the goal entertainment films ought to achieve. To evaluate entertainment films, the highest standard to apply is its entertainment value; that is, if an audience gets real psychological and physiological pleasure when viewing a film, then the film has realized its aesthetic value.

To judge an entertainment film, we should grasp its aesthetic dynamics instead of merely taking it as a static entity. An entertainment film is a continuously realized process in which lies aesthetic value. It is in this process that this kind of film realizes its aesthetic value, by providing its viewers with a spiritual pleasure and release. In today's society, the activities designed to entertain are diverse: fashion shows, tourism, sports and so on. People have their own ideas before going to a movie, since they now have many options available and to see a film is only one of them. A film must offer something to attract them.

In our country, if we want to do a good job in making entertainment films, we need to clarify several ideas in theoretical terms. First of all, we must define their position in terms of cultural ecology. The ecosystem of filmmaking is comprised of three parts: avant-garde films, serious films and entertainment films. In this ecosystem, entertainment movies dominate. This doesn't seem to be any problem for production. As Shen Jiming said, more than 70 percent of the products of the studios are entertainment films. However, they lack a theoretical status that matches this high percentage. This must be clarified theoretically, or film theory is derelict. I guess since our film industry hasn't developed along this natural track, we must not have made any really high quality entertainment movies. Today, as we discuss movies made to entertain, we should sense a crisis in both theory and practice. In our recent film culture there's been a strong sense of crisis for the avant-garde. This doesn't help us. In a word, we ought to give entertainment films a high status and assure their dominance. With their status verified at the highest theoretical levels, we'd essentially change our minds about the entertainment movie.

To study entertainment movies, we should study the understanding of entertainment, since they're made in accordance with a psychological need. To do further research into entertainment requires us to trace its cultural origins. For reasons both subjective and objective, entertainment films in

China have been poor in both quantity and quality. Historically, as most directors well understand, Chinese film has been evaluated in political terms and brought into line with politics. It's a tradition. When making *A Difficult Couple* (1983), Zheng Zhengqiu understood this clearly. The purpose of filmmaking was to civilize, "to rectify social maladies and set the public mind straight." Film was burdened with the responsibility for social advancement. Such a tradition inevitably made one ignore movies when seeking entertainment.

The use of film for propaganda and education replaced its use as entertainment. When this was taken to the extreme, film became a political tool at the command of a minority of people, and degenerated, in the end, into the instrument the Gang of Four used in their attempt to usurp Party leadership and state power. This traditional concept, as a result of the technical development of film, exaggerated the functions of film as an instrument of propaganda and education to such a degree that it gave the illusion that the medium could guarantee the prosperity and security of a state! Its existence as a means of entertainment was totally ignored, which directly affected the development of art and literature.

The fact is, our need for entertainment and enjoyment is not at all decadent or philistine; it is a natural and healthy awareness of life, based on the existence and demands of human perceptions. Someone suggested that a new perceptual world be built that is pregnant with and surpasses the rational, and Freud uncovered the pleasure principle. We should uphold the human need for entertainment and enjoyment on the basis of the perceptual and value highly the entertainment film made in accordance with this psychological demand.

The first functioning of entertainment films is to release the emotions and feelings that people can't satisfy in reality. If a society is to maintain its existence, it is impossible for its people to do things only according to their instinct for pleasure, so they create many cultural disciplines to stabilize and restrict themselves. However, repressed human emotions and desires simply cannot vanish into thin air. Instead they accumulate in our hearts. According to Freud, literature and art provide people with a channel for catharsis. Movies made to entertain are, of course, designed to release repressed desires. This helps people, especially those in modern society, adjust their thinking and achieve a psychological balance. If not released in this way, these desires could become a socially destructive power. That's terribly frightening. If we really paid enough attention to entertainment films and let people find their release by enjoying various films with grotesque and breathtaking plots, it would significantly help to maintain the stability and balanced development of society.

Shen Jiming: It's said that the two cities in China with the lowest crime rates are Shenzhen, which has comparatively more channels for people to rid themselves of stress, and Qufu, which is the hometown of Confucius and restricted by traditional moral codes. This cultural phenomenon is worthy of study.

Rao Shuguang: Some consider the entertainment film a negative escape from reality. As a matter of fact, the entertainment film has a positive value for social construction, though its world is different from the real world. It's not simply an imitation or representation of reality—it represents stressed emotions and unfulfilled desires in reality, through images which have the illusion of external reality. In the perceptual world of the entertainment film, people can sense the values of happiness and life and achieve a kind of satisfaction. This can arouse in people the love and pursuit of life, and the real passions in their hearts. On this significant level, people can not only find peace of mind, but also liberate their passions and maintain them with a kind of vigorous creativity.

Modern psychology values highly the study of creativity. The results of creativity and perception can only be found in an environment where feelings can be totally liberated and released. The entertainment film does this very well, bringing people beyond their perceptions to total self-satisfaction. One thus becomes complete, with one's entire nature one's own. From this notion, the entertainment film, as well as the pleasure-seeking consciousness that it tries to fulfill, has exceptional value, a positive and constructive significance to people living in a modern industrial society. The human being is complete if able to play, and only if complete can one play. Watching films can be regarded as a high level of play which provides us with a complete awareness of life, full creativity and lively passions.

Shen Jiming: In the last dialogue, someone mentioned that film, including the entertainment film, is a kind of game. We should elaborate on this, for the concept of film as game actually concerns the origins and characteristics of all art. In the past, when we spoke of games, we belittled their value. In traditional Chinese culture, games and entertainment had no importance and were ignored by the dominant culture. Craftsmen and artists were given a low classification and scriptwriters could only be listed in the "ghost book." Since the earliest Chinese film, entertainment has never been treated fairly, because of tradition and the depreciation of entertainment on the theoretical level.

Song Chong: We should give theoretical emphasis to the following statements: (1) Entertainment films form the major body of production. (2) Entertainment is not necessarily vulgar. (3) Entertainment should be treated as an end, not a means to an end. We should lobby for entertainment within theoretical circles. As filmmakers, we should study the rules which govern the entertainment film, and with the help of theorists, establish some general principles so as to improve their quality.

Zheng Dongtian: Song Chong included the four main elements of the Hollywood entertainment film in his director's notes for *A Deal under the Gallows Tree*. Such an open statement on the adaptation from Hollywood is rare in

Chinese film history. That's very interesting, for his statement is rational and tells, through his unique understanding, which is above simple advocacy, how to make entertainment films. But lately a question keeps coming into my mind: Although everyone says that the entertainment film should have entertaining qualities, why don't other directors assert openly that the purpose of these films is to entertain, rather than try every possible means to give them an ideological content?

For example, critics praised Zhang Zien's *Magic Braid* (1985) as the first entertainment film to combine ideological reform with the martial arts. After seeing it, I don't agree. I think people attended the film to see the Braid, not for instruction about reform. The Chinese already have too many models to follow. The Braid may be an object of worship, yet it cannot compete with foreign guns. Thus the hero cuts his pigtail and takes up arms. The concept of reform here is shallow and has nothing to do with enlightenment, even if the audience can sense it.

The construction of the entertainment film cannot consist of deeper levels of ideological significance, yet every director tries hard to achieve them. This confuses me. Song Chong replied to my question by stating that any ideological significance is due to the directions of Chinese aesthetics currently in demand. In truth, the matter is more complex. Moral instruction in art and literature not only limits creativity, but also accustoms the audience to such instruction. That's why the contemporary audience won't accept a film lacking it. Then why don't we make entertainment films with ideological content, rather than entertainment alone, since pure entertainment cannot survive in China?

A year ago, after *The Thief of Emei* was released, I introduced the several levels or types of entertainment films it inspired in an article for the *Chinese Film Times* in Shanghai. Recently I had been giving more attention to the gap between entertainment and art films, in terms of their functions as entertainment and in physical stimulation. Though there has been pressure to produce more and more entertainment films, their qualities need improvement. *The Thief of Emei* made something out of the lowest level; it shifts from the monk fighting the Taoist priest to policemen fighting thieves, sometimes with guns, sometimes with martial arts, and the battle is located on the roof of a modern hotel instead of at a temple. Because of this, 300 prints were sold, which is reasonable, for it caught a basic principle of commercial film, which is the constant demand for new stimulation.

The audience drinks the first cup of water because it is thirsty, but is unwilling to drink a second; if you add some orange juice, it is happy to have it. A director once showed me a script, telling me he suffered because he was unable to develop his characters well. I told him his script had no basis for such development and that he should instead focus on fresh and attractive action. This seems to be our only option. On another level, we need interesting characters, as we have seen in most commercial films from

Japan and the United States. In a given environment, certain types of characters will be generated.

On an even higher level, we can see that entertainment and pleasure function in relation to sociological and humanistic themes such as friendship, peace, love and trust. Spielberg's *E.T.: The Extra-Terrestrial* (1982) and Arthur Heller's *Love Story* (1970) excite and satisfy their audience without enlightment or reflection. The cores of these films are their production values, without complicated connotations. Their purpose is to entertain.

There can be good films on all three levels. The director must be clear about which level he's working on, so he can control the amount of ideological content that goes into the film and be aware that by trying to include everything, he might exclude the necessities.

I think we can develop the entertainment film on the third level, since the pure entertainment film is deprecated and neither money nor high technology are available for their production. With certain ambiguous genres and some instructional content, the third level of entertainment film may satisfy the audience and gain approval from the authorities as well. The combination of form and content in *Magic Braid* is fine, but only if the things that are combined are proper and there is a clear distinction between form and content.

We are now correcting the idea of pure entertainment established over the past two years. We hope that on this basis, Chinese directors and their audience can work out ways of producing entertainment films. Whatever direction is taken, filmmakers must first learn from the experiences of others. If you want to make entertainment films on a high level, then study Alfred Hitchcock.

One other element should be noted: the nature of the audience. American films pay much attention to this. Scientific research gives constant feedback to the filmmakers.

The dialogue with directors continued on December 25, 1986, at the Beijing Film Studio, where Yao Xiaomeng, from *Contemporary Cinema*, spoke with Director Zhang Huaxun about martial arts films.

Yao Xiaomong: Among entertainment films, martial arts films play an important role. After the fall of the Gang of Four, the release of *Mysterious Buddha* (1981) and *The Will of Warriors* opened the history of martial arts films in the New Era. The debate over these films has become highly significant.

Zhang Huaxun: Making entertainment and martial arts films is very difficult in this country. After I made *Mysterious Buddha* and *The Will of Warriors,* I got pressure from all sides. After the release of *Mysterious Buddha*, people criticized me, first for going after box office profits, though people now recognize the importance of profits, since the film companies survive through them, and second for the amount of bloody terror. Perhaps the eye-slicing scene is too realistic, but compared to scenes in *First Blood* (1982), the bloodiness in our film is far less graphic. Third, I am accused of pandering to low tastes and pursuing an unhealthy mood in the audience, which is nonsense. When *The Will of Warriors* was released, it was classified as a film that could not be openly publicized. Today we can say that, in terms of art or politics, making a martial arts film at the beginning of this decade was equivalent to making experimental narratives.

Yao Xiaomong: The criticism of martial arts and entertainment films at that time coincided with social and cultural circumstances. Nowadays, it's fashionable to talk about the "dominant ideology." The dominant ideology at the beginning of the decade was that entertainment should contain moral messages. I think this is a question of the function of film. The idea that the function has been changing during the New Era is thought-provoking. At first the function was educational and the audience was the student; as the concept changed, the audience became the god, and then the friend, of the filmmaker. Recently, some have claimed that the audience is the enemy. Today we understand that different genres have different functions. If you (Zhang Huaxun) were criticized earlier, it indicates that you were a pioneer in matters of the function of film and that you had a perceptive concept of the medium. So you needn't be resentful.

Zhang Huaxun: The question of martial arts films is a matter of Chinese culture, which includes knowledge about the nation, culture, philosophy, ethics, history, traditional medicine and so on. It's not easy to make a really good martial arts film. Some refer to martial arts films as fighting films and kung fu films, which is incorrect. Martial arts is a combination of acrobatic fighting and artistic skill. It is not blind combat.

Yao Xiaomong: In "Chinese Acrobatic Fighting Films and American Westerns," I questioned why westerns have been so popular internationally, since besides the fact that they form a genre, they are also entertainments. Bazin says the western tells the history of America. I think martial arts films should reveal Chinese culture.

Zhang Huaxun: *Mysterious Buddha* was very popular in eastern Europe. When I asked people there why they were interested in the film, they said they saw Chinese culture in it and understood the greatness of the nation. Chinese martial arts films bear strong imprints of our culture. In ancient China, both civil and military achievements were valued. The great heroes in our history were masters of the martial arts. Chinese martial arts favors martial morals, which is related to ethics. *The Legend of the Three Kingdoms* makes this very clear.

The acrobatic fighting of each character in *The Will of Warriors* is carefully designed. For example, He Dahai uses Xing-Yi boxing to show his rudeness; the henchman uses Eagle-Claw boxing; Magic Palm Li, a mysterious master of martial arts, uses Eight Diagrams Palming to indicate Taoist characteristics. I've tried hard to make martial arts films contain characteristics of Chinese culture. These days, the study of Chinese martials arts is popular all over the world. China has long treasured civil and military virtues. The martial arts are rooted in China and developed here, so why don't we use our martial arts films to promote our culture?

Yao Xiaomong: Filmmaking, including martial arts films, is an international activity. We make martial arts films not only for the Chinese audience, but for everyone. That's why we need to express Chinese culture in our films. For example, it is insufficient to represent Shaolin boxing only through the combat between the monks, without emphasizing the allegorical Buddhist content, since that extends far beyond the region and the concrete images. A particular chapter in *Secrets of Shaolin Boxing* talks about the "extremism of the Chan Sect." If we could represent that in our films, it would be wonderful.

Zhang Huaxun: Film is beyond doubt the best means of representing the strong actions of martial arts, since the moving camera and editing can show them best. A sharply thrown punch, for example, is best exaggerated by intercutting between frames. Making martial arts films is different from making normal films. The number of shots is often twice that of a normal film, and they emphasize sound effects and visual actions. In *The Will of Warriors*, when Dong Fangxu at the last moment unleashes his unique skill, the camera catches this from several different angles, since the audience has been waiting for the final action and the different angles represent their viewing angles. This delays the actual action, thus intensifying the release of suppressed emotions.

Yao Xiaomong: The final scene of *The Will of Warriors* is very successful. I saw this film twice and got very excited each time. The audience was yelling along with the characters. Such motivation is a great success.

Zhang Huaxun: When I made this scene, I paid special attention to the accumulation of emotions. Dong Fangxu has a unique skill, yet the ethics of the martial arts forbid one from using such skills. He repeatedly controls himself, as the feelings of audience get more and more heated and they beg him to use it. At that point, Dong Fangxu hits his opponent's hand, then his legs, and then knocks the foreign devil out, finally using his skill to completely overpower his enemy. The development progresses gradually until the audience is pushed to a climax. When the film was shown in Eastern Europe, the audience cheered wildly, maybe because they feel hostile toward the Soviet Union. I plan to make several more martial arts films after I complete the art film I'm working on, and once I start shooting, they will be better than *The Will of Warriors*.

11

The Entertainment Film: Dialogue III

Rao Shuguang
Translated by Wang Xiaowen

Participants:

Chen Huaikai: Director, Beijing Film Studio

Shi Xiaohua: Director, Shanghai Film Studio

Tian Zhuangzhuang: Director, Xian Film Studio

Wu Yigong: Director and Chair, Shanghai Film Bureau

Xie Tian: Director, Beijing Film Studio

Xu Yinghua: Screenwriter, Shanghai Film Studio

Yang Yianjin: Director, Shanghai Film Studio

Chen Huaikai: In recent years, more and more people have been talking about the functions of film, and as a result, the functions of film have seemed to increase greatly and now include education, culture, philosophy and wisdom. Apparently film is responsible for all social functions. Isn't that a heavy burden for the medium to bear? I don't think film can.

In the past, we thought too highly of the political and moral functions of film. Although film does have a variety of functions, I'd say that its major function is aesthetic pleasure and entertainment. Premiere Zhou once said that the educational function of film lay in its ability to entertain. As a matter of fact, we shouldn't expect as much as we do, as though film could serve every social purpose. The major goal of film is to meet our needs for entertainment and aesthetic pleasure.

I suggest we reclassify our films. In the past, we only were concerned that film serve political ends, and most films were not much more than illustrations of political policies. Though it is clear that film cannot be separated from politics, I think we should first of all admit that film is an art, like music and painting. I favor variety, and for this reason, suggest we reclassify film into different categories.

As I see it, there are three categories: (1) the entertainment film, which satisfies the needs of a mass audience; (2) the art film, which has been under attack in part for neglecting audience psychology; and (3) the propaganda or educational film. Filmmakers in my generation educated the majority of our current audience, and the movies we made contained a great deal of political propaganda and moral teachings. Performances at the time were highly dramatic, which is why that audience, whose aesthetic model was established by traditional films, feels alienated from contemporary films, which have weak plots and mediocre acting, and finds them tasteless. This is also why a number of experimental narratives, or art films, have failed at the box office despite their high aesthetic values. Nonetheless, these films have influenced the entire industry in matters of composition, image structures and sound-image relationships. Those making entertainment films cannot ignore them. The real issue, then, is that of popularity and elegance combined.

China produces proportionally few art films. Of an annual production of about one hundred and fifty films, only three or four are art films. There's no reason to fear that; it's not a matter of their shortcomings. Their aesthetic concepts can be found in most entertainment movies. I support the experimental narratives and art films, because their creative explorations are beneficial in the long run. Society is rapidly changing, and audiences will continue to change their ideas. Filmmakers must look ahead to this. The third category, those called political propaganda, which I'd rather call educational films, are needed by the contemporary Chinese audience.

Of these categories, the entertainment film is the most difficult to make. In the first place, the ambiguity of the term, only recently introduced, confuses many people. In the past, the concept was never mentioned. Furthermore, today many people look down on entertainment films, as though making them would be beneath their dignity and is in bad taste. This disdain is a result of the traditional idea that "virtue" supersedes "profits." Others erroneously underestimate the difficulty of making such films, and consider them mere trash. Making entertainment films is not an easy task.

In past years, we maintained a six-to-three-to-one proportion of the themes of films scheduled for production. For every six films with contemporary themes, which directly served political and propaganda purposes, three others centered on revolutionary history in order to educate the younger generation, and one, outside the dominant directions, was designed to entertain. The entertainment film was considered harmless, yet profitable. During that time, I filmed a traditional Chinese drama; I was warned that this would damage my reputation. Such films, it was claimed, were only made to serve the peasantry. But the truth is, such films, from a contemporary point of view, are a form of entertainment.

I believe we must enlarge the scope of the entertainment film. Those of the past two years are primarily detective stories, horror films and martial arts movies. Yet ordinary stories can be entertainments. Xie Jin, a master of the entertainment film, proves this. Well-made melodramas are a form of entertainment which provides much aesthetic pleasure.

Is it not possible to bring directors and theorists together to make an in-depth study of the entertainment film? Theoretical preparation for film-making has been very poor thus far. But first, it might not be a bad idea to develop a theory of entertainment. If we don't have sufficient theories of our own to draw from, we can adapt foreign theories to meet our ends. A study of Hitchcock might prove helpful to us. The first thing we should do is refute from a theoretical position the notion that films made for entertainment purposes have little value.

Xie Tian: Entertainment should cultivate noble virtues. Clearly the entertainment film is different from an aesthetic experiment, but it is a genre and as such is worthy of extended study and serious treatment. We shouldn't ignore or underestimate it. It is nothing to joke about.

Some comedies stink like dirty socks, or farts, or cesspools. That's a very poor reason for making films. As a genre, the entertainment film should provide healthy aesthetic pleasures, and those who make them should have a clean conscience. Some argue that entertainment has no other purpose than to entertain, to make people laugh and celebrate the misfortunes of others. Films which do this are meaningless. Certainly laughter is healthy and makes you feel young, while depression adds to your age, but more important is what you are thinking at the critical moment the laughter dies down. That lingering taste is what the director is after.

Comedy is the hardest kind of film to make. A director puts three times as much effort into it as goes into ordinary filmmaking, for comedy requires more skill. It's difficult to make others laugh and at the same time make the laughter significant.

I made two comedies starring Zhao Ziyue: *Good, Better, Best* (1962) and *Road of Fortune* (1984). Although the latter had a few faults, yet as comedy, besides making people laugh, it also expressed the advancement of technology and advocated economic reform in rural areas and argued against conservatism. While we didn't want to appeal to major issues, we did want the audience to get something out of the film. We all feel good when we've really accomplished something.

Some films force their audiences to laugh, but that can be done well or badly. To force laughter is foolish enough, but when it's poorly done, it's unbearable. When I made my films, I reminded myself not to be too vulgar and cause adverse side effects. Most people don't enjoy nasty things. On the other hand, if a comedy is too profound, the ordinary audience will have a hard time understanding it. That's also unacceptable.

Chinese comedies should contain some truth. If you want others to like your film, and to laugh sincerely, you must tell stories based in truth. A joke demands reliability. Everyone knows the great comedian Charlie Chaplin went through three phases of creativity, the most outstanding of which was the middle phase. In his early phase, Chaplin, who later rejected that period, was primarily a clown. Chaplin, who came out of the lower class and had a deep understanding of it, is called the King of Comedy because of the deep life experiences he conveyed during his middle period. His films are entertaining, but his entertainment has significance. Generally speaking, comedy cannot be separated from real life or people. Life itself is a character, and a character is real life. That's what makes comedy count.

Wu Yigong: Recently, after I completed *The Adventures of the Young Master* (1987), people asked why I made it. The reason is simple. I made it because I loved it. Of course there were other motivations, for it is part of the current trend. Yet it is difficult to make an elegant film with a good return at the same time. Initially, I failed to mobilize others to follow the trend, but when I became its leader, some found it reassuring. "Well," they said, "the general manager is already making this kind of film, why don't you?" or, "The general manager doesn't want to be an artist anymore. Do you?"

Another reason for making this film was to break into the international market. In the past, all we could bring to the international scene were films like *Yellow Earth* and *My Memories of Old Beijing*. Though they earned a good reputation, they appealed primarily to the art film audience, which is limited. Now we aim to break into international commercial circles, to achieve international audiences rather than international awards. I think this is important. Of course I wasn't afraid to make this film, because the original novel had so much to offer. The theme is unique. Casting also required careful thought. In the past, we only had two major types of comedy, one of which was the light comedies which developed from the comic dramas of South China. I was determined to experiment with Chinese comedy. That's why I was determined to make this film, intending to make a realistic comedy, as I saw it, of China.

I made this film self-consciously and willingly, not because there was anything to fear, nor because it offered a way to relax and escape my routine as a studio manager, which people assume means attending meetings from dawn to dusk every day. I needed to make a film like this for a change. A lot of people wanted to know what I was going to say in this film. I didn't want to say anything. "You must be after something," they persisted. The truth is, in this film I didn't intend to create a deep structure for people to analyze.

The current trend in world cinema is a combination of breathtaking action and comedy. Comedies are relaxed. They don't force you to think deeply. Film is film, not philosophy. The audience can ponder it if they wish, but they don't have to do so. A filmmaker needn't force others into deep thought. It's wrong to think every piece of art must be profound.

The entertainment film is difficult to make, unlike the art film, which depends on the personal concept of the filmmaker. The entertainment film is concerned with its effects upon the audience. In a comedy, for example, when the audience laughs at a specific point, the laughter continues for a short time, obscuring the dialogue. The filmmaker must delay the dialogue and slow plot development without the audience realizing it, which takes a bit of brainstorming. The filmmaker must not only anticipate such effects, but also anticipate the way different audiences will respond to the same thing.

Sound was given special attention in this film. I instructed the recordists to boost the voice levels, making the sound too loud for a small auditorium but proper for a cinema, since it's impossible to expect an entire audience to remain silent throughout a screening. People laugh or talk if they feel it necessary. It would be terrible if everyone kept deadly silent. Such matters cannot be gauged by aesthetic standards of truth.

Comedies can never be true to life. We shouldn't expect them to imitate reality, but to find ways to be creative. A dialogue at night between the hero and heroine would be spoken very low in reality, but we can't do that in a film. We have to make technological adjustments. A few people found some of the scenes too brightly lit, but it was impossible to keep these scenes dark. Some were already too dark. In terms of realism, they should have been dark, but such a style would be unsuitable for comedy. Comedies must be brightly lit. In art films, the filmmaker must consider light and shadow, natural lighting as well as darkness. Such considerations are useless in the entertainment film, though objectively, you do try to take everything into consideration. Sometimes the entertainment film requires things to be exaggerated. A bathroom in a film might be much larger than such a room would be in reality because a display of martial arts takes place in it. There must be room for it. The audience won't think this strange or unrealistic. You cannot pursue truth or falsity in the entertainment film.

People have criticized me for putting everything into this one movie: horseback riding, driving, martial arts, a heartbreaking fight, comic effects. I meant to do this, because this kind of film is designed to make its audience laugh and relax. In a word, it's a kind of experiment. Maybe that's not quite the way to put it. Maybe we should simply say that the entertainment film is the real experiment.

Tian Zhuangzhuang: When we speak about entertainment films, we really need to sit down and talk about how to make them. If you think it's easy, you are making a ridiculous error. It demands a great deal of knowledge. You must know how to handle the pace, develop the plot, and put the audience at ease. The wonders of the entertainment film must be unexpected but reasonable. That's a hard job.

Shi Xiaohua: There's a kind of comic drama in Shanghai which I once thought vulgar and didn't want to see. I thought it lacked artistic value. Later, three events astonished me and made me change my mind. After the Cultural Revolution, when Chaplin's films were re-released, they were so popular that even the worst cinema was packed. Most those in the audience were poorly educated, old workers who spent most of their spare time playing poker. When the French film *Narrow Escape* was shown, my son wouldn't miss a show and went to the cinema ten times. One Sunday, when I finally made him stop because he had a test on Monday, he cried bitterly. I was surprised that a kid had such enthusiasm for comedy. Recently, at the Berlin Film Festival, I saw many films from different countries. One American film, *Tootsie* (1982), starring Dustin Hoffman, who played a woman, was immensely popular. The well-educated and art-conscious audience also enjoyed comedy. This universality is rare in China. We can say that healthy and progressive comedies are welcomed by both domestic and foreign audiences.

Rao Shuguang: In Western countries, comedy is popular and has high aesthetic value. It merits special attention.

Shi Xiaohua: Comedy isn't necessarily tasteless. Audiences, sophisticated or not, like it. However, when some Chinese comedies are shown in China, they are accused of being unrealistic—yet when the same plot shows up in a foreign comedy, the same people become involved and laugh, and it becomes acceptable.

Certainly comedy is different from melodrama and has its own principles. We can't judge it by the principles of normal dramas. But though comedy has its own presumptions and thus cannot be measured in terms of realism, there can be a comic rendering of reality based on true experiences. It is after all not reality and lies above it. Why then should we judge it on the basis of unreality, or falsity? Why do we always criticize domestic comedies for these reasons?

Rao Shuguang: What comedy pursues is not superficial reality, but aesthetic reality. This aesthetic truth should be identified with its creative characteristics. As you just said, comedy creates a unique effect, the comic rendering of reality.

Shi Xiaohua: This unique effect reveals life on another level. If comedy is a deep expression of life, we should accept it. Artists feel very hurt that we measure comedy in terms of realism, which kills originality. It's an old story. In the German comedy *King of Kings*, the plot of Hitler's imaginary sister is historically untrue, yet the audience accepts it—but if something similar were done in a Chinese comedy, the film would be accused of altering history and severely criticized.

I think there are two ways to render reality in comedies: one is, to express the comic elements of real life; the other, to satirize a phenomenon through an artistic treatment which transcends reality. The latter is rare here, and theorists, leaders and audiences find it hard to accept. That's why Chinese comedy cannot achieve a higher level, and that's tragic.

Rao Shuguang: It's ridiculous to use truthfulness as the criterion by which to measure any kind of film. The concept of truth itself should be open. For some films, what really counts is the aesthetic reality they create, which is defined not only by the truth of realism, but by special aesthetic principles.

Shi Xiaohua: It is very hard for people here to accept the idea that we might have a higher aesthetic overview of life, which would allow us to pursue a higher aesthetic truth, as does the *King of Kings*. All we do now is reflect upon the same level of actuality, rather than generalize about life on a higher aesthetic level. Artists need the approval of theorists, the authorities and the audience in order to do what they want to do. We hope there are no accusations of lying when an artist isolates himself from the general trend.

Xue Yinhua: When Marx talks about the dialectic relationship between production and consumption, he takes the critical position that consumption determines production. But in the film industry, production always determines consumption. We've never done any demographics and have no accurate figures for the market. When we talk about the entertainment film, we must depart from this. We should understand the needs of the market and predict on that basis. Film production should also be determined by consumption, so that film may develop as well as it possibly can. From this point of view, our conversations on the entertainment film have theoretical value. Otherwise they're just nonsense. The TV drama *Ji Gong* now has been given widespread national coverage. One can see its ads and hear its theme song everywhere.

Yang Yianjin: The theme of *Ji Gong* has won great popularity. It is very entertaining. The director seized on this theme, though he could have made a better production.

Xue Yinhua: Why don't our most well-known directors make films like this?

Yang Yanjin: It indicates that some directors are misdirected by the theorists. Theorists use the battlefield of public opinion to make a mess of their own minds. As a result they lose opportunities to seize good stories.

Xue Yinhua: Film is not only an art, but a commodity. It takes money to make films. Where does that come from? From the marketplace, of course. That's why film should take over the market. We should realize this rather than ignore it. Our films are made for our audience. The withering of the market means our films are lifeless. We will confront the problem of the withering market when we address the entertainment film.

Rao Shuguang: This is what motivated us to arrange these dialogues, and through them we hope to find a key to regaining the market.

Xue Yinhua: We need consider which films have both aesthetic and economic value. It isn't necessary to mention the word "entertainment"; we can improve the potential of film to attract an appreciative audience. Film must have this potentiality to achieve both aesthetic and economic value.

Yang Yanjin: We have a narrow view of entertainment. We consider it vulgar and pandering to low taste.

Xue Yihua: Entertainment isn't easy to come by. There is no outstanding co-median, and there are no alternative actors or actors with special skills, even in a big studio like Shanghai. The quality of normal productions is substandard, to say nothing of the quality of entertainment films.

Rao Shuguang: To be honest, film is a cultural commodity. It survives by its customers. That is to say, the audience is the food, clothing and parents of film. Film cannot exist without an audience. If you want to satisfy the audience, you should first understand its aesthetic needs.

Xue Yinhua: Take a simple example. If I give a lecture on philosophy, I state eight or ten points to illustrate my views; but if I want to make my points interesting, I have a problem. Culture is not as profound as philosophy. Coca Cola is a form of culture which is popular throughout the world. Hollywood films are also internationally popular.

Rao Shuguang: Actually, the popularity of a film is a positive expression of the film's value no matter how the critics rate it.

Xue Yinhua: When they decide the Golden Rooster Awards, why do they exclude those belly-filling films which have made high profits? Why do they ignore the directors of those films?

Yang Yanjin: The position taken nowadays is that film is the teacher of its audience, an engineer of the soul. But as a matter of fact, all audiences, including the authorities, are customers.

Xue Yinhua: It seems the audience can be human only after you have taught them. That's ridiculous.

Yang Yanjin: People spend their time and energy going to the cinema to get a lesson from you. I don't think that's what they want to do.

Xue Yinhua: We used to emphasize the study of themes instead of the study of forms. I think the making of films is the making of forms. The audience goes for the forms. Those who go to Shanghai opera won't go to Beijing opera, and those who go to Beijing opera won't go to Shanghai opera. Yet the forms haven't developed much. The Golden Rooster Awards only iden-tify with one form.

    The richness and diversity of social necessities determine that film has to be rich and diverse in form. It is here that the discussion of the enter-tainment film takes shape, and the discussion gains theoretical value and significance. China's theoretical studies should not depart from Chinese reality, because Chinese directors should work for Chinese audiences. We shouldn't ignore Chinese directors. When we talk about Chinese film these days, we use foreign films as examples. It seems we have a clear and logical view of foreign films rather than Chinese films.

Xue Yinhua: We have very few genres, yet the more genres we have, the better our films will be. It's like fashions. When you have more styles of clothing available, people have more choices.

Yang Yanjin: That's competition. Competition generates elimination. Those who make films which don't attract audiences and earn profits, should be removed.

Xue Yinhua: Ticket prices should float. If you attract a larger audience, the price should go up. *Superman* (1978) and *Midnight Singing* (1986) got as much as five kwai per ticket.

Rao Shuguang: Here we should also abide by the laws of economics.

Xue Yinhua: The audience is willing to pay for what it really wants to see.

Yang Yanjin: It's considered absolutely right to say "serve the people," yet it seems incorrect to say "serve the audience." Isn't the audience made up of people?

Rao Shuguang: To serve the audience means to serve the people.

Xue Yinhua: We can only serve the audience. If one doesn't go to the cinema, how can we serve him? We should promote the slogan, "Serve the audience."

Yang Yanjin: The audience fosters, feeds and clothes us. We creative people and you theoretical people are all living off them.

12

A Response to the Issue of the Contemporary Entertainment Film

Shao Mujun
Translated by Fu Binbin

In recent years I published a series of arguments on the entertainment film *Counter To Common Thinking*, including "On the Complete Nature of Film," "On the Duality of Film Categorization," "Against Frowning on the Refined," and "On the Three Stages of New Chinese Cinema." Since these arguments conflict with today's common understanding of the entertainment film, I have not been surprised to have had a number of questions thrown at me. Since such questions lead inevitably to rebuttals, an argumentative dialogue is naturally constructed, which, put into writing, might be called a style of refutation. Here the querist is a fictitious person, based on reality, represented by the letter "A," while the respondent, indicated by the letter "B," represents my point of view.

A: Currently, under the sudden heavy pressure of commerce, Chinese film has to change its direction in the making of entertainment films. Almost all 22 studios, taking the entertainment film as a panacea, are marching tacitly, yet decidedly, toward the desperate end, "Kill to the last man." Sadly, some excellent directors have given up their aesthetic ideals and started, against their conscience, to cook up movies on such fashionable subjects as drug trafficking, AIDS, robbery, murder, rock 'n roll and hijacking. This is distressing; Chinese film is in danger of serious degeneration of its ideological and aesthetic qualities. As theorists and critics, it is our responsibility to turn the tide and call for a return the exploratory spirit and realistic style we established during the New Era (1979–1989). We'd be making a great mistake if we merely chimed in with others, worshiping entertainment films as the mainstream of filmmaking, and allowed the insane wave of entertainment films to engulf socially realistic films like *Hibiscus Town* and experimental narratives like *Yellow Earth*. Contemporary Chinese film is burdened with the task of cultural enlightment. What constitutes its mainstream ought to be filmic works which cut vigorously and courageously into the realities of life and represent images of new socialist characters. Our film should reform its audience, but shouldn't lower its quality, compromise for money and ultimately let the audience reform it. In this regard, your view that, while the Chinese economy is in a period of transition, we should emphasize and restore the "social nature" of film as popular entertainment, and that the flood of entertainment films conforms to the laws of film development, is totally wrong and detrimental.

B: At present, entertainment films are poor. Rough and slipshod productions clutter the screen, and as statistics demonstrate, many films, though made for profit, haven't even regained the original investment. In this regard, your anxiety, frustration and anger are quite understandable. But what has caused the current predicament, and where is the way out of it? Your "prescription" is to negate the nature of film as popular entertainment, to reform the demand of the masses for it, and to turn the cinema into a classroom for cultural enlightenment. Although your intentions are noble, they're impractical. Even before the flood of entertainment films, the audience had started to decline. Since 1979, the rate of decline has been a billion viewers per year, and it's getting worse.

The issue of the entertainment film began two or three years ago, when the economic crisis in the film industry became evident and people began to realize that they had to make more films to meet the demand for entertainment, despite criticism from theorists and critics. The issue was raised with the usual traditional Chinese disparagement of commercialism: "We want to shoot some movies for profit, not for face." Why not "for face?" First, because we cannot "gain face" from theoretical or critical circles. Second, since "not for face" is explicitly stated, styles, techniques, character configurations and the like are no longer given consideration. Therefore, we only need third- or fourth-rate directors to handle such movies. The entertainment film apparently has nothing to do with art or culture. Toward the end of last year, when the economy of the film industry was on the brink of an abyss, there was a sudden rise in the number of entertainment movies, but the theoretical and critical circles refused to even talk about it.

It is evident that we made a major error from the very beginning on the issue of whether or not film should provide entertainment. To make a profit means to lose face, and to entertain means that one has no face. It is here that the root of the problems in the development of the contemporary Chinese entertainment film was planted. This commonly accepted, classical definition leads to a continuous identification of entertainment movies with sex, violence and buffoonery. Since this definition is still in common use, the theory which considers entertainment movies the mainstream of contemporary film has been fiercely opposed.

Indeed, if entertainment movies can only be martial arts films, detective stories, comedies and the like, intended to stimulate the senses, and if those which have the power to move us through finely designed, painful stories and strong casts are not regarded as entertainment films only because they have serious subject matter and lack what is fashionable, then even a moron, not to mention someone with insight and vision, would oppose the proposal to embrace entertainment films as the "mainstream of film."

I'm not denying that appealing to human instincts is an act of amusement; however, it is not the only content of entertainment, nor is it the only entertaining ingredient a film can provide. Entertainment means to provide one with a feeling of pleasure (relaxation, comfort, ease and satisfaction) and to free one from feelings of unhappiness (distress, fatigue, dullness and loneliness). There are many ways to achieve this other than sexual provocation and strong stimulation. *Gone with the Wind* (1939), *The Sound of Music* (1965), *Waterloo Bridge* (1940) . . . all these well-known films present neither murder nor sexual exhibition, nor do they present foolish shows and sensual stimulation. The films of Chaplin in his later period became more and more serious (*The Great Dictator* [1940], *Monsieur Verdoux* [1947], etc.). Should these films be relabeled serious, social realist or art films merely because they do not conform to the classical Chinese definition of entertainment movies?

I doubt anyone would deny that the American westerns are entertainment movies. Everyone, from presidents and college professors to vendors and peddlers, loves westerns, because they are devoted to the American spirit of adventure and pioneering. The fact that John Ford is regarded indisputably as a master and *Stagecoach* (1939) has become a classic, inseparable from any history of film, shows clearly enough that entertainment movies are related to art and culture.

A: In your articles and speeches, you have repeatedly described your dualism of film categories, that is, film as entertainment or non-entertainment. According to you, the line of demarcation between these categories lies in whether or not a film was made to please its audience. There are unjustifiable contradictions in this statement. For instance, films made for an audience are not necessarily made to please. *Hibiscus Town* was designed to expose the reactionary nature of the Cultural Revolution through the fate of an individual. How can it be put in the same category as *The Thief of Emei* (Er Mei Fei Dao) or *Yellow River*, with its great chivalrous hero Huang He Da Xia?

We can hardly imagine a film that wasn't made for the audience. Experimental films are admittedly inferior to martial arts films in terms of box-office value, but they are certainly made for an audience, although the audience is specialized. I can hardly imagine that under socialist circumstances filmmakers of ideological consciousness would waste the people's money to make movies merely for personal ends. If entertainment movies come to be understood in such sweeping terms, won't the present debates, such as whether or not entertainment films should form the main body of contemporary Chinese film, or over the quality and principles of entertainment filmmaking, lose their value?

B: Categorizing films into entertainment and non-entertainment is done internationally. Entertainment movies, or commercial and dramatic movies, to use other names, aim at a vast audience through commercial distribution. Therefore, as I pointed out in "Questioning,"[1] the third kind of film, the entertainment film, is different from non-entertainments in three ways. (1) The two types of film have different structural elements. The basic elements in an entertainment film are the cast (stars), the story and the power of emotional motivation, while the non-entertainment film emphasizes a filmmaker's individual features and ideas (art film) or undertakes the explicit, accurate task of political propaganda and education (propaganda and educational films). (2) Entertainment films make no attempt to conceal their commercial nature and profit motive, while non-entertainment films stress their non-commercial nature and do not consider profit-making as an end. (3) Entertainment films use genres intended to simplify the audience's understanding of content; these genres constitute the films' essential theoretical foundation. At the same time, great attention is paid to cinematic grammar, audience psychology and marketing. Non-entertainment films in most cases draw upon the theories of other art forms (art film) or take a nation's policies as their guide (propaganda and educational films).

My classifications obviously do not contain judgment values; however, that doesn't mean that all films of a category are equal. Therefore, when I claim that both *Hibiscus Town* and *The Thief of Emei* are entertainment films, I don't mean to say that they are of equal quality. Although *Hibiscus Town* is a film of great ideological charm and critical power, its non-entertaining elements are packed with entertaining elements, like the painful love story of the female protagonist and the maximized emotional elements in the narrative. It is this that allows the ideological content of the film to access a large audience. Any entertainment film strives first to attract an audience, to capture people's interest to such an extent that they cannot help but see it, and at the same time, always to keep them happy. On the basis of this premise, a series of specific rules for scripting, narrative techniques, placement of highlights and character descriptions takes shape.

Art films do not follow any established rules. On the contrary, they strive to break the rules, to be different and unique. Therefore a French director called art films "film noir," to best sum up their essential features. In this term, "noir" means personal and creative individuality and experimentation in art. All established rules must be discarded, and there is no need to consider whether other people can accept or understand the film.

In our present discussion of the entertainment film, the basic issue should be how to strengthen the filmmakers' understanding of the audience so that they can plan their work more seriously. We could learn more about how to make good martial arts and action movies, because currently audiences are interested in these genres, just as audiences in Hong Kong today prefer comedies; European and American audiences are intoxicated with action and adventure; and Indian audiences ardently love song-and-dance films. It is normal for the audience to prefer a certain genre in a certain period. When the audience prefers a genre, producers immediately go after it and make films of that genre like mad. When the audience becomes bored, producers go on to something else. ("Going after what's hot," in Western film, refers to this). It seems this is common everywhere except in those countries where films are made under the direct control of a central government. Thus the present increase in martial arts and action movies here is caused by the law of supply and demand, and should not be criticized by saying, "The Chinese like to do things like a swarm of bees."

If the concept of entertainment movies were so broadly defined, would this lead to the making of only one kind of film? I don't think so. Diversity is not by type of film, but by subject matter and style. In the broadly defined concept of entertainment movies there is the potential for making films of diverse subject matter and styles. The definition does not go against diversification, any more than dividing literature into the serious and the popular will make it less diverse.

A: I don't oppose dividing film into the two categories. However, I disagree with you on one point. You emphatically claim that they shouldn't contain value judgments, that films ought to be treated equally and the notion of a hierarchy in this matter be opposed. However, since you emphasize the social nature of film as a form of popular entertainment, you have actually elevated the position of entertainment movies in the ontological sense, because the art film, as a representation of a unique individual experience, obviously does not expect general acceptance and therefore goes absolutely against the so-called social nature of film. Yet when evaluated in terms of "the overall nature of film," entertainment movies are substandard, because they, as products of comparable craftsmanship, are far from, even counter to, the artistic nature of film, which requires that a specially constructed set of signs be used to represent special life experiences. You have emphasized again and again that entertainment movies do indeed have something to do with art, and that those who make them ought to pay attention to improving their artistic qualities. Furthermore, you have repeatedly referred to a few so-called "masters," like Hitchcock, as examples to encourage those filmmakers. I feel that this indicates that you haven't gotten down from the high horse of a theorist. Now that you are promoting entertainment, there's no need for you to chat about art anymore.

On the issue of entertainment and art films, I propose not only that films be categorized and a clear line of demarcation be drawn, but also that the task of filmmaking be divided and everyone make his own films. The reason to make entertainment movies is to satisfy the desires of the general public—in Freudian terms, to satisfy sexual desire and the desire for violence. Therefore, entertainment movies cannot exist without sex and violence. In this regard, those who make entertainment moves can learn from those tabloid newspaper writers who aim only at attracting their readers, without considering such things as literary qualities, profound themes or complicated characters. Right now, the major trouble with Chinese entertainment movies is that there aren't as many of them as there are tabloid newspapers. Vulgarity is vulgarity. Don't ever hope to be a little more elegant, once you've entered the realm of vulgarity. It is impossible to appeal to both elegance and vulgarity at the same time.

Those who devote their lives to art films shouldn't be pushed to make entertainment movies. Everyone has his or her own aspirations, but that doesn't mean that everyone can make art films. Besides, in the present economic situation, it's become more difficult to make them. Nevertheless, what represents the level of a country's film culture is undoubtedly its art films, not its entertainment movies, just as what marks contemporary Chinese literature and art cannot be a tabloid newspaper on the streets.

Consequently, I cannot agree that what dominates the international film history is entertainment (commercial) movies, not art films. I must admit that for nearly a century more entertainment films than art films have been made, but only in a world history of film in which every movie ever made were included could entertainment movies dominate. In a history of film art, entertainment movies could hardly be included; the ones who would be included would be Eisenstein, Ingmar Bergman, Antonioni and the like—not Hitchcock, because Hitchcock had nothing to do with art. He was a craftsman. His excellence in creating suspense, or whatever, can hardly be regarded as art.

B: I appreciate your frankness, though our views are totally different. We could never agree on some issues, such as what is or is not art. Therefore, you can well claim that entertainment movies have nothing to do with art—art as you see it. You may well negate the artistic position of Hitchcock and the like, and you may well go on reading that history of film art on your own, although no such history has ever been published.

At present, the film circle holds basically three attitudes toward entertainment movies. The first is contempt, taking entertainment movies as a sacrifice one makes to cater to others and obliterating a filmmaker's individuality. The sole purpose of making an entertainment movie is to coax the audience into buying tickets.

The second basic attitude is to underestimate it; this course is taken mainly by the filmmakers who complain, "It's not as easy to get rich (by making entertainment movies) as I expected," or who break with the models and rules in their first attempt. Certainly, to make entertainment movies requires innovation and experimentation, but the rules for making them were gradually formed, through countless reciprocal film movements of "from the audience, to the audience." Breaking the rules before starting the game is a bit too hasty, and the hope of success is certainly slim.

The third basic attitude is enthusiasm, that is, engaging in the creation of entertainment movies with a serious and earnest spirit, and analyzing and evaluating them in the same fashion.

If the making of entertainment movies was treated in the same way as any other creative act, would filmmakers be led in a wrong direction and their films be neither fish nor fowl, neither vulgar nor elegant? In the 1988 meeting of the Golden Rooster Awards, I proposed that an issue of "frowning on the refined" exists in the making of contemporary Chinese entertainment movies. By that I meant that in an environment where public opinion generally favors experimental films, creators of entertainment movies improperly insert refined and elegant elements, such as the discontinuity, unusual angles and strange compositions, required of non-narrative, philosophical language into their work. Because they feel inferior, they want to raise the quality and artistic level of their films and gain praise, or at least to avoid the castigation of theoretical and critical circles. This doesn't add lustre to their works; on the contrary, it makes them as distasteful as foreign phrases mixed up in a Peking Opera, or sweet and sour sauce mixed with coffee. However, my opposition to this doesn't mean I oppose paying attention to quality, nor do I want to drive entertainment movies out of the realm of art, as those who would turn them into tabloids preach.

The representation of individuality is emphasized in contemporary art. This is a strong correction against the mechanical aspect of mimetic theory, and the inevitable result of the industrial revolution in the West near the end of the last century. Today, except for some key people who strongly oppose the consumer culture of the West, the representation of individuality is favored but hasn't been generally understood. Too many filmmakers believe it must be taken to an extreme, must break away from the general public, in order to be art. This notion seems especially ridiculous in the field of film, which is naturally geared to the audience.

Many people speak ill of the assembly-line productions by Hollywood in the 1930s and 1940s because they completely eliminated individuality. However, we should see that assembly-line filmmaking is itself a product of the great studio system of Hollywood. After the disintegration of this system in the 1950s, assembly-line production came to an end, but Hollywood movies didn't lose their audiences. As we can see, then, assembly-line production is not necessarily related to the creation of entertainment movies. Also, even in Hollywood in the 1930s and 1940s, truly talented directors could still make distinctive films on the assembly line. Proof can be found in the batch of Hollywood directors, primarily Hitchcock, proposed by the French New Wave critics in their auteur theory.

My concept of art apparently belongs to the vulgar; therefore, I should not only oppose looking down on the refined, but also turning entertainment movies into tabloids. I have been trying hard to pull entertainment movies into the palace of art and at the same time prevent them from becoming enchanted and falling into company with the refined. If this is riding the high horse of the theorist, I'll never get down from it.

A: You've published a lot in the past, singing praise for the experimental film. Now that experimental filmmaking has met a serious economic barrier, you're pushing entertainment movies and claiming you'll sing a holy song of peace to soothe the soul of the experimental, and denouncing the years when experimental narratives grew vigorously, as a period of art for art's sake. A theorist must avoid treating theoretical work pragmatically, currying favor with the powerful and advocating one thing today and another tomorrow. I clearly oppose traditional films, commercial movies, and therefore propose to sing a song of success for experimental narratives. In the present situation, we should not stop shouting encouragement for experimental narratives merely because of financial problems. We should appeal to the Party and the government to support them for the future of our national culture.

B: I have held a consistent position on the experimental narrative and entertainment films. I have neither advocated one thing today and another tomorrow, nor supported one while negating the other. I have argued with a lot of comrades over the years, with both those who support and those who oppose experimental narratives; with those who support and those who oppose entertainment films, because I hold some unique positions about the position, function, structure, value and the like, of both experimental narratives and entertainment films. I must admit these opinions of mine have rarely received support from theoretical and critical circles. Either I am considered too Westernized, or confined too much to the traditional. For example, my support of commercial movies is based on my understanding of the social nature of film. I support the art film in the hope that it will help find talented personnel for commercial movies, so as to elevate and perfect them. Once out of this orbit, I will be on the opposite side. You think I advocate one thing today and another tomorrow, because you haven't understood clearly the reasons why I support or oppose these things.

Chinese experimental narratives belong to the art film. I did applaud and sing a song of success for them, but at almost the same time, I warned the theorists and critics not to follow in every film movement in the West, which has constantly taken potshots at the nature of film as popular entertainment and elevated film to a pure art, an inappropriate position obviously divorced from the masses.[2] I pointed out clearly at that time that the contribution of the art film should lie in the new energies it can bring to commercial movies and its ability to foster new talent.

After the incessant criticism of the Xie Jin model, I published "The Road of Innovation of Chinese Film" and "Surpassing Does not Depend Necessarily on Negation,'' pointing out emphatically that to be anti-tradition is not the road to innovation, that revolt and breakthroughs should be done only on the basis of a deep understanding and free control of tradition, and that in filmmaking, to praise oneself for being lonely without keeping vast audiences in mind actually reveals one's incompetence and shallowness.[3]

When the winds praising experimentation and denouncing entertainment were blowing harder and harder in the theoretical and critical circles, and when the tendency to frown on the refined and the disease of artistic vanity became more and more evident, I blew my trumpet in a correspondingly higher tone to praise commercial films. At the meeting for the Golden Rooster Awards in Shenzhen, I expounded the history of film in New China from the point of view of the audience. After affirming the positive results achieved in the period "in which film served art," I proposed that attention should be paid to the negative influence of this period. In the New Era, what is most influential and talked about is undoubtedly the vigorous rise of the theory and practice of the art film. To characterize this stage of Chinese film by this feature doesn't imply an overall evaluation of all movies produced in this period. Therefore, there was no need to rush to the defense of the ignorance and paucity of the artistic spirit represented by Xie Jin's films.

Right now, the art film in China is facing an extremely hard economic situation. The artists, who lived long in a paradise of film, where box-office income was simply not a consideration, are perplexed by the sudden rise in commercial pressure, like children who have not learned the skills of survival who suddenly lose the parents who fed and clothed them. The problem the studios now face is no longer the dilemma of making money or saving face, but the demand that they make money. The art film, no matter how "indispensable" it is theoretically and how "reasonable" the theory of division of filmmaking, is left hopeless without investment. Therefore, considering the present situation, whether to sing a song of success for experimental narratives (to encourage film artists to continue to hold aloof from the world and look at people from a bird's-eye view) or to sing a song of peace to soothe their souls (to hope that the artists learn how to make movies for the audience) is a matter of life and death for Chinese film.

What puzzles one is why some of our comrades who are eager to sing a song of success for experimental narratives are unwilling to change their tune and care more about the entertainment film and about how to enhance its quality. They insist on dividing filmmakers into two groups: the intellectual aristocrats, who sit leisurely in their ivory towers, and the philistines, who are in charge of satisfying the sexual desires and desire for violence of the audience and making money from it. Zhang Yimou's *Red Sorghum* has proved that an entertainment movie can accomplish a lot in terms of art and can represent a nation in the realm of international cinema. From both Zhang Yimou's own account and the film itself, *Red Sorghum* cannot be considered an experimental narrative.

In terms of world cinema, those who preach and shoot art films, with few exceptions, are all outsiders—painters, photographers, novelists, architects, lawyers and teachers—as well as young people who have not found the road into the profession. They have only two purposes: to try to reform film using the laws of other arts, and to attract attention through their unconventional ways, in order to open the door into the realm of film. Actually, that our experimental narratives became a hotpot of creativity during the first decade of the New Era was the result of a special historical condition which will disappear in a twinkle and cannot be regained. "The theory of film as film was discarded. . . . The arts were in desperate need of innovation. . . . The issue of entertainment movies was still forbidden territory and the film market was superficially prosperous."[4] It was natural that film be restored to normalcy, that is, be made for the general public. Theorists and critics who have a sense of responsibility for the prosperity and development of Chinese film ought to consider this easily recognizable reality. It is quite improper to consider oneself aloof and elegant, or to try to please the public with claptrap.

In the long run, it is necessary to make a small number of experimental narratives which do not take money-making as their end, so as to find and foster new talent and to experiment with uncommon representations and the imagination. But the argument that entrusts the elevation of the artistic quality of film and its international recognition to experimental narratives, the theory of division "which divides filmmakers into explorers and tabloid writers," must be denounced and rejected. Considering the present situation and the filmmakers' general ideological level, cultural quality and artistic competence, what's at stake is to require or even compel filmmakers to strengthen their awareness of the audience, to try their best to study it, and explore the right way to its heart. Now, the mentality of frowning on the refined hasn't faded; the subcurrent of criticizing the Xie Jin model is still flowing, and things such as "the classical definition," "tabloid tendency" and the "theory of division" are seriously affecting the healthy development of entertainment movies. It is beneficial and does no harm to talk less about, or even temporarily ignore, experimental narratives.

A: We are thus involved in the issue of how to treat the sublime and popular culture, or the refined and the vulgar. I agree that what represents the cultural level of a country or nation must be the sublime (refined) culture, not the popular (vulgar) culture. Entertainment films unquestionably belong to popular culture. It is unimaginable to use them to represent Chinese film art. Films are expensive and therefore rely on a large audience to sustain them, but to negate the position of film in the sublime culture for this reason is philistine. Everything should be decided by the demands of art and culture, not by those of profit or capital. The government should help foster art films, since this concerns the level of Chinese culture. We should continue to appeal from the highest theoretical levels for help from the government, instead of just letting it continue to negate the necessity for the existence and development of art films.

B: There are many things the government should do besides foster art films. The entire industry should be totally reformed. A mechanism of competition should replace the big pot, the iron rice bowl, and the iron post of power. A law of film should be formulated, and so on. I'm willing to appeal for the realization of all of these.

However, on the issue of fostering art films, I think we must understand one thing clearly, and that is the motive and purpose of our appeal. In this regard, my opinion is fairly clear. As I stressed earlier, the primary purpose of my hope that the government invest in art films is to find and foster talent. In a number of countries in Western Europe—France, for example— the government takes a certain amount of money from the box office to support maiden works of young people who aspire to make films. I appreciate this. At some film festivals—Tokyo, for example—an award is given to directors who have made a brilliant first works, so that they may continue their profession. The purpose of such an award is to foster talent. Instances of investing much in art films other than to discover and foster new talent are in the least rare, if they exist at all. As Vincent Canby, the American film critic, says, there's not a single capitalist in the United States who would spend $7 or $8 million to collect an art movie. To appeal for the fostering of art films out of a dislike of entertainment movies is even more unreasonable.

One reason given in the appeal for art films is especially debatable. Someone apparently thinks that since the Chinese audience, fated to be structured in feudal times, still contains the sediment of backwardness in its thinking, films made for it inevitably pander to its moral tastes. For instance, the Chinese are acutely aware that they were the subjects of feudal rule; therefore, entertainment movies have to satisfy them by depicting a "wise king" or an "upright magistrate," and the like. According to this line of reasoning, the Chinese are born meek; therefore, they need powerful characters in martial arts movies to maintain their psychological balance. Because of this, more entertainment movies will inevitably weaken or even eliminate an artist's spirit of social criticism, and anesthetize the audience.

This is putting the cart before the horse and may even be an argument intended to humiliate the Chinese people out of ill will. The entertainment movies of the West are indeed intended to anesthetize audiences, to let them forget their problems and feel at ease, to escape reality. This has been normal for Hollywood thus far. There have been inferior Chinese entertainment movies which promoted an awareness of feudalism, but is there enough evidence to prove that the problem was not caused by the ideology of the filmmakers? Is there evidence to prove that the filmmakers were indeed forced to make such movies? I'd rather believe the American scholar who pointed out that the reasons Hollywood makes a lot of films intended to satisfy rather than trigger a demand for action, or to arouse sympathy and fear rather than cause a revolt, is that "they are made to serve the ruling class, to help sustain the present situation, to soothe the oppressed and to induce those who dare not to take action because they lack organization to merrily accept the absurd solutions to the various economic and social conflicts provided in genre movies." Here, the audience is a victim. Further, is there sufficient evidence to prove that the audience would dislike entertainment movies with both great charm and a strong spirit of social criticism? Before Liberation, China had many well-made, progressive films for entertainment, such as *The Spring River Flows East* and *Crows and Sparrows* (1949), which made a spectacular stir, not to mention classic instances, such as Chaplin's films, readily found in foreign film histories. On the other hand, can we say that art films, which represent an artist's individual, unique experience of life, must be spiritually uplifting? Haven't we seen enough Western art films, which publicize religious mysticism, pessimism, and sexual liberation?

To put it bluntly, I think it utterly groundless to think that films made for vast audiences must cater to feudal, backward notions and primitive desires in the minds of the majority. It is even more ridiculous to consider the appreciative psychology of the Chinese audience as something special. People invariably cherish the true, the good and the beautiful, and despise the false, the evil and the ugly. Therefore, the success of an entertainment movie lies in nothing more than its ability to coincide with a certain moral mentality that humans share (good will be rewarded with good, evil with evil), to satisfy human desires (a harmonious family, a happy marriage, a rich life), to arouse a certain curiosity shared by humans (uncommon customs, natural mysteries) and to trigger a common idea of idols (a hero and his beauty, a unique talented figure from time immemorial). These are not all feudal and backward things, nor are they only Chinese.

In my conclusion, I'd like to say something about the issue of the so-called elegant and vulgar cultures, the sublime and the popular.

Issues of culture are complex. Works on the subject by emminent scholars, both at home and abroad, are numerous. A careful study shows that some terms used in recent writings, about elegant culture and vulgar culture, leave room for debate. The two extremes of a culture, in general, exist throughout history and in all countries and regions. However, the division of elegance and vulgarity, the sublime and the popular, has different meanings in different times and places. Within the same category there are also differences between the high and the low, the progressive and the reactionary. I do not intend to do an historical analysis of the limits of culture, nor do I want to talk about the concerns of other countries. What I want to do is give my own observations about the relationship between film and culture in the present stage of development of the Chinese economy.

Are there two extremes in Chinese culture, the elegant and the vulgar? Of course. But the elegant and the vulgar we're talking about are obviously not a simple evolution from the feudal dynasties of the culture of the royal court or officialdom, on the one hand, and the culture of the marketplace, on the other. Nor are they a reprint of the sublime and consumer cultures in the developed countries of the West. The elegant and the vulgar in contemporary China are not antithetical, but are learning from each other and making up each other's deficiencies. The difference between the elegant and the vulgar lies only in that the former can only be enjoyed by a minority at any given time, whereas the latter reaches the majority. In this respect, whether one is able to enjoy a culture and appreciate it or not depends on one's cultural accomplishments and interests. There's nothing more complex about it. Both serve the people and socialism, but they adopt direct and indirect ways of doing so. The line between them is often ambiguous, since the elegant culture in contemporary China is unlike the sublime culture of the West, which opposes commercialism without separating from it. The elegant culture in China also does not sidestep reality and place social life outside its creative perspective.

The elegant culture is generally viewed and evaluated from the same point of view without great divergence, except that one or two people equate it to the sublime culture of Western, developed countries. The problem is how to view and evaluate the vulgar. A common pitfall is to define the vulgar as philistine, uncultivated and boorish without justification, and thereupon be accused of frowning on the vulgar. The theoretical and critical circles of film are especially liable to fall into this. Looking at the actual situation, it is obvious that the products of the vulgar, as cultural products for the general public, are qualitatively different in terms of ideological content and artistry, but it is not true that all of them are tabloid literature and bathroom art. Low-quality and crudely made works, strictly speaking, have nothing to do with culture. They are merely a heap of junk, like those bad imitations of goods which lose their attributes as commodities because they have no practical value. All good works created for the general public in the modern history of Chinese literature and art should be considered outstanding representations of the modern vulgar culture of China, whether they inherit the May Fourth tradition or carry forward the tradition of revolutionary literature and art. These days, whenever someone wants to talk about the vulgar culture, he must omit Lu Xun and bring forth Zhang Henshui, omit *Red Sorghum* or *Hibiscus Town* and bring forth entertainment movies "designed to earn money and lose face." This is indeed a distorted understanding.

So I am not worried in the least that if the production of experimental narratives decreases or even comes to a halt, Chinese film will lose works that represent its cultural level in international circles. As long as the film circles devote themselves to the elevation of the ideological and artistic level of entertainment movies while trying their best to create a good working environment, Chinese film will continue on its way in the world. What's more, if the mainstream of Chinese films are really those works intended "to make money but lose face," then even if several experimental narratives win a few international awards, where does the glory of Chinese film lie?

NOTES

1. Shao Mujun, "Questioning the Third Kind of Film."

2. Shao Mujun, "To Gain Aesthetic Enjoyment from Entertainment Movies," *Wen Yi Daily*, February 1, 1986.

3. Shao Mujun, "The Road of Innovation in Chinese Cinema," *Film Art*, September 1986; Shao Mujun, "Surpassing Does Not Depend Necessarily on Negation," *Guang Ming Daily*, November 27, 1986.

4. *Chinese Film Daily*, September 5, 1988.

13

Contemporary Chinese Entertainment Films: A Summary of a Symposium

Zhang Wei
Translated by Fu Binbin

As the 1980s drew to an end, at a time when the Chinese economy and culture stood at an important turning point, our ideas about filmmaking and film culture were undergoing a great transformation: Entertainment was replacing propaganda and art, and gradually taking the dominant position. During the 1988 "craze for entertainment films," every studio produced a few fairly good ones; however, many others were barely satisfactory, and roughly made works could often be found. Attitudes toward the craze varied widely, both inside and outside of film circles.

In December 1988, in response to the controversy, *Contemporary Cinema* held a symposium on the contemporary Chinese entertainment film, to define its role, both positive and negative, within the overall culture. The participants first viewed a number of entertainment films made both at home and abroad, among them such domestic works of 1988 as *Troubleshooters*, *Rock and Roll Kids*, *Crazy Singer*, *He Chose to Murder*, *Arrest Deferred*, *Cop Hunting*, *Huang Tianba*, *Goddess of Revenge*, *Brutal Desire* and *Crazy Bandit*. The symposium, presided over by Xu Zhuang and Shen Jiming, deputy chief editors of *Contemporary Cinema*, produced a variety of speeches, dialogues, debates and arguments.

In his opening speech, the editor-in-chief, Chen Haosu, said, "Our lives are devoid of entertainment. This is not a sign of progress, for entertainment satisfies the advancement of society and civilization. In the past, entertainment was positioned at the low end of the scale because of poverty and political turmoil. It's time to change this. A film can educate people and make them understand their anxieties; however, this is not the sole responsibility of film art. A monotonous overemphasis on propaganda or art may lead us to underestimate entertainment and entertainment films." Chen Haosu thus advocated that an artist should foster entertainment, and make high-quality entertainment movies. In his opinion, it is proper for the audience to release its feelings and achieve catharsis with the help of entertainment. Entertainment films should dominate, but this doesn't necessarily mean there's not room for other types of films.

The symposium launched its discussion by centering on the background and significance of the current craze for the entertainment film. Some pointed out that it was the inevitable result of the development of Chinese history and culture. As they saw it, the rise of the entertainment film represented an important transformation in the development of Chinese film culture and its idea of film, since it emerged together with the overall transformation of the Chinese economy and culture. Within film circles its significance surpassed even that of the restoration of order in the New Era, out of the chaos wrought by the Cultural Revolution.

In the opening discussion, some filmmakers found it difficult to decide whether entertainment or art films were better. The reason why domestic entertainment films are of a poor quality was obviously related to a tradition which emphasizes education while it despises entertainment, and to the disdainful attitude held by some studio leaders who, more often than not, refuse to assign the most talented directors to entertainments, thus hindering the creative development of such films.

Theorists, who often flock to experimental narratives, muddle their criticism of entertainment films and may even find them unworthy of study. Critics not only refuse to get down off their high horses, but also refuse to let artists get down off theirs. After Zhang Junzhao shot *The Lonely Murderer* (1985), he was called "degenerate"; Tian Zhuangzhuang, after making *Rock and Roll Kids* (1988), was considered "lost"; and Teng Wenji, after *Hurricane Operation* (1985), was labeled "shallow." Therefore, filmmakers who had already made outstanding entertainment films (Zhang Huaxun, for example, who had made *The Will of Warriors* and *Mysterious Buddha*) began to make art films because of the lower status of entertainments. They surrendered what they did well for what they did poorly. Others, who lacked good scripts, turned to pretty compositions and cinematography to compensate. Their movies hit the mark by a fluke, for they were praised for their "desalination of plot."

Some theorists argued that it is entirely wrong to think that only art films should be preserved in history, since art and educational films do not constitute the main body of production in any country. Film history, they pointed out, is primarily a history of entertainment. Still others argued that entertainment films had their own masters, like Chaplin and Hitchcock. Spielberg may have won no Oscars, but he remains a great master of film art, known to all.

Many participants proposed that the concept and semantic meaning of the entertainment film be clearly defined. Some thought that two approaches could help in this: the theory of subject matter and the theory of purpose. The theory of subject matter holds that genres such as murder mysteries, detective stories, martial arts films, musicals and comedies belong to entertainment film, while movies with serious subject matter, aimed at social criticism or education and propaganda, have nothing to do with entertainment. The theory of purpose, on the other hand, holds that movies made to express individuality and personal experience are artistic, while those made to please audiences are entertainments. The theory of subject matter was generally considered untenable, since the same subject matter can be treated in either an art film or an entertainment. The theory of purpose was considered more scientific, but an opposing opinion insisted that the theory of purpose could not distinguish entertainment from non-entertainment. The line of demarcation, they argued, ought to be drawn in philosophical terms. Films which provide a way to self-contemplation are art films, while those which supply self-enjoyment are entertainments.

As the discussion intensified, the participants had to compare the differences and similarities between art and entertainment films. Entertainment films, they pointed out, belong in the realm of popular culture and conform to the grammar of language, while experimental works are part of high-brow culture and inherently counter to the norms of language. The entertainment film identifies with mainstream ideology, while the experimental film runs against it. Entertainment films value the importance of story and stress causal relationships, while art films are anti-narrative and break cause-and-effect relationships. An entertainment film follows traditional morality, but an art film goes against it. The audience of the entertainment film identifies with the film, whereas the audience of the art film is distanced from it.

Considering the scope of entertainment films, a number of participants thought that all features except experimental narratives belong in the realm of entertainment. One opposing opinion insisted that a third kind of movie, realistic films like *Hibiscus Town* and *In the Wild Mountains*, does not belong in the world of entertainment.

With regard to the relationship of entertainment to art, some filmmakers proposed that the thick wall between the two kinds of film should be removed, and that entertainment and art should be blended in a single pot. To make entertainment films on a high level, one must put one's personal ideas, experiences, enthusiasm, emotions and the whole of one's heart into them. Opposing this idea, several theorists suggested that one should think solely of oneself and not the audience when making an art film, but that if one wanted to shoot an entertainment, one had to emphasize the audience without considering one's ego. One opinion held that movies for entertainment should have ideological connotations, and that these connotations should be plain, yet fresh. Another suggested that an entertainment film is not supposed to bear the weight of philosophical theory; the task of education and enlightenment should be shouldered by works specifically designed to do so.

As the discussion progressed, one participant argued that the entertainment film primarily offered a substantive way to sexual satisfaction, through which the spectator could relieve suppressed emotions, that when the audience purchases tickets it actually buys the opportunity to relieve its desires. The question then is to what extent this should be allowed. Entertainment films should evade sexuality.

Following some discussion, someone noted that a film representing sex shouldn't strip everything away leaving nothing left for the imagination. On the contrary, it was argued, a film should have sexy characters, men and women with especially sexy features. Another held that it was not necessary to strip to attract an audience, and not necessarily true that only by displaying sexuality could a film make money. The key to success is a good story. Beautiful cinematography, songs and dances, and locations can also provide sensual pleasure.

A third participant suggested that the entertainment film should provide new values and capital, thus making the cultural marketplace alter its orientation. Some stressed the need for a high level of cultural quality and artistic style, and proposed decreasing the number of murder mysteries while increasing other genres.

Analyzing the development of domestic entertainment, Song Chong, Head of the Beijing Film Studio, pointed out that "in the fifties, our heroines were Red; in the sixties, they were blue, women of morality; in the eighties, gray has dominated—female singers, prostitutes, and thieves. Now the so-called 'riff-raff' culture has appeared." He suggested that entertainment films produced by the Beijing Film Studio reinforce the heroic spirit of the Chinese nation, diminish vulgar tastes and foreign flavors, and strengthen the healthy trends of the Reform Era. The open-mindedness of a large studio should advocate the ingenuity of an artist and reduce the clumsiness of a craftsman.

Song's speech initiated a comparison of Chinese and American entertainment movies, which yielded seven points. (1) Ideology penetrates into the films of both countries. (2) American film emphasizes both political benefits and economic profits, while in the more than thirty years since Liberation, Chinese film has stressed political functions. (3) American films, with high investments, aim at a global market, while Chinese film, with low investments, targets the domestic market. (4) The Americans use entertainment to realize ideologies, wheras the Chinese use education. (5) American film draws upon multi-form and modular genres, while Chinese film is uniform and synthetical. (6) Though both industries make dramatic films, the Americans stress miraculous images and a great deal of external action, while the Chinese give priority to interior action, emphasize dialogue and pay more attention to screenwriting. (7) With regard to aesthetic effects, American film seeks the release of desire and audiovisual pleasure, while Chinese film places particular emphasis on moral evaluation and emotional purification.

With the deepening of the discussion, the participants concentrated on how to elevate the quality of entertainment films and attract the audience. Some thought that the quality of entertainment films would improve as China learned more about genres. What we need to study first is how to standardize the way we shoot different genres. Then we need to enrich our musicals, song and dance films, comedies and youth movies, which are our weak points. Many pointed out that an important reason we are losing our audience is that too many domestic films have failed to adhere to the grammar of genres. A filmmaker should master the rules first, before breaking them and going off in a different direction.

To change the face of entertainment films, many professionals also proposed that we first strengthen our screenwriting, since screenwriting is the first baton in the relay race of filmmaking; failure of the first leg in the race will adversely affect the whole thing. Some suggested that a screenwriter of entertainment films should follow the principles of popular literature, the principle of two "do's" and three "don'ts," for example. *Do* link all segments of the plot together, and *do* use unique effects, but *don't* make a character complicated, *don't* make the dialogue artistic, and *don't* take an abstruse philosophy as the theme. However, others responded by saying that this method of screenwriting or filmmaking, indigenous to China, would ultimately ruin the quality and reputation of Chinese entertainment films.

A number of filmmakers pointed out that an entertainment film should be well packaged, that is, have good cinematography, sound, editing and so on. Everyone agreed that an acting institute should be established, where actors and actresses could get special training in the various genres.

In a discussion of criticism, several participants maintained that theories constructed around non-entertainment films cannot be applied to the criticism of entertainment films, and that a special effort must be made to study theories of entertainment, such as genre theory.

The seven-day symposium, which launched a fierce debate, is expected to have a positive influence on the quality of entertainment films.

Part V

The Debate on New Chinese Film Theory

By the late 1980s, the trend against tradition in new Chinese film theories was intensely criticized. One of the major criticisms came from the Changchun Film Studio, the oldest filmmaking base of the Communist Party. A group of editors from *Film Literature*, a magazine published by Changchun, issued a dialogue in *Film Art* (November 1987), the major theoretical journal published in Beijing, complaining about the new theories. The dialogue began with a criticism of the way the entertainment film was being discussed, and focused on the inconsistencies of the radical theorists. In the early 1980s, these theorists had criticized the traditional concept of film as a form of drama and called for the modernization of film language; In the mid–1980s, the same theorists advocated the works of the Fifth Generation. They apparently wanted to advance the art film movement. However, in the later 1980s, these theorists suddenly changed their position in favor of the entertainment film. The editors of *Film Literature* believed that the inconsistency of the theorists, especially in their discussions of the entertainment film, had caused confusion and frustration in filmmaking circles.

Those who advocated the new film theories did not waver in the least in defending their own positions. However, they did it, not from consistent film aesthetics, but from consistent theoretical methodology, which they argued was based in science. They held that the methodology of traditional Chinese film theory is essentially one of ethics, consistent with the spirit of the traditional culture. However, they failed to define what film is or is not, but instead proclaimed what film should or should not be, from a strong official political position. In contrast, the new theorists tried to treat film as an object of scientific understanding and tried to define film through an independent, academic position. Using this point as their base, they established the consistency between the developments in Chinese film theory in the early 1980s and those that came later in the decade. In these statements, they did not avoid in the least the relationship of new film theory with Western theories, and declared that their scientific methods derived from Western theories, mainly from those of Bazin and Kracauer in the early 1980s, and from more contemporary theories in the late 1980s. Indeed, some of them borrowed directly from Western theories, defining mainstream Chinese film as "ideological myth," instead of reflections of reality and truth as portrayed by socialist realism. Here we can see clearly that the radical film theorists were consistent, not only in their methodology, but primarily in their critical attitude toward traditional culture. The paper by Li Shaobai, a reputable film historian, represents the moderate view of older scholars.[1]

This debate, with the discussion of Yingxi, presents an important development in Chinese film theory in the New Era; this development is the reexamination and reevaluation of theory itself, its methodology and philosophical fundamentals. If, on the one hand, the traditional mythology and its relationship to traditional culture were criticized in the discussion of Yingxi, on the other hand, the new methodologies and cultural characteristics of film theory were explored in the debate on the new theory itself. This development represents the self-criticisms and modifications of film theory in the modernization movement and cultural changes in China in the 1980s.

NOTE

1. Li Shaobai, "Scattered Thoughts on the Value of Film Theory," *Film Art*, January 1988.

14

The Inequities and Biases of Film Theory

Zhou Yu, Li Chao and Zhao Baohua
Translated by Wang Xiaowen

When our film theorists claim that Chinese film is facing a crisis, do they realize that theory, too, is in crisis?

Zhao Baohua: Since the beginning of the New Era, Chinese film theory, no less brilliant than Chinese filmmaking, has opened the doors of the field to the entire world. On the one hand, film theory has started to introduce us to the development of international film studies; on the other, it has started to look inward upon itself. The diversity of recent theory and the variety of schools of thought indicate this direction.

Li Chao: The major achievement of film theory in the New Era also lies in its concern for the relationship between film and reality. Theorists now pay considerable attention to the relationship between film and audience, and to the qualities of the medium itself. The sincere study of cinematic language and form and the nature of the medium, as well as the introduction of foreign schools of thought, style and technique, has pushed forward the development of Chinese film and improved its quality.

CONFUSION CAUSED BY A SHIFT IN DIRECTION

Zhao Baohua: Film theory has been very active during the New Era; yet veiled behind its activity has been a chaos which dominates production and film-making practices.

Li Chao: In the first few years of the era, the theoretical circle was crazy over the discussion of the "new film concept." Many theorists presented their opinions of this, but others only offered casual ideas. At the time, theorists were uncertain, as can be seen in their conflicting positions toward the experimental narrative, at the beginning of this period, and the entertainment film, at the end.

In the past, many considered the new concept as a documentary style with a simple plot, but just when realistic aesthetics was reaching a peak and study of the experimental narrative was on the rise, theoretical studies took a sudden turn and the entertainment became the hot target of research and debate. This rapid shift of interest has led to major conflicts. Not only are the theorists confused, but so are the filmmakers. The emergence of this new interest has something to do with declining box office returns, but it is also a move away from the lack of balance between past theory and practice.

Zhou Yu: This sharp reversal reveals the problems of film theory. The chaos in theory is most harmful to the filmmakers, for the contradictions and unevenness deprive practitioners of a clear direction. In the past, theorists advocated a documentary style which diminished plot, character, theme and expression. They denied the Hollywood model, considering it a matter of dramatic style rather than of film art. Today, however, they have reevaluated Hollywood and advocate learning from it. In the past, some regarded plot as something vulgar and ugly; today, critics advocate the entertainment movie, which puts plot in the most critical position. The contrast is obvious. People feel confused, doubtful and resentful, especially when the contradictory opinions are given by the very same person.

Zhao Baohua: All of a sudden, every director wanted to be a Wu Yigong, to make the same kind of film. Everyone favored the deemphasis of plot. Unfortunately, this caused an deemphasis of profits as well. The crisis at the box office confused the theorists and led them to turn to discussions of the entertainment film. Where they once fervently pressed for a documentary style, now they began pushing the entertainment film just as fervently. The result, in general, has been two extremes and twice as much confusion.

Zhou Yu: The de-emphasis of plot creates films like *On the Hunting Ground* and *Horse Thief*, hardly a print of either of which was sold, revealing the crisis of this position. If *Horse Thief* were a documentary, it would be excellent, but defined as a narrative with not much of a plot, it loses all quality as a feature film.

Li Chao: If Tian Zhuangzhuang failed to clarify the theoretical concept of his film, theorists also failed to clarify the concept in their debates.

Zhao Baohua: The theory of a new concept of film led, on the one hand, to total failure at the box office; on the other hand, it put film artists into an awkward situation. Wu Yigong moved on to *Sister* after his first film, *My Memories of Old Beijing*; after his first film, Tian Zhuangzhuang went to *On the Hunting Ground* and *Horse Thief*. Zhang Huaxun made *The Mysterious Camel Team* (1986). He didn't want to make any more films after *Mysterious Buddha* and *The Will of Warriors*, because he feared the theorists wouldn't recognize him anymore.

Li Chao: There should be a separate category for films like *Yellow Earth, On the Hunting Ground* and *Horse Thief.* As experimental narratives, they're fine, since they needn't be concerned with the box office. But film theorists should be clear-headed when they evaluate these films. They should be especially cautious when giving advice to filmmakers. There was nothing wrong about Chen Kaige and Tian Zhuangzhuang making these films. What was wrong was that when the theorists discussed them, they thought of them as epoch-making works, real films, and the films which preceded them as pre-films, non-films.

Zhou Yu: When they drew their conclusions about the films of the New Era, a number of theorists considered the experimental works to be the best and neglected the realities of the marketplace. Even when experimental directors were confused and felt that their works were unwelcome to the audience, these theorists insisted their films were the only true films.

Li Chao: The style of *Yellow Earth* is good, but it isn't the only good film. We can't say that *Yellow Earth* was good and *The Will of Warriors* was not, or vice-versa, since the entertainment film is now in high favor. In his "Dialogue on the Entertainment Film," Li Tuo says, "Currently, some people deride us for having advocated the new concept of film and experimentation, but now we've come to the end of our tether and must return to the entertainment film. There's something to this notion." (See chapter 9.)

Zhao Baohua: The madness surrounding both the experimental and the entertainment film has its extremes and prejudices. Apparently if certain theorists favor something, it becomes the ultimate truth. They always want to create waves so others can follow the trend. As a result, their authority is sharply reduced and practitioners tend to doubt them.

Zhou Yu: Actually, we should be tolerant of both experimental and entertainment films. Although experimental works add a great deal to film language, other films also make original contributions, which enrich the language and at the same time nourish the experimental. The things that come out of the experimental, in turn, feed other art films. The process is circular. In the past ten years, experimental films have achieved a lot, yet why do some people dislike them? It's because the theorists have gone to an extreme, overestimating the experimental while looking down upon other films. The truth is, among the non-experimental are plenty of films worthy of praise that have not been given proper evaluation, an omission that is damaging to the development of Chinese film.

Zhao Baohua: What should you think after seeing the title, "The Emergence of Fifth Generation Directors Marks the Beginning of Cinematic-ness in Chinese film?" Apparently there were no true films before those of the Fifth Generation. At the least we had *Street Goddess* and *The Lin Family Store* (1959). Whoever concluded that only pre-films existed before *Yellow Earth* probably hadn't seen many films of the past. Also, the quality he mentioned belongs only to theories concerning ontology and the nature of film.

CONFUSION CAUSED BY DIFFERENT AESTHETIC STANDARDS

Li Chao: The crisis in theory relates directly to the uncertainty of aesthetic standards.

Zhao Baohua: To begin with, the irresponsible definition of aesthetic standards can be blamed on the once famous article, "On Mediocrity," by the Beijing Young Film Critics Society.[1] They made the directors of films they considered mediocre their targets, and included a number of excellent films among those which didn't suit their tastes. What they really favored were the experimental narratives, for they thought only such films could lead to a new direction. As a matter of fact, they don't know what mediocre means. They only used the term so they could conveniently define things according to their own tastes.

Zhou Yu: They consider themselves more intelligent than everyone else and refuse to debate with others on an equal level. They don't think it's important to study film seriously theoretically and with high intelligence. They simply concluded that the "Changchun Film Studio is a major source of mediocrity" and that the "Shanghai Film Studio should shut its doors."

Zhao Baohua: The Changchun Film Studio has made a number of mediocre films, but if we can find the core of this mediocrity and treat it, the entire film industry will benefit. People wonder why the society considers comparatively good films mediocre. The major reason for the society's criticism is that Changchun hasn't produced films that fit into the trend. Well, what is the trend of Chinese film? What are the films which lead the trend like? They never define it. Maybe it's buried in their minds.

There are other inequities in Chinese film theory. First, theorists pursue the works of only a few select directors and ignore an overall study of Chinese film. Second, they give more attention to a learned audience and neglect the larger, primarily rural and uneducated audience. They stress "elegance" and ignore "vulgarity."

Zhou Yu: This issue came out of the film society's conclusions about the films of the New Era, which some divide into three phases. Their point of departure is invariably the experimental works, which form only a small portion of a studio's production. If they want to undertake conclusive research, they should include the other films, which constitute the majority made during this decade and which have brought aesthetic pleasure to their audience and supported the entire industry. Some of these films were actually better than the experimental narratives. It's impossible to get a real look into the New Era without a large-scale study.

Li Chao: I think there's more than one approach to this matter, including, for one, the different opinions brought on by the overall estimation of Chinese film, such as the view that Chinese film as a whole is of poor quality. Most people, audience and theorists alike, seem to agree with that, and everyone wants to improve it. Yet some theorists focus only on a few, presumably excellent, films, ignoring the production level of Chinese film as a whole as well as the tastes of the audience. They show no interest in improving the quality of other films, but simply pass them off as mediocre. This is harmful.

Zhou Yu: That's why some theorists are worried. They advocate "reeducating" the audience, dragging them closer to their point of view, but the audience refuses to listen. They spend their money to see movies, not for reeducation.

Zhao Baohua: Some contemporary theorists are rather exclusive, believing that only what they advocate can be correct. Audiences have low and high tastes; film has different genres. Since there is diversity in taste, there must be diverse film styles.

Zhou Yu: The relationship between filmmaker and audience is not one of educator and student. It is ridiculous to advocate educating the audience. We should adjust our films according to its tastes. You can't expect to always be on the same level. Sometimes you are on a high level, sometimes the audience is. Film improves through a continuous process of give and take, a dialectical relationship, an equal relationship.

Li Chao: Audience appreciation and artist's creation form a relationship between consumption and production, in Marxian terms, which is basically the same as that in the commercial world. Consumption stimulates production; otherwise production is aimless. Marx said that the art object creates an audience with aesthetic ability, the ability to understand it. This applies to all products. So production not only creates objects for its subjects, but also creates subjects for its objects. If you believe in Marxism, you should be confident. As long as your film is good, the audience will like it and improve as your filmmaking improves. You don't have to reeducate them.

Zhao Baohua: The imbalance in aesthetic evaluation is also represented by the tendency to separate theory from practice. Too many theorists create a labyrinth, using obscure terms which others can scarcely understand. One can see this in the articles written about the New Era.

Li Chao: Some theorists use "imagistic" film to define the evolution of Chinese film in the New Era, speaking of it as the period of the imagistic film.[2] There is no proof of this.

Zhao Baohua: That conclusion is unscientific. The end of film theory is to serve practice, and to be accepted by practitioners.

Li Chao: People often assign arbitrary titles to a period. To call *Yellow Earth* imagistic is incorrect. All films contain images, after all. Film can't exist without them. It isn't proper to separate "image" and "imagistic."

Zhou Yu: Chinese film theorists always expect their ideas to direct the practice of others, but they don't relate their theories closely to filmmaking and solve its real problems. That's why so few filmmakers pay any attention to theorists.

Li Chao: You hit the nail right on the head. Too many theorists are eager for quick success and an instantaneous return.

Zhou Yu: They hope to propose something startling and make it the banner of the times. Things not under their flag are not in the troop.

Li Chao: Another inequity of aesthetic standards is that theorists favor space more than time. We should note that Chinese film hasn't emphasized space for some time. Many directors know well how to tell a story, but know less about matters of space. That's what makes the introduction of Kracauer and Bazin, as well as Western expressionism and aesthetics, quite beneficial. Through their emphasis upon spatial configuration, our theorists and the Fifth Generation have made a significant contribution, but there is some confusion. They overemphasize the aesthetics of the image; they ignore montage theory; and they propose a theory of "spatial thinking," elevating the function of spatial composition to an improper height.

It's fine to divide aesthetics into the aesthetics of drama and the aesthetics of the visual image, following a comparision between Chinese and Western aesthetics. Traditional Chinese film aesthetics is based in drama. It's necessary to propose an alternative concept in order to make people recognize and study the ontology of the film image. But it is doubtful that an aesthetic based on the film image can replace the traditional concept based in drama. It is true that the aesthetics of film-drama pay less attention to images than to narrative, even though narrative is restricted by its dramatic qualities. Yet the limitation of the aesthetic of the image is that it ignores narrative. On the structural level, film has both aesthetic qualities, which, together and inseparable, form the overall structure of the medium.

Zhou Yu: Actually, montage theory has a strong concept, which is the construction of space. Ever since Griffith and Eisenstein, the concept of constructed space has been there. When, for example, a shot of two people is cut with a shot of only one of them, a space is created. That's common knowledge, yet apparently some people don't agree with it. If we consider the long take, it isn't only about space. We simply can't define the long take as an aesthetics of space.

Li Chao: In the same way, we cannot simply call montage theory an aesthetics of time. To do so would be improper, for it would separate time and space. Time and space cannot be separated, no matter whether it is physical, mental or aesthetic. Such a separation would be harmful to both Chinese filmmaking and its theory. Yet another inequity in Chinese theory is exaggeration of the aesthetic potential of space. While the expression of space in film is unlimited, its potential can only function if combined with the potential of time. Our theorists ignore or belittle the functions of time and plot, at the same time that they emphasize space and composition. This leads them to ignore the most important element of film—the narrative. The function of narrative is an important subject of both classical and contemporary film theory. When it is ignored, theory becomes separated from practice, and the development of Chinese film is seen as backward.

Zhou Yu: Since film developed from photography, composition is unquestionably an important element. But film differs from photography because it deals with time; it adds motion to space. If we ignore time in film, we do ignore the narrative, which I agree is its most important element. The basic cause for the neglect of time can be found in the debate on plot. Since plot cannot exist without time, diminishing the time element would diminish the elements of narrative: character and theme.

Li Chao: Ignoring the narrative element would not only cause confusion in basic theoretical issues, but also would have an adverse effect on criticism. Consider the criticism of *Sun Zhongshan* (1987), a very good film, especially in its uses of space, but with many problems in time-space relationships. According to the director, Ding Yinnan, "The film is structured in terms of space. A theorist noted that the film is a successful, thorough and complete example of spatial thinking. It is second after *Yellow Earth* in the exploration of the aesthetics of space. *Sun Zhongshan*, overall, is structured and controlled by spatial composition."[3] We should enhance our understanding of filmic space, since it is a weak point in our cinema, but we shouldn't in the process weaken the functions of time and plot, nor ignore narrative structure. Attempting to move away from narrative structure and structure an entire film in terms of space would lead to a weakening of the relationships between the narrative elements. That's what's wrong with the first part of *Sun Zhongshan*. We see the four uprisings and their failures only through images and compositions, not through motivation, purpose and signficance. The film lacks causality.

Zhao Baohua: We only see an extremist's consciousness in this film because of the unilateral theory. Since the director meant to ignore and weaken the narrative functions, the inner motivation of Sun Zhongshan is obscure. What impresses most are the extravagant and delicate scenes of the daily life of this historical figure, rather than his character.

INEQUITIES AND BIASES CAUSED BY THE LOSS OF FILM ONTOLOGY

Zhao Baohua: We have said that the biases of film theory are caused by the fact that a few theorists focus on only a handful of directors and neglect general research into Chinese film. Though there are a few studies of Chinese film, they are biased. Wang Yichuan studies the overall history and the current situation of Chinese film.[4] He believes there has been a replacement of perceptual ontology by rational ontology. What on Earth is film ontology? We should make a study of this.

From the point of view of a mass medium, the ontology of film should be that of the audience. If film loses its audience, it loses its ontology. Wang Yichuan's ontology is based in the study of culture.

Li Chao: That's a sociological point of view. He thinks Chinese film since its inception has been a tool for moral instruction and has thereby lost its perceptual ontology.

Zhou Yu: I think Wang approaches the ontology of art and film from a philosophical position. As far as I can tell, he draws several conclusions. First, perception is a basic human quality; second, active perception is a basic quality of art; third, perception is also a basic quality of film; and fourth, the center of film is found in perception, the perceptual film and entertainment. The definition of film as pure perception denies that it can reflect the spirit of the times and advance consciousness. Purely perceptual film eventually ends in the expression of personal feelings.

Zhao Baohua: Self-expression is irrational, merely perceptual, instinctive and subconscious. It divorces film from contemporary times and from the realities of life.

Li Chao: We need to study Wang's theory in terms of the entire system of film theory. His theory is not an isolated case and cannot be removed from the current debate over the entertainment film. It is a part of it. From this point of view, Wang's theory does not coincide with the advocation of catharsis in the debate. From a purely theoretical position, it obviously has problems, but from a realistic point of view, it has its merit. In the past there were strong waves of irrationality in art and literary circles, and in the film circle, this irrationality blended with the wave of entertainment films, which complicated the issue. We need to be careful when we borrow from irrational Western theories. We cannot study the entertainment film in terms of such Western theory, for this would misdirect it.

Zhou Yu: According to some theorists, the entertainment film does not rest entirely upon catharsis, but also has an instructional function. Charlie Chaplin, the famous comedian, makes the best combination of entertainment and moral instruction, yet some will argue that instruction in entertainment is an obstacle to its development. That's ridiculous.

Zhao Baohua: We agree there should be guidelines for the entertainment film and for the study of it. We also agree that film should be entertaining and are willing to make efforts to see that this happens. We even agree that film has a cathartic function and should pursue a certain degree of pleasure. However, making the pleasure principle of Freud the primary principle of the entertainment film is highly questionable.

Li Chao: Art includes both entertainment and instruction. This combination forms the complete aesthetics of art, though the ratio between them may vary. We may emphasize one aspect, entertainment, at this time, but we cannot make entertainment the only aesthetic principle.

Zhou Yu: It may be true that catharsis can reduce the frequency of crime, but it isn't essential for all films to have a cathartic function. Films containing sex and violence function not only as a catharsis, but inductively as well. After all, entertainment films work on different levels. Some people enjoy nudity; others find it vulgar.

Li Chao: The question is how we define healthy, as opposed to vulgar, entertainment.

Zhou Yu: Noble and healthy entertainment comes together with good feelings and makes people feel pure and optimistic; vulgar entertainment only satisfies perceptual instincts. There's a difference between the two.

Zhao Baohua: We can't simply understand entertainment as the satisfaction of perceptual instincts. There is rational satisfaction in entertainment.

Zhou Yu: I think Chinese theorists should study Chinese experiences of entertainment for the past several decades first, before they study the contemporary entertainment film. They should seek out models appropriate to Chinese film rather than follow the Hollywood model.

Zhao Baohua: The biases of studies of the entertainment film prove once again that the study of film ontology is incomplete. We cannot define film as perceptual simply because it might satisfy the need to be entertained.

Li Chao: In the same way, we cannot define film as imagistic simply because the basic element of film is the image.

Zhou Yu: If we did that, we'd certainly lose the ontology of film.

Li Chao: Since we are in an era of informational, systemic and control theories, we needn't follow the older method of metaphysical thinking. We should study every possible aspect of film ontology.

ESTABLISHING A SYSTEM OF CHINESE FILM THEORY

Zhao Baohua: The current crisis and confusion in Chinese film theory stems from a long-standing underestimation of its value. Film theorists have been given little respect; theoretical studies have been difficult to publish; theorists have not been well trained; filmmakers have given little attention to theoretical knowledge and have tended to be non-academic.

Zhou Yu: Especially our film directors. There is an historical reason for this. Many filmmakers working during the war years were stage directors, unaccustomed to theoretical approaches to their work. They were satisfied so long as they had an audience. In this respect, the directors who graduated from the Beijing Film Academy have had an advantage. Another reason is that for a long time we had little communication with the outside, other than the Soviet Union, as far as theory is concerned, which limited the visions of both theorists and practitioners. The debate on the qualities and values of literature in film, for example, reveals the weak basis of Chinese film theory. During the New Era, we translated several Western theories, but in comparison with the number of theoretical studies in the world, the translations are really few. That's one reason why Chinese film is biased and inequitable.

When Seigfried Kracauer's *Theory of Film: The Redemption of Physical Reality* was translated into Chinese,[5] a wave of filmmaking in a documentary style came into fashion, though the book had been published in the West a number of years before. The book has had its influence on theory, yet after all, it represents only one of a number of schools of thought. Since our view of theory is limited, we tend to treasure the few theories available.

Zhao Baohua: We have a painful suspicion that Chinese theorists and translators haven't made adequate introductions of the Western film studies they've made available.

Zhou Yu: It's not easy for a translator to be a theorist. A translator must study Chinese film while making the translations and must be able to relate the material to filmmaking in China. Otherwise mistakes will be made. We tend to shape our filmmaking through one theoretical study. If the practice fits the shape, it is acceptable; if not, it is not acceptable. This tendency denies the past tradition and practices even in China, as well as abroad. This is a major malpractice.

Li Chao: There is an inborn weakness in our theorists. They ignore the basic and systematic study of philosophy, aesthetics and literature and focus only on film. The so-called perceptual ontology is the result of a lack of basic knowledge of aesthetics. The reason to study foreign theories is to establish our own theory. We cannot restrict ourselves to a single theory, but must broaden our knowledge. We need an army of film people, as good at film studies as at filmmaking.

Zhou Yu: There are plenty of theorists, especially young theorists, who are giving less attention to Marxist theories. Their ignorance and lack of understanding of Marxism makes them poor judges. This is one of the major reasons for the confusion in film theory.

Li Chao: Lack of an understanding of Marxism is only one part of the reason; the other is the lack of a careful study and understanding of the aesthetic habits of the Chinese audience, the tradition of Chinese art, and the current situation in China.

Zhao Baohua: We hope we can establish an army of film theorists who can absorb the essence of foreign theories on the basis of Marxism and who can establish a theoretical system with Chinese characteristics, based on modern methodologies.

NOTES

1. "On Mediocrity," *China Film Times*, July 26, 1986.

2. Chen Xihe, "The Tendency of Film Waves in the New Era," *Contemporary Cinema*, June 1986.

3. Wu Houxin, "Spatial Thinking in *Sun Zhongshan*," *Contemporary Cinema*, July 1985.

4. Wang Yichuan, "The Replacement of Film Ontology," *Film Works*, March 1987.

5. Seigfried Kracauer, *Theory of Film: The Redemption of Physical Reality* (New York: Oxford University Press, 1960).

15

What Is Film? A New Look at the Question

Li Tuo, Zhong Dafeng
and Hao Dazheng
Translated by Sun Jianrong

1

Knowledge and science receive the least understanding in the film industry, in spite of which theorists attempt to study film as a science. Such an attempt raises the inevitable question: What is cinema?

—Li Tuo

Li Tuo: Many of the debates in film theory extend beyond the film industry and reflect a significant historical and cultural background, yet because of the constraints of traditional/cultural perceptions and the complexity of the contemporary political situation, the content and value of theory remain unclear. A fundamental principle of theoretical research, which is that theory should have practical applications, proves inadequate. Theory itself is highly complex. Though some theories may be practical and should be categorized as applied theories, applications of pure or basic theoretical research may not necessarily work, as has been proven in the development of natural science and thinking in the West.

Practice does not have a direct relationship with many of the principal propositions in natural science and the liberal arts. This scientific view of knowledge has a direct link with the ancient Greek tradition of knowledge for its own sake (''art for art's sake'') advocated by Plato and Aristotle. The cultural conception of ancient Greece had a strong impact on the West and eventually enabled it to divide theoretical knowledge into applied and basic. Applied theory, fully developed by America and Japan, has benefited the social production and national economies of these nations in many ways.

Of course, when he first established his theory of relativity, Einstein did not think of its practical applications, but only regarded it as a scientific inquiry into the vast mysteries of nature. Scientific research of this sort is still common in many parts of the world, and many scientists devote all their energies to it. In such research, human beings and nature are studied objectively as a humanist activity; the pleasure in discovering truth is totally beyond the search for material recognition.

The pervading view in China that learning must be practical has been sharply criticized by Taiwanese scholars, who point out that the Chinese sense of learning refers only to technology, not to science. For example, the Chinese have been concerned primarily with the application of the four great inventions (the compass, gunpowder, paper and paint), but never question the reasons they were invented. While no one doubts the significance of these inventions, the debate over the difference between Eastern and Western cultures has gone on since the Opium Wars. The argument has been that the concept of science has never existed in China in the strictest sense, and that the Chinese respect neither science nor knowledge. Unfortunately, this claim remains ignored and unrecognized by Chinese theorists. Because of such ignorance, a variety of misunderstandings have occurred in the film industry. Many find it difficult to accept the idea that, strictly speaking, theory is a matter of knowledge.

Hao Dazheng: Film has always been regarded as an instrument and a means. What makes it scientific? Do theoreticians care whether a film makes money? It is a matter of opinion whether film is a political tool or a subject for scientific study. Do not assume that film is an art to be commonly accepted; there is still a problem of theoretical and conceptual thinking. How can film be defined before the social position of film theory and film for cultural purposes has been clarified? We cannot debate film as an art without first having a basic knowledge of the concepts of science.

Li Tuo: In traditional Chinese culture, concepts of virtue as the core and of mortality as the norm conflict with science. On the practical level, Chinese traditional culture is rational, but on a higher level, in its general attitudes toward human beings and the universe, it is anti-rational. This creates a negative force in Chinese culture which makes it difficult to promote a scientific attitude. Chen Xihe and Zhong Dafeng touched on this question in their essays about shadowplay theory,[1] but unfortunately did not expand their discussion and had little response.

2

Every time an original work or new theory arises, judgments are made. What is more, such judgments invariably claim to be absolutely authoritative, creating self-contradictory questions later. This has been the case since the 1950s.

—Hao Dazheng

Hao Dazheng: At the beginning of the 1980s, such negative attitudes and styles were illustrated in the criticism of Bazin's theory without an overall view of "irrationality," or existentialism. The fact is, the only part of Bazin's work known in China was full of energy, helping the emergence of a number of progressive films. What was all the fuss about? It made no sense to assume that mere mention of Bazin's forerunners had defeated Bazin on the philosophical level. This clearly illustrates the ancient simplistic and unrealistic treatment of criticism.

Zhong Dafeng: What happens now is that other scholarly views are denied and other scholars are criticized without knowing anything about them. Freud, Jung, Sartre, and Husserl are often discussed, but how many in the film industry have read them or understood their scholarly opinions? Not many. Bazin's theory is complex, but his views in *What Is Cinema?*[2] reveal a scientific approach lacking in our own theory and criticism. It's therefore amusing to see that while to utilize Bazin is scientific, the criticisms cite phenomenology, irrationality and the like.

Hao Dazheng: Those who claim that Bazin is irrational are irrational themselves. The importation of Bazin made more of us aware of the evolution of modern theory after the birth of semiotics, because these theories, from the viewpoint of the dramatic film, emphasize science, making them even more difficult for some of our professionals.

Li Tuo: Theorists arguing the Yingxi approach to film are anti-scientific, because they approach film in terms of its function and ignore the issue of film as the object of a scientific approach. They cannot accept scientific approaches because they have not established a concept of science in their minds.

Zhong Dafeng: In fact, many Shadowplay theorists have only a superficial understanding of film on its technical level, but fail to touch upon the question of "What is cinema?" Emphasis has been placed on Bazin's scientific spirit, yet it is there that criticism of Bazin begins. The criticism lies away from his perceptions of art and the value of knowledge, and away from his questions about film in which social functions are replaced by audiovisual images. Semiotics, structuralism, psychoanalysis and ideological criticism, that is, in-depth, high-level study of social consciousness in film, are increasingly criticized, regardless of the differences between ideological criticism and Marxism. The former attempts to interpret film and to study society through a nontraditional approach to bourgeois literature.

What is considered Marxist in the West is absolutely the opposite of the official (accepted) ideology in China.

It's interesting that some of the critics use bourgeois philosophy of the eighteenth and nineteenth centuries to criticize those who opposed it, which paradoxically makes their criterion a criticism of their criticism.

Hao Dazheng: For a long time, it has been assumed that whenever two types of theory emerge, one must be against logic and therefore wrong. This is ridiculous. Decisions are made in such a way that whoever takes a position is always right. Communications break down when two different views on the same subject, one scientific, the other political, arise. Even if one were indeed right and the other wrong, we'd only find out in the end—and since in China no progress was made in history and culture for a number of years, it's hard to make clear whether some scholarly approaches were right or wrong. If one is ignorant of new ideas and approaches, one should make an effort to learn about them. It's never too late to consider how to evaluate them, after a thorough understanding had been achieved. Marxists always stress "study, study and more study" and never claim that some are born knowing everything. Nevertheless, the so-called Marxist theorists make judgments without seeing any evidence. This is against the scientific concept of Marxism.

Li Tuo: Whatever theories and opinions we criticize, we should have reasons, evidence and analysis. Although it's less troublesome to criticize a person by using concepts of bourgeois philosophy, existentialism or phenomenology, it's anti-scientific. I'm against worshiping new theory. Chinese people have a tradition of authoritarianism; when their trust in one theory is lost, a replacement has to be found. This is a value in traditional Chinese culture which can be criticized and reformed, but not with an anti-scientific approach.

3

Within the entire film industry one needn't look to others to find a God, but instead should develop oneself and one's own God.

—Zhong Dafeng

Hao Dazheng: Since theory can serve practice directly, why can't theorists draw upon practical experience to serve theory? By such cross-cutting, theory and practice could develop together, side by side. The relationship between them is a two-way communication.

Li Tuo: It's commonly understood in China that theory serves practice, yet some theories have almost no impact on practice. We must admit their existence.

Zhong Dafeng: I think that learning just in order to know about something is one of the spiritual treasures of humanity. In the course of the evolution of civilization, what kind of theories can be said to have no significance? From the point of view of development, any kind of spiritual work has significance, but some work is practical, some is not. The key point is whether we can admit that some theoretical thinking has no practical value.

Li Tuo: True, although the idea that it is practical knowledge makes the Chinese feel even more the importance of theory. I asked some French directors if they were interested in Althusser and Lacan, and they said no, that Lacan, especially, was quite remote from them, that directors should study art, while Lacan was a theorist and a thinker. They had a different view of Bazin, because he is accessible. Our filmmakers and directors have shown too much interest in Freud and Li Zhehou [a well-known contemporary art critic] and have tried to apply them immediately to filmmaking.

Hao Dazheng: In the past, our filmmakers, like our theorists, tended to rely upon the ideas of others, rather than on their own. They constantly hoped to find a backbone on which they could depend. This backbone was supposed to be a prescriptive and instructional theory which became one's central policy. One had to follow it. But the situation is different now, in the face of economic and political reform. Film theory is beginning to reveal its original function, to get rid of past political and authoritarian marks, and therefore it no longer has that magical or instructional power. It would be ridiculous to go back to a policy-making theory.

In recent Chinese films, the trend toward rationality is a reflection of self-consciousness, of social awareness, a progressive phenomenon, but at the same time, it is also a serious weak point, because there is a contradictory relationship between rationality and the audiovisual (sensory) characteristics of film. In the past couple of years, good films have often revealed this theoretical trend. In fact, film theory was empirical first, not purely theoretical. The director who looks for ways of filmmaking from Lacan, Althusser, Sartre or Freud may find himself lost. It may be of more help to study the filmmaking of Francis Ford Coppola and François Truffaut.

Zhong Dafeng: Relying on an important director can give confidence. This is done throughout the film industry. I think the entire film industry should be confident that one can create by oneself, become the God, instead of looking to others. Every filmmaker may have opinions close to certain theories, but an artist has to have a unique view of life and be able to express it.

We advocate a rational, scientific approach to deal with theoretical problems, but not with the creative act itself. To study film as a scientific subject is not the same as to make films into scientific essays or observations. These are different concepts. It is bad enough for a theorist to rely on an artist, but it is even worse for an artist to rely on a theorist.

Li Tuo: There's no doubt that filmmaking can benefit from theory and criticism.

There are countless examples in film history. But as mentioned by Hao, the key question is in what way. To me, the most terrible and stupid act is the attempt to use a philosophical thought in making a film.

Hao Dazheng: It is a traditional error in our filmmaking to directly visualize ideas and dismiss the important process of conceptualization. This was the case in the 1950s, and it's still the case, with the accumulated ideas and new graphic concepts in the present progressive films. Every artist should have an independent mind and way of creating. The transformation of ideas into conceptualization is not filmic yet. Only when conceptualization in its logic obtains socially oriented, feasible and direct audiovisual elements can it become film conceptualization. The reason these processes are not given attention in modern film theory is that it is taken for granted that they have already been assumed by every modern filmmaker. More than one set of experiences in contemporary film has already become theory, and therefore there's no need to put all the processes into a comprehensive film theory. One needn't start from zero every time. This is why there's a division of labor between critical and practical theory. What would be the value of filmmakers if theory were directly visualized? There would certainly appear to be a tendency to visualize theory without considering the difference between filmmaking and particular principles described by theory. It is inappropriate to blame "new theory" for this. Philosophers and artists have their own unique yet distinctive ways of thinking, although both can manifest unique thoughts.

Li Tuo: We oppose the visualization of philosophy, as well as the denial of choice. In fact, contemporary filmmaking is confronted with the need to make many decisions based upon various possibilities. If interested in understanding the nature of film, one should study fundamental theories; if interested in the representative devices of film, one should stress applied theory and questions concerning the technology. This itself is also a matter of making decisions—deciding how to approach a given theorist, or choosing between some philosophical and artistic ideas. In fact, decision making already exists, but its concept is not yet popular. Many people still hope that decisions will be made for them, from the philosophical to the aesthetic. Many filmmakers even hope for a theory they can immediately adopt in their filmmaking.

Hao Dazheng: That's what is considered a lack of decision making. The so-called decision making refers to decisions by an entity. Filmmakers and theorists are separate entities, as is the audience. The leadership is also an entity which can and should make decisions. The decisions made by others and the ones we are talking about here are different. What's more, there is no relationship between decisions of filmmaking and those of theory.

Zhong Dafeng: The power of theory lies in its ability to destroy the way of thinking to which we are accustomed. Every new theory is comprised of the thoughts of many people from different perspectives. Modern theory is different from classical theory, different from Eisenstein and Bazin. The latter teach you montage and the use of the zoom; the former, what cannot be used. It's your own decision when it comes to this "what cannot be used." The area in which the filmmaker can create lies in what he does not need. Modern theory tells us what is out of date, what is not out of date, what has been put to use in Hollywood.

If you don't want to know these things, then don't take this approach. This is something, unfortunately, that is not described by the theorists. Why did the New Wave emerge after Bazin's objective aesthetics? Bazin made a thorough description of objective aesthetics. If you don't want to follow objective aesthetics, turn in other directions and other new waves will appear. If you don't want to follow Jean-Luc Godard or Antonioni, then try other directions, but never go back to Hollywood.

To come out with something original requires an original direction. To a great extent, theory, in relation to filmmaking, tells you not what to do, but what you should not do. When everyone is talking about what film is, Christian Metz, instead, is talking about what film is not. In the end, he doesn't know what it is either. Film needs creativity, and making films relies on many people. Metz's ability is limited. We are all limited. Perhaps none of us have understood what film is, but theory keeps on advancing.

Li Tuo: The advance of theory is sure to have a destructive impact on thinking.

4

There is no way. It is hopeless. Not only film theory, but all humanity in China is in a state, which I call the soft-bone disease: we matured too fast, but lacked calcium in the bones.

—Li Tuo

Zhong Dafeng: The circle of film theory faces an embarrassing situation. Every theorist wants his views to be accepted, but most theory-oriented people don't hope that people pursue the theory directly in making films, since some theorists are against it. The circle of filmmaking has the opposite view. The former "wakes up" after a film has been completed, realizing that it may be wrong to make films according to a certain theory, for when this is done, theory becomes "nonsense" and makes a mess of filmmaking.

The Chinese have a habit of talking about theory on the applied level. This tradition in Chinese film theory has already become the basic thinking pattern, that the use of sync-sound, for example, is generally for narration.

Hao Dazheng: Everyone admits that film is an audiovisual art, but there is disagreement when it comes to specifics. Does narrative, for instance, function as a structural element which plays a role in the audiovisual system of film, or does this audiovisual art serve this main structural element? Quite a number of people get lost confronting this question. China lacks research on pure theory, but wants to treat every applied theory as pure theory. Politics, literature and film are all systems, each with its own systemic qualities. If any one of them enters another system, it loses some of its original qualities and gains new ones; that is, it becomes modified. To understand this, one does not need to understand systems analysis, though this may not be clear to people. The overall ideological system is different from that of film, or the latter can be considered a subsystem of the former, but they are not the same. Why in the past did we ask for the impossibility of matching the value of the ideological system in film with that in politics? Compared with pamphlets and brochures, the ideological impact of art is not that powerful or direct. The impact of ideology in film has its own mechanics, silent and subconscious, but it is profound. Film has its own criteria for the position and impact of ideology, which does not deny the existence of political and ideological elements in film, but film must have complexity and delicacy. Were the complete set of mechanics and functions of the ideological system to enter film, film would, like water bubbles, expand and explode.

There does not exist a simple and direct relationship, as was once thought, between an artist's work and politics, its ideological progress. Art has its own independent principles. What is needed now is to put aside the concept of direct equivalency and restart scientific research on this relationship.

Li Tuo: What we recall now, however, is that the importance of importing Bazin's theory into China was not the rise of objectivity, or the entrance of Chinese film into a phase of objective aesthetics. I think its real importance lay in its raising the awareness of the issues of cinema in Chinese film circles and helping Chinese filmmakers begin to treat film as a scientific object. This was not realized then, because some of those who introduced Bazin and his theory did so from the practical side. Currently our films have many problems, but to solve them we have to solve the question of understanding film in a scientific way. Then we can talk about treating film as art. There is a lot to explore in *What Is Cinema?*

Hao Dazheng: The question of what cinema is was raised after the import of a scientific consciousness into film theory. Don't think that Bazin was referring to the length of shots when he raised this issue. It isn't Bazin's fault, it's ours.

Zhong Dafeng: It is quite different to ask "What Is Cinema?" after Hua's talk on the nature of film in the 1920s and the introduction of the theoretical school of the pioneers in the 1930s. The reason why this issue was never resolved is that the point of departure never changed. It took narrative as the core and treated the audiovisuals of film as a technical issue, and never went beyond the basic thinking pattern, function and purposes the audiovisuals serve. Film required a new thinking style.

Li Tuo: Criticism and reassessment of shadowplay theories must be strengthened, or it will be very difficult to strengthen the scientific study of film.

Zhong Dafeng: Chinese film is not yet beyond the shadowplay stage in general, although signs of development beyond the theatrical stage have already appeared. We must realize this sufficiently. We did not thoroughly understand classical theory before semiotics. We did not complete the "tests" of classical theory. It's not yet time, having taken only one step in modern theory, to claim that it has been completed. So what should we do?

Li Tuo: There's no way. Not only film theory, but all humanity in China is in a state which I call the soft-boned disease: we matured too fast, but lack calcium in the bones. This is a cultural phenomenon, and there is no cure for it. We entered the area of modern film theory, for example, in psychoanalytic and rational criticism, before we had a grasp of classical film theory. If we fail to grasp theory well, we will not have good results. Fortunately, a few people are devoting themselves to a solid study of modern theory, which is better than was done in the past. Scientific study should be strengthened. The psychology of film, for example, has hardly been studied thus far, nor has any commentary been made. The psychology of film is important. In fact, it is now a basic subject of modern film theory.

Hao Dazheng: For lack of a fact-seeking spirit, abstract overgeneralizations are favored. There's a constant tendency toward Althusser's macro point of view instead of a careful search for facts, which is a thinking disorder among us. We shouldn't feel self-satisfied, since we have a lot of weaknesses and a lot of room for improvement.

Li Tuo: To some extent there is truth in the criticism of the film industry. We should carefully analyze ourselves so that we can move toward scientific and specific theory. There are weaknesses in the structure of our theory. It may be asking too much to bring up this question, but every theory has its subdivisions. Abstract overgeneralizations prevent our theory from dividing scientifically. Each individual study tries to cover everything. It always excites us to read Rudolf Arnheim's books, though some seem too technical to the Chinese. The truth is, this is what we lack. Studies of these specific scientific subjects are the bases for the development of film theory. We are not yet aware of this. Although we supply this lack now, we should be on the alert.

I think a self-review of the theory circle should consider four aspects: (1) the constraints on us derived from tradition; (2) those derived from recent political history; (3) the specific cultural environment, for the sudden "openness" has fully exposed our weaknesses; and (4) the lack of an atmosphere in the film industry conducive to scientific research. What's wrong with Shao Mujun's "The Road of Innovation in Chinese Cinema"?[3] Why make such a fuss about it? It's only a theoretical explanation, a historical evaluation. Shao Mujun's conclusions may or may not be right, but there should be room for discussion, since this is a scholarly issue. There is no need to attack science and democracy unscientifically. If science in film theory needs to be strengthened, then the democratic spirit should not be ignored. This also includes studying Xia Qian's pattern. If we can study Lu Xun and Maxim Gorky, why shouldn't we study Xie Jin?

There's another point that needs clarification. The recent development of film has been referred to as the period of "objective aesthetics" while it actually is a period of neo-objective aesthetics. I think both designations are false.

Zhong Dafeng: In terms of theory there is such a trend, but such a pattern has not formed in filmmaking. In its openness, film theory is highly remote from theory in the other arts. This is true of both basic and applied theory. The demands of film theory have remained unchanged. Film theory has never been treated as scientific, but instead has been attached to political theory, or seen as a footnote to practice. I think whether theory has helped the overall development of film, as the criterion of the value of theory, can only be seen in a broad and abstract sense. Film theory has far less impact on society than a calendar with holidays marked on it, since the calendar can be found in every household.

Li Tuo: In the severe criticism of film theory there have been three issues: (1) the mythification of theory; (2) the separation of theory and practice; and (3) the lack of clarity in theory. What has been discussed thus far can be said to have partially answered these criticisms. The lack of clarity in theory and criticism is also an objective reason that leads to these criticisms. Film theory and criticism should be sub-categorized and have a reasonable structure and design. This is an urgent task. Philosophical theory in film is different from general theory, which can also be subdivided. Applied theory differs from basic theory. Both are within the scope of film theory, but on different levels.

Hao Dazheng: This is because basic theory is not concerned with the mechanics and processes of filmmaking. Basic theory, in the abstract, becomes pure theory. Basic theory provides the essential materials for a pure critical theory. By combining basic theory with the mechanics and processes of filmmaking, we obtain applied theory. Our lack of basic theory and solid materials makes our critical theory weak and immature. We only have adaptations; for example, we don't have solid research into the material aspects of celluloid and shots, resulting in a vicious circle of nothingness.

Li Tuo: Many issues in film criticism are worth our attention. For a long time, our criticism has had dual duty: criticism and theory (in the narrow sense). Criticism was theory, and the critic was a theorist. Until recently there was no dividing line between the two. This is not to say that theoretical research cannot touch upon criticism or vice-versa, but one should be clear about what is being discussed, theory or criticism. To understand the connections and relationships is to formulate the rules of the game, which can help the game go smoothly, assuming one cares about one's role.

Hao Dazheng: The trend toward specificity in film research is the result of ongoing studies of film culture. Today people can read audiovisual images fairly accurately. Accordingly, we now want theory to use a scientific approach in studying and regularizing every reaction between us and image. The birth of scientific approaches seems to have systematized art, but in fact it is a trend toward a larger unity, based on a deep sensitivity for film and an understanding of film culture. If film is seen as a system, there should be a theoretical system to generalize, explain and analyze it. This is natural. It is also a requirement for historical development, and is not under human control.

NOTES

1. Chen Xihe, "Shadowplay: Chinese Film Aesthetics and Their Philosophical Fundamentals," *Chinese Film Theory: A Guide to the New Era*, George S. Semsel, Xia Hong and Hou Jianping, eds. (New York: Praeger Publishers, 1990), pp 190–192.

2. Bazin, André, *What is Cinema?* 2 vols., Hugh Gray, trans. (Berkeley: of University at California Press, 1987, 1971).

3. Shao Mujun, "The Road of Innovation in Chinese Cinema," *Film Art*, September 1986.

16

Film: A Myth with Hidden Ideologies

Yao Xiaomong and Hu Ke
Translated by Fu Binbin

Hu Ke: The question, What is cinema? is originally a classic issue in the domain of film ontology. Comparing contemporary film theories throughout the world, we find that the theoretical study of Chinese film is in need of new perspectives. Today we are not going to discuss the ontology of film, but will address ideological criticism.

Yao Xiaomong: Film theory in the West took a great leap in the 1960s, and in the 1970s, the theory of ideological criticism emerged. Not merely a combination of linguistics and psychoanalysis, it absorbed Althusserian Marxist theory, including industrial and social analysis, and at the same time related itself to feminist film criticism.

Chinese theoretical studies of art have always emphasized political and ideological criticism, but since such criticism was not based on the framework of linguistics and psychoanalysis, it differs from the ideological criticism we're talking about now. This criticism, consisting mainly of theme and character analysis, was greatly influenced by Russian schools and the bourgeois trend of critical realism in the nineteenth century. We have always insisted that our criticism of art and literature rest on historical and dialectic materialism and the methods of our own Marxism, but have ignored two issues. (1) Classical Marxist theorists differ in viewpoint and methodology from the progressive bourgeois literary theoreticians and critics of the nineteenth century. We were aware of their differences in global perspectives but failed to see the differences in textual analysis. (2) When using Marxist theory, we emphasized more often than not the ideological content of the specific work and evaluated it ideologically as a social phenomenon; consequently, we failed to make an ideological analysis of the process and means of expression by which the content was conveyed. More simply, we failed to make a Marxist analysis of the grammar and rhetoric of the art work itself. Since we have long been devoid of a clear understanding that language itself is ideologized, we broke into the work discussing content and form separately, thus removing Marxist theory, to some extent, from structural analysis.

In 1979, the modernization of cinematic language was initiated in the theoretical circles. This discussion itself suggested two possible directions. (1) It could pursue the techniques of filmic expression so as to accelerate the development of the artistic and aesthetic aspects. (2) It could approach the ideological content in terms of linguistic modes. Looking at it now, the discussion leaned in the first direction, being consistent with the then general atmosphere of aesthetics as a whole. Another important phenomenon emerged later, when Chen Xihe and Zhong Dafeng published a series of articles on the aesthetics of Yingxi, which played a positive theoretical role though they contained a fatal problem. Research into Yingxi theory in effect dodged the issue of film language and returned to the traditional analysis of themes. The methodological significance of Yingxi theory is that it uses literary and artistic means to carry out social principles, thus emphasizing again the ethical taming of the artistic work. In my opinion, the study of Yingxi is significant in terms of aesthetic theory and historical research, but the discussion has limitations in methodology and thus unconsciously counteracts the modernization of cinematic language. It's a great pity, for it caused a setback in the development of film theory.

Hu Ke: You think that China had a chance to develop ideological criticism but failed to do so. The issue of the modernization of cinematic language itself, in fact, had an ideological background. It is only by using such a roundabout way of "talking art" that one can avoid political restraints. We can hardly say that this is not an ideological act. The re-enhancement of "art" had dual importance at the time. First, Chinese film lacked artistic techniques, and an emphatic call for "the artistic" was necessary for its development. Second, the emphasis on art met a political need to strive for the right to speak in society, under the cover of art. As we know, politics in China is a kind of power, but there are other powers, too. Knowledge is a kind of power. One who wants to gain the right to speak in society or in film circles, but who has no political power, can undoubtedly find a way to do so. That is, in any field, if you possess knowledge, you have a certain right to speak in it, and this power can partially counteract the power of politics.

Yao Xiaomong: Contemporary progressive theorists in the West hold that art is a hidden apparatus of ideology. Since art is bound to exercise a healthy influence on the human heart, it has a definite function of education.

Hu Ke: It's completely wrong to think that art has no relationship to ideology. In fact, all kinds of ideologies can be disguised as "pure art" and filter into the minds of the audience. We have a generally accepted standard in art, the so-called criterion of truth, beauty and goodness. Everyone, whether political leader or ordinary reader, theorist or artist, holds the identical attitude toward art, and thus the criterion of "truth, beauty and goodness" inevitably becomes a myth. In this situation, we step into a phase of realistic aesthetics, and everyone is expounding on reality because it is commonly accepted that what lies behind reality is self-evident, needs no proof and is above suspicion. Consequently, reality also turns into myth. One who "possesses" reality takes a dominant position and is able to promote the sale of his ideology under its cover. Film, in some leaders' eyes, is an excellent instructional tool for the masses; therefore, works of art should be created according to "life," as they define it, and conform to their educational needs. Reality, then, is idealized, and people discuss it not in terms of art but in accordance with the different needs of ideology. In this regard, realistic aesthetics depends for its success on ideology rather than art. It extricates itself, to a certain degree, from the control of leftist theory with the help of "realism." This attempt to break away from leftist ideology is reasonable, since if film is always dictated by politics, its artistic side will unquestionably be at a standstill.

Now, we should admit that film has a close relationship with ideology, and that ideological criticism has ample scope for its abilities. To propagate a pure art, beyond ideology, is merely to advocate a myth. It would be better for those involved in film theory to confront and study ideology than to try to avoid it. Ideological analysis is ruthless and sober. There may be no ideal human under its light, and evil may also be a motivating force which pushes history forward.

Yao Xiaomong: As Chinese film moves toward art and aesthetics, the problem of how to encourage further development arises, because although we have imported Bazin's aesthetics theory, the theory of the long take, it is a Western product of the 1950s, with existentialism and phenomenology as its philosophical base. A discussion of this theory in China in the 1980s obviously requires an international academic background.

Hu Ke: That's an important point. Chinese film theory needs an international background. Our theoretical studies should align themselves basically with modern film theories abroad, in terms of their theoretical framework, but use different objects for research. That would provide a universal standard, and we could have an international dialogue and communication.

Yao Xiaomong: Ideological criticism is one of the major critical modes in the West. We should strive to conform our research to the international scholastic background through meticulous scholarship, to make it possible for us to exchange knowledge with others. From a sociological viewpoint, the development of Reform and the open-door policy, and the gradually increasing cultural exchanges, account for the rise of ideological criticism.

Ideological criticism requires a combination of scholarship and ideology. To analyze others by ideological methods is itself a kind of ideology, concerned with the issue of standpoint and principle we've talked about.

Compared with general academic and aesthetic criticism, ideological criticism demonstrates one's position in a more direct and daring way. Academicism is another side of ideological criticism that cannot be ignored. Constructed on linguistics, psychoanalysis, Marxism, structural anthropology or some other basis, ideological criticism has a complete set of concepts and categories and its own analytical method. Therefore, ideological criticism is a scientific mode of academic criticism. Internationally, the so-called ideological criticism refers mainly to Marxist criticism. Development of ideological criticism in China, a socialist country, would be well received.

Ideological criticism has a subversive nature, a certain political purpose, which is to overthrow the capitalist system, just as feminist theory aims at subverting the phallo-centric social system of capitalism. But it's worth noting that ideological criticism adopts the political propositions of Marxism, not those of anarchism. Unlike anarchism, this kind of criticism doesn't want to oppose and subvert any social system except capitalism.

We have long been separating Marxism artificially into Chinese, Western, revisionist and so on. There are of course different schools and different opinions inside Marxism, but in general, Marxism is a unified entity, an international theory. We should oppose the narrow-minded view that only in China can real Marxism be found.

Hu Ke: The subversive nature of this ideological theory, to put it frankly, is to expose the very inside. In capitalist countries, bourgeois ideology is expressed subliminally by the filmic narrative and by means of sound, light, electricity and chemistry. The film audience subconsciously accepts ideas which they would be unwilling to accept. Ideological analysis, then, tries to study how bourgeois ideology is conveyed through filmic means and inculcated into the audience, under what conditions the audience is fooled and accepts it, and in what way the capitalist system of production is maintained. The task of ideological criticism is to expose this process. There are many non-Marxist things that should be subverted into films at the initial stage of socialism; therefore, our use of the subversive aspect of ideological criticism for reference abroad is proper and appropriate.

Yao Xiaomong: Film itself has the mechanism to produce daydream-like fantasies in the process of viewing. A cinematic signifier bears no actual object for reference, and thus is particularly suitable for myth-making. In this sense, ideological criticism is different from phenomenology and viewing aesthetics. It doesn't attempt to create an artistic and aesthetic whole; on the contrary, it is a critical deconstruction, aimed at revealing the inherent emptiness, absences and gaps in the completed work, since every work is bound to bring with it the political, economic and historical contradictions and antagonisms of its society, which causes them in its language of expression. Thus we should see that what's important doesn't lie in what a movie tells us, what it exposes and what it eulogizes, but in the fact that the structure itself bears an ideological nature. The difference between ideological and artistic or aesthetic criticism is that ideological criticism is more Marxist in nature and bears a more revolutionary character. The two kinds of criticism, to a certain extent, are contradictory. Aesthetic criticism stresses the content of the work itself, while ideological criticism places emphasis on the contextual and social-historical relations which lie outside of the content, in the text.

Hu Ke: Ideological criticism should be used with great care. It's easy to destroy a thing in China. A theory's finished as soon as everyone's talking about it. Systemic theory was destroyed in this way. At the time, everyone was talking about "systems," but now someone who brings it up is considered a fool. On the other hand, never take ideological theory as dissident and harmful. It's a most important weapon in the development of the reform and the open-door policy.

Yao Xiaomong: You're obligated to clarify your own positions in terms of scholarship, but you're not responsible for asking anyone to believe you. Therefore, I don't expect everybody to consider ideological criticism the best method. That would be impossible. This kind of analysis, however, is essential, because it's necessary to display the contradictions, gaps and voids in a text. For instance, are there elements of machoism in the text of *Red Sorghum*?

Chinese film does have a problem of artistic quality. The reason can be found either in the use of cinematic techniques or in the organic nature of capital. The Chinese film industry does use a great deal of capital. The proportion of what we invest in equipment and machinery to the variable capital we pay for labor is comparatively high, and correspondingly, this determines our mode and scale of production. A production crew on location will get room, board and everything else. It's like a big family. This inevitably dampens creative energies and the scope of artistic creation.

Another reason comes from ideology, with which quality has a close relationship. Some even considered the latter of crucial importance to the former. *Chun Miao* (1974), by the great director Xie Jin, shows great skill in camera movement; however, it's made totally within the Cultural Revolution discourse. A product of the Cultural Revolution, this kind of language may seldom be found in movies made in the future. In the scene where she struggles the most fiercely against the capitalist-roaders, Chun Miao and other positive characters stand on the top of the stone steps with the camera shooting from a low angle, while President Du and Doctor Qian, standing below, are shot from a high angle. This states an ideological position.

From the narrative discourse of *Chun Miao*, we can perceive that the Cultural Revolution must be carried on, but it is in the tactfully hidden subtext that the audience is subconsciously poisoned by the ideological thoughts of the Gang of Four. Viewed in terms of the motivational function of narrative, Chun Miao as the heroine has behind her a supporter, an

equivalent of the wise man in mythology: the party secretary of the production brigade. But the secretary is only a signifier of a signifier, since
there is still someone else behind him. When Chun Miao is in great difficulty, the secretary emerges at the most crucial moment and tells her that
Chairman Mao has given a directive: "The emphasis of medical and health
work should be on the rural areas." The party secretary helps Chun Miao,
but the one who provides the real help is absent.

Xie Jin knew exactly what he wanted to say. His cinematic language
fully represents his ideological thoughts. Immediately after the party secretary finishes speaking, we see a low-angle shot of a bamboo forest and
the sun. Where is the one who really helps her? He is absent, but at the
same time he is everywhere. At the time, Xie Jin could not have avoided
being influenced by the various forms of extreme leftist thought. His skillful
means of expression combine with the ideological content to constitute the
language of *Chun Miao*. Consciously or subconsciously, Xie Jin pandered
to the dominant ideology of the time, throwing in his lot with the wrong
one.

Since we have a different system of film, our movies must first meet the
needs of the leaders. If the leaders do not nod agreement, a movie will
have no chance to meet its audience. The leaders want to see in a movie
the ideological elements they need for their own ideological satisfaction.
However, the ordinary audience can seldom identify with them. On the
surface, this non-identification seems to be a problem of lies or imperfections. Thus we understand better why some films receive praise from the
leaders but fail to attract ordinary people, and why some films are hailed
by artists, but not by the masses. A few days ago, the issue of satisfying
both refined and popular tastes with a single work of art was raised. Since
this is an attempt to unify all the ideological thoughts in the society, the
issue will inevitably receive political support.

Hu Ke: In my opinion, film undoubtedly has a cathartic function, of which we
had long been unaware or avoided speaking of under political pressure. If
analyzed carefully, even films made under the rule of the Gang of Four
contain elements of visual pleasure, elements to satisfy one's desire. Nobody
wants to see a movie which cannot do this. Among the model plays, people
didn't like *Fighting on the Plain* (1955), but loved *Sha Jia Creek* (1971),
The Story of the Red Lantern (1970), and *Taking Tiger Mountain by Strategy*
(1970). The "battle of wits" scene in *Sha Jia Creek* was well-known to
all. To put it bluntly, the battle of wits is in fact a woman's flirtation with
a man, ingeniously disguised. For instance, Sister Ah Qing's clever struggle
with Diao Deyi by using Hu Chuankui as her shield is analogous, in a
sense, to the loose woman scene of a Hollywood movie. Sister Ah Qing is
a woman poised between two men, Commander Hu and Instructor Guo.
She has once saved Hu Chuankui's life, and when she turns to Instructor
Guo, we unconsciously accept the "revolutionary" thought the author in-

tends to filter into our minds. Sister Ah Qing's choice of Instructor Guo is a disguised political choice. When the audience identifies with her choice of man, it also identifies with her political choice.

What's ingenious in *The Story of the Red Lantern* lies in the relationship between Li Yuhe and Tiemei: they are father and daughter, but not by blood. They could be lovers. The relationship of father and daughter and lovers is well worth seeing. Therefore, one always views with a knowing eye the scene in which Tiemei acts like a spoiled child before Li Yuhe. Here the relationship of "father-daughter and non-father-daughter" easily makes one indulge in fantasy. Similarly, when people concentrate on the screen and identify with Tiemei, Tiemei's pledge—"Dad is carrying a thousand jin; I, too, want to carry eight hundred"—becomes their determination. On the surface, the pledge is strongly sermonic, but the audience, in fact, can find pleasure in the scene.

There were no channels for catharsis at that time, since it was a very harsh period; however, the audience could still find a way, though it was well disguised. In fact, it is because it is well disguised that the audience feels relieved. All the female leads in the model plays are beautiful, as the audience, of course, expected, but beautiful women cannot be seen at no cost. You have to pay for that, because when you are viewing beautiful women, you have already accepted the ideological thoughts of the Gang of Four and submitted to the then dominant ideology.

We should, on the one hand, note that film satisfies desires, and on the other, realize that this might be used to infiltrate certain ideological thoughts. Filmmakers cannot use "education" alone. If you want your audience accept your thoughts, you have to give them something in exchange. You must fulfill their desires.

Yao Xiaomong: What a spectator dreams via cinematic means is not a simple dream, but a daydream. When you are allowed to dream a sweet daydream, the bourgeoisie is making a myth. What cannot exist in reality exists in movies. What is ugly in actual life turns acceptable in films. This myth ought to be broken, the daydream deconstructed, and its very nature exposed.

The relationship between daydreams and the subconscious is worth studying. You mentioned that what ideological criticism exposes can even be the subconscious; moreover, it can be the subconsciousness of the filmmaker. I think it's quite right. The key point of penetrating a daydream is to expose the subconsciousness in the depths of the filmmaker's psychology, and to analyze it contextually.

The Last Emperor (1987) tells a story that spans 80 years, but actually creates a myth about contemporary China. The movie embodies Bernardo Bertolucci's ideas about politics, power and sex in China in the 1980s. It also includes his opinions of the relations between Japan, England, the United States and China. This is an unintentional display of his subconscious, not a conscious expression of his thoughts.

The author of *The Building for Couples* (1987) has a similar display of his subconscious: the men in the movie do not want to be fathers; there are no fathers in the movie; and there is no paternal position in the familial structure. This movie doesn't avoid sexuality; however, sexuality is represented, not for the purpose of fathering, but for sensual pleasure. To oppose patriarchy is to oppose the hierarchical notion of feudalism. What's noteworthy in the film is the patriarchal notion in which all the male characters are competent, be they painters or factory directors, while the women characters are dependent upon men. The filmmaker reveals the relationship between competence and power, and expresses at the same time his opinion of the issues of reform in the 1980s.

Red Sorghum relates a story of the 1930s at the same time that it represents the author's modern mentality. In his understanding of society, the one who is competent is a king, a man who can actualize his life, provided he has the desire to conquer. "My grandpa" in the movie holds "my grandma" in an inverted configuration, itself rich in significance. This has a contextual relationship with the fact that, these days, people from all walks of life have a chance to show their competence and wisdom on the basis of competition in an open society.

Subconscious ideas of this kind will sometimes appear repeatedly in the works of a given author. Xie Jin's portrayal of womanhood, for example, is safe and secure for men. The development of the plot and the operation of the narrative makes men the primary motivating powers. Examples abound in *The Red Detachment of Women* (1961), *Chun Miao* (1974), *The Legend of Tianyun Mountain*, *Garlands at the Foot of the Mountain* (1984) and *Hibiscus Town*. Men advance the unfolding of the plot, while women are just there to be seen. Womanhood in these movies is flattened and desexualized, the womanhood men desire. From a feminist point of view, a woman is not a castrated man, and the female characters in a movie constitute the most dangerous signifiers of eroticism to men. However, in Xie Jin's films, women are harmless and not a threat. What's more, they are totally dependent on men. No matter how harsh Chun Miao is, she has to turn to Doctor Fang for instructions. Therefore, the men in the audience could fulfill their desires in a carefree manner. When making his movies, Xie Jin probably never thought about this, but it is a revelation of his subconscious. As Laura Mulvey puts it, the male subconscious constructs the visual pleasure of films. In this sense, we could take a film as the author's discourse, as his psychic being. No matter what subject matter a film represents or when the story takes place, it always creates a modern myth.

In the past, we did apply Marxist theory to film studies, but whenever we talked about cinematic language, we considered it in terms of art and failed to integrate Marxism with techniques. Marxism was merely used to analyze themes and characters. Later, people seldom talked about Marxist theory. What we intend to do now is apply ideological criticism and Marxist theory to the analysis of cinematic language. This job has its potential and is well worth doing.

Hu Ke: All issues of cinema have an ideological background and contain a potential claim on politics. This is even true of the writings solely about film art and its structure, and development. We're often in a bad spot when dealing with these ideological factors. Should we expose them, or let them remain hidden for a while? It's hard to decide. Perhaps we still need some tolerance.

17

Scattered Thoughts on the Value of Film Theory

Li Shaobai
Translated by Fu Binbin

The editorial department of *Film Art* recently put forth a compelling topic for discussion: the value of film theory. This certainly is an issue that is worth addressing.

Basically, filmmaking in China began to be in sync with the development of film theory at the start of the New Era. The filmmakers' achievements must at least in part be credited to the contribution of film theory. The discussions on the modernization of film language, the nationalization of film, the literary value of film and the nature of film, and the importation and introduction of various film schools and sects from abroad have not only invigorated scholarly thought and the academic atmosphere in film circles, but also directly or indirectly influenced filmmaking. Naturally, the influence of theory upon practice does not produce instant results. Theory, however, can exert a gradual and imperceptible influence on creative thinking, and consequently affect practice. Because of this, when we note the achievements of our theory, we must at the same time not lose sight of its defects. These defects vary from arbitrariness and prejudice in film criticism, and theoretical abstraction disjointed from reality, aimed at bringing the diversified phenomena of art creation into a personally defined model, to elevating half-truths to the position of the whole while rejecting any other possible generalization. Those of us involved in theoretical work, having been accused of leading practice in the wrong direction, should take a long, hard look at what we are doing.

The significance of film theory, excuse me for being blunt, thus far has not attracted much attention, especially from the leading body responsible for film. Movies have to be made, since this is an inflexible task, while film theory, since it is considered unimportant, is, of course, not indispensable. Every year we hear of meetings to be held to discuss filmmaking, but are seldom told there will be conferences on film theory and criticism. We often hear of conferences overseas on the state of filmmaking in a given year, but we hardly know the situation of film theory during the same time. Emphasizing production at the same time theory is despised could be said to be a long-standing bias in the field of film.

Film theory, in my opinion, functions upon film practice in at least three ways. First there is the influence of elementary theory of filmmaking, the function of which is easy to understand. One cannot shoot movies without having some rudimentary knowledge of cinema, let alone mention that film is a complex creation involving a synthetic art, modern technology and industrial processes of production. Therefore, training in elementary theory appears essential to cinema. Kuleshov's *Fundamentals of Film Directing*[1] is so helpful that we don't know how much many of us have benefited from it. However, such books on elementary theory as we have written have been rarities of rarities until recently.

The second influence of theory is on the level of practical application. The direct summation of our predecessors' experiences, and the crystallization of previous painstaking creation, it can play a direct role in our filmmaking. Xia Yan's *Several Problems of Screenwriting*, for instance, has greatly benefited many of our screenwriters.[2]

The third is theoretical abstraction on a high level. Research into film ontology and the aesthetic characteristics of film, for example, are part of this category. Its functions were ignored in the past, since it was considered too abstract and too remote from reality to affect practice. The introduction of the long-take theory and the advocacy of documentary aesthetics which began in the New Era greatly influenced the creation of some film works, so people have been giving highly abstracted theory more attention. Still, research into this, in my opinion, is still the weakest.

There are many comments on the rights and wrongs, successes and failures of film theory and criticism. This might not be bad, for this is the theory of theories. Similarly, regarding theory itself, if there were not different schools of thought, there would be no contending arguments. Academic research cannot be intensified, and the progress of theory cannot be realized, without arguments. Of course, advancement of theory ultimately depends on the development of practice; but arguments are always an effective means to intensify research.

In my opinion, the value of film theory does not lie in its utilitarian properties, but ultimately rests in its scientific truthfulness, in its ability to make a correct or almost correct objective explanation of the phenomenon of cinema, to answer the questions raised from experience, and to scientifically predict the future development of film. The most fundamental standard by which to measure the value of film theory is its truthfulness. But truth is complicated. In the first place, it is not concrete, but in constant flux. It develops parallel to practice. What is considered a truth at one time may turn out to be incomplete or even false at another. Also, truth is absolute at the same time that it is relative; it is the unification of its absoluteness and relativeness. One can hardly imagine a single theory which could achieve the very end of cinematic truths, and yet remain unchanged. In a word, film theory is the generalization of film practice and a consideration of the essential nature of the objective phenomenon of cinema; it comes from practice and is at the same time tested by practice.

To "let a hundred schools of thought contend" and to encourage and tolerate the free expression of diverse scholarly viewpoints, to argue and exchange with one another, has no other purpose than to constantly clarify our understanding of truths through argument and, furthermore, to discover and develop the truthfulness of cinematic science. This process makes one more free and conscious in the mastery and creation of film art. Consider the debate over the nationalization of film. Since this question was raised in a meeting of film directors in 1980, many articles have been published. Both its supporters and their opponents have stuck to their own points of view. There even have been different ideas and reasons within each group, and uniformity in discussion can hardly be reached. But through this discussion, our understanding of this issue has been greatly elevated and deepened, and it no longer remains at the same level as seven years ago. Therefore, we should neither hold a blind attitude toward film theories, thinking every theory good and correct, nor treat them as something devoid of a single redeeming feature, without dealing with each case on its merits.

To elevate and intensify film theory in the light of the present situation, I think it is necessary to strengthen research in the following ways.

1. We should study film theory as a whole. Film has not only an aesthetic nature, but also has entertaining, ideological and economic properties. That is, it can provide entertainment and moral education as well as aesthetic enjoyment. Until recently, however, all these have been actualized through its distribution as a commodity, as the audience pays for its tickets. In this regard, not a single one of the artistic, entertaining, ideological and economic attributes of film can be dispensed with, though different emphases can be laid upon them to meet the demands of a specific movie. Viewing theory as a whole, it is not hard to evaluate the half-truths and biases revealed in the diverse arguments and discussions in recent years about experimental narratives, entertainment films, the need to emphasize art alone and the domination by the audience. If one takes the aesthetic attributes of film as having a lesser importance, one can discover that cinema is a synthetic art and, furthermore, a synthesis different from drama, opera, ballet and other arts. As a synthesis with a principal body, it takes moving pictures as its name, while fusing and absorbing artistic elements from literature, drama, music, fine arts, photography and so on. Although in making a specific film work the artist can draw from the other arts, thus emphasizing music, painting, literature or drama, film after all can never become music, painting, literature or drama. Overall, the degree of truthfulness in some of the expressions used in the debates of recent years, such as "throwing away the walking stick of drama," "the divorce of film and drama" and "the literary value of film," should be specifically defined.

2. We should study the consistency of film theory. If one dissected and analyzed film

as a whole, one would see its various aspects, parts, levels or angles. For example, if cinema were considered an economic phenomenon, one could not help but see what is put in and what comes out, as well as its distribution processes, from which come film economics and its branches: production, management and marketing. If cinema were taken as an art, one could not ignore its relationship with society, its historical and cultural roots, its aesthetic mechanisms and features, and the relationship between filmmaking and appreciation, out of which come film sociology, the science of film art and the science of the audience. The rest can be reasoned on this analogy. In a word, the consistency of film is objective. If we want to gain a deep understanding of the phenomenon of film and fully master it, we have to pay great attention to this study. The theory of the "box office value of film," since it was raised emphatically by Zhong Dianfei in 1956, has gone through all kinds of hardships and frustrations, being in vogue at one time and out of favor at another. The reason for this, besides political situations, lies also in that theory didn't develop a comparatively complete and theoretical explanation and interpretation. The value of the truthfulness of certain theories lies only in their consistency.

3. We should study the interrelationships within film theory. There are always points where different attributes, dimensions and levels penetrate and join with one another. For instance, there is always a relationship between the artistic and economic phenomena of film, between filmmaking and film appreciation, between the entertainment and educational functions of film, between the different departments of filmmaking (screenwriting, directing, acting, cinematography, music and art design, etc.) and between various departments of production and distribution (studios, distribution companies, theatres, etc.). This relationship is the point where they meet each other. These junctions are important in various branches of cinema, and some them are the subjects of new interdisciplinary studies.

Our study, by dividing film into different levels and segments, gradually helps to put the science of cinema into a disciplined, systematic orbit. The distribution of film profits has long been a problem argued back and forth by studios, distribution companies and units in charge of film release. The problem remains unsolved and brings great harm to the balanced development of film. Sharp contradictions are often revealed between the entertainment function of film and its aesthetic and educational functions. Films of a high entertainment value might not be effective in education, and movies with a strong educational function may not have a high aesthetic value, or vice-versa.

The Thief of Emei, an often-criticized movie, had three hundred prints distributed, ten times as many as *Yellow Earth*, a highly praised film which won international acclaim and is, in my opinion, excellent in its innovation and creativity. Although the number of prints distributed does not necessarily indicate how much the audience liked a film, and is also not tantamount to its entertainment value, it more or less illustrates some problems in this matter. This is the difference between economic and artistic value, and between a film's aesthetic effects and its function as entertainment. But can we unify the different values and functions effectively? This is the question film theory must answer.

NOTES

1. For an English translation see Lev Kuleshov, *Kuleshov on Film*, Ronald Levaco, trans. (Berkeley; University of California Press, 1924).

2. Xia Yan, *Problems of Screenwriting* (Beijing: China Film Press, 1989).

Part VI

The New Era and Afterward

Conclusion

The New Era, the exciting historical period which began in 1979 and survived for a decade, was put to an abrupt end when the PLA fired its first shots at the students demonstrating for democracy in Tiananmen Square on June 4, 1989. In its ten years, Chinese film, both in theory and practice, made major advances and achieved unprecedented heights, and gaining widespread international recognition for the first time. Having been extremely politicized since the founding of the People's Republic in 1949, when the Communist Party took control of the central government, we should not be surprised that China immediately responds to changes in the political system and its regulating policies and by modifying its overall economic and cultural policies, including those affecting literature and the arts.

Drawing the lines of demarcation for the New Era remains a complex task under discussion among historians and sociologists, as well as film theorists. In the present study the decade (1979–1989) can only be classified on the basis of the most influential and dominant ideological issues within the larger political and economic context, and by the developments in Chinese film from its revival in 1979 to its later prosperity.

THE EMANCIPATION OF THE MIND

The New Era was unprecedented and vitally important, not only in Chinese filmmaking and film studies, but in politics, economics and social ideology as well. In Chinese film history, the number of important, high-quality films released during this period was beyond all expectations, and heated debates over cinema studies, launched one after another, filled the pages of every journal given to the subject. Enthusiastic and energetic theoretical research into the young, still evolving art seemed intent on verifying Bazin's observation that five years in cinema equals the output of an entire generation in literature. In a way, the changes and developments of filmmaking in the ten years of the New Era more than equalled those of all past generations. In the outstanding productions of the earlier phase of the New Era, films like *Yellow Earth* (1984), *Old Well* (1987) and *Evening Bell* (1987), or in *Red Sorghum* (1989) and *Judou* (1990), made later, as the New Era ended, one found few traces of the naivete and roughness of films made in earlier times.

Yet we have concluded, as we did in our initial volume of translations, that what was once thought crucially important is no longer sacred, that debates once exciting to all no longer arouse the same enthusiasm. What was once serious and intellectually stimulating turns out in retrospect to be naive, and at times foolish. Nonetheless, whatever happened has an historical existence which bridges past and present. As we look to the future, however, we should note again the major reasons for the rapid rise of filmmaking and film studies in the New Era, and the tremendous changes in both.

In 1979, as the now-famous Third Plenary Session of the Eleventh Communist Party Central Conference came to its end, the participants established the "emancipation of the mind" and "open-door" policies in politics and economics in order to promote and guarantee for literature and art that a hundred flowers would indeed blossom, a hundred schools of thought would contend. With the Party shifting from class struggle and socialist revolution to economic construction and reform, the basic themes in social ideology and culture, liberated from their 30-year sentence in the penitentiary of politics (1949–1979), turned to economics and technology. Filmmaking and film studies, too, shifted from their unilateral ideological orientation to an exploration of technique and form.

Filmmakers and theoreticians, mostly the middle-aged and the young, confronting international cinema for the first time after China reopened its doors, immediately grasped the comparative backwardness of their national cinema. With a strong sense of historical mission and social responsibility, they encouraged and helped each other as they doubled their efforts in exploration and research. In the process, they made a significant contribution to the revival of film studies and filmmaking after the Cultural Revolution, and laid a solid foundation for those to follow. The Fifth Generation rose out of this atmosphere.

The Fifth Generation filmmakers not only injected fresh blood into filmmaking but also strongly encouraged film studies on a new and more sophisticated level. Their seminal works enlarged the range and potential of filmic expression through innovative uses of cinematography, time and space relationships, and sound as well as color, changing forever, without question, the face of Chinese film. They clearly challenged traditional Chinese film theory and practice and ultimately stimulated further development in both directions. As a result, Chinese theoretical circles came to maturity, and in every critical and theoretical area, a new batch of talented young graduates emerged, especially during the latter half of the decade. Contemporary Chinese film theory and criticism grew more profound, richer and more diversified than all that had preceded it.

At the same time, a large number of contemporary Western films and film theories were introduced and popularized. Translations of Bazin's *What Is Cinema?* and Kracauer's *Theory of Film: The Redemption of Physical Reality* were quickly followed by studies in semiotics, structuralism, formalism, psychoanalysis, ideological and feminist criticism and put to use in the study of literature and art. The works by Bazin and Kracauer, as well as works by Mitry, Roland Barthes, Claude Levi-Strauss, Jacobson, Metz, Foucault, Benjamin, Althusser, Fredric Jameson, Andrew, Bordwell, Nichols, Nick Browne, Mulvey, and Ann Kaplan, brought numerous new approaches into the field and, in contrast to the past, heavily influenced Chinese film studies.[1]

CHINESE THEORY AND THE WEST

With these observations in mind, what critical conclusions and evaluation, then, should we make about the significance and achievement of this period, which lasted ten years and so recently came to its end? We must first note that in ends and means, Chinese film theory has always distinguished itself from that of the West. Invariably oriented toward practice, it stresses its instructional function, thus developing an aesthetic closely related to practical criticism and film techniques. Even during the New Era, the theoretical study of film ontology was more often than not integrated with criticism and techniques and did not evolve into abstract thinking. Consequently, a basic characteristic of Chinese film theory is its cooperation with and integration into film practice. In turn, practice applies theory and improves it by raising new questions. This unique interaction not only pervaded the New Era, but also runs the full course of Chinese film history. Even more intriguing is the number of practicing filmmakers who, like Zheng Dongtian, Xie Fei, Zhang Nuanxin and Han Xiaolei, are themselves theoreticians, and the number of theoreticians who, like Lin Hongtong, Chen Jianyu and Ni Zhen (who wrote the script for Zhang Yimou's most recent film, *Raise High the Red Lantern*), endeavor to make films.

The West, in contrast, taking a philosophical approach, emphasizes the study of film theory in itself, pure and independent of practice. Generally, Western film theory does not depend upon or instruct filmmaking, and most filmmakers remain unconcerned with theoretical issues. At the annual conferences of the Society for Cinema Studies (SCS), the major organization of film theorists and scholars in the United States, discussions of theoretical issues attract established scholars from the United States and abroad, but filmmakers rarely participate. From a methodological point of view, the Chinese have proven adept at handling the objective world, with direct perception and a sense of unity, while Westerners have excelled in understanding phenomena through analysis and abstraction. The difference is primarily a matter of culture, for the Chinese have long treated aesthetics axiomatically, whereas the West has taken an epistemological approach. It is this which has given Chinese film theory and criticism its unique oriental flavor.

A significant turning point for film study in China was marked in 1979. Throughout the decade which followed, the study of film shifted for the first time from the external to the internal, from the superficial at the beginning to profound research, in which many interconnected issues came under discussion. Under the stimulation of Western film, the study moved away from the uniformity typical of Chinese film to the pluralistic, and progressed from naive observations based on the enthusiasm and excitement of filmmakers to mature, scientific study, from barren dependence upon traditional ways to the prosperity of multiple approaches. Finally, we must understand that the discussions and debates on film in the New Era were unprecedented—something that had never happened before in the history of the People's Republic, nor in the years which preceded Liberation.

Profound and effective or not, the phenomenon itself was exciting enough to provoke film circles out of their long silence. No matter how much or how little was known about Western film theory, the theoretical forum at least indicated that people had cast their eyes on the rapidly changing modern world outside of China. Whether or not the Chinese film circle had made up for its "innate deficiencies and postnatal dislocation," as one writer put it, or changed its loose habits and became less isolated, the concept of film as a scientific subject, a betrayal of tradition, a new awareness of film theory arose and was put into practice.

THE LIMITED VISION

The characteristics of the development of film theory in the New Era also can be seen through a comparision between the first and second phases of the decade. The primary direction theory took immediately after 1979 aimed first at investigating, developing and establishing film as an art in itself apart from literature and drama, and later shifted to its pluralistic relations with society. In the middle of the decade, as the political and economic reform advanced and the society moved toward modernization, film theory, while continuing to explore the medium, began to shift focus to its multifaceted relations with society, going far beyond film itself and into much broader issues.

If film theory in the first phase of the New Era shifted from the external to the internal and concentrated on ontological studies, toward the middle of the decade, it turned outward again to external considerations, refocusing on the relationship between filmic means of expression and the social and political background, as well as the cultural and ideological context. Film study, on the surface, had come full circle, having moved from considerations of content to considerations of form, and back again to content. This did not mean that theoretical study negated the intrinsic values of the medium. On the contrary, when film studies turned back toward external, social considerations, they did so with self-confidence and understanding. The theoretical studies in the second phase preserved the achievements in film form of the first and pursued a more sophisticated, modern approach. Under these circumstances, during the New Era theoretical circles began to reflect upon such issues as innovation in social ideology, a new understanding of filmmaking, traditional culture and theory, new genres and new relationships between theory and practice.

The dramatic changes in the field of film were the inevitable result of the economic reform and pursuit of modernization China undertook at the time, which demanded that film treat society from a modern viewpoint and that society treat film with equivalent perception. To do so would promote the merger of the trends in film with those of the overall culture.

Looking back on film theory and criticism in the New Era and reviewing the values of every development, Chinese film theory progressed from content to form and back to content, and filmmaking moved from its superficial political position, deeply into a new social consciousness. In every stage along the way, the film world preserved its past achievements while it continued its drive toward higher levels and diversified in both form and function.

Theoretically and historically, however, probably because the issues were too loosely defined, Chinese film theory never focused selectively enough on specific, concrete problems. The discussions were extensive, but not scientific and systematic. Thus, in the end, they reveal the limited vision and knowledge of contemporary Chinese film theorists. The advances and limitations of the debates presented here illustrate the path of Chinese film during a decade filled with difficulties, excitement and restlessness in every significant intellectual or aesthetic movement; however, it does no good to celebrate these debates with simple optimism, any more than it would to reject them with blind pessimism. Chinese film theory continues to develop, but needs to go much further.

AFTER TIANANMEN

The tragic events in Tiananmen Square on June 4, 1989, not only caused China to regress politically and economically, but also darkened the prospects for continued cultural development. The tragedy serves as a pointed reminder of the anti-rightist struggle in 1957, as well as the damaging chaos of the Cultural Revolution. With the memory of films made under a dictatorial government still fresh in people's minds, film theory circles began to sing once again the time-worn refrain: we need to create a socialist Chinese film. The debates and arguments within film theory, which had created a new and exciting decade for film studies, fell silent once again. Political propaganda now dominates both filmmaking and film studies, with severe criticism leveled especially at the works of the Fifth Generation and at the theories and practices of the entertainment film.

After June 4, 1989, one continuation of the directions of the past decade has been the study of films made in the 1950s and 1960s, now considered "classics" of the Communist Party. The investigations focus on the close relationship between these films and their political and ideological context, but are cautious in their evaluation. Though once considered political and aesthetic masterpieces, these films were negatively criticized in the 1980s for their close relationship to politics. Among the new writings which rewrite history and revise the theory of history are Li Yiming's "The Place of Xie Jin's films in Chinese Film History," Wang Hui's "Politics and Morality: Mysteries of Displacement: An Analysis of Xie Jin's film," Ying Yong's "Glorious Twilight of Classical Writing: On Xie Jin and Familyhood in His Films," and Dai Jinhua's "History and Narrative: On Xie Jin's Films," all recent articles in *Film Art*.

A second significant development, which comes from another direction, is the increasingly loud voices critical of Chinese film theory in the 1980s, especially in the latter years. The theory and practice of entertainment, the first targets, were condemned in the official newspapers as the thoughts and practices of bourgeois art. "It needs to be pointed out," Gao Honggu, president of the Guangxi Film Studio, criticized, "that the rising issue of the entertainment film is not accidental. It is an inevitable result of the desalination of the instructional function of socialist ideology and ethics which has dominated film in recent years. The bitter fact of film practice has already proved that the scantiness of objectivity in entertainment films has been negative for Chinese film."[1] The Fifth Generation has been called a myth which never actually existed, but was conjured up by film theory in the 1980s. In 1990, *Film Art*, an important forum for theory in the 1980s, was first reduced to a bi-monthly "for lack of funds" and, more recently, has ceased all publication. In 1991, the editorial board of *Contemporary Cinema* was also reformed. A former director of the film bureau was named editor-in-chief, and a campaign to promote socialist film with Chinese features was initated by the new editorial board. These developments put an end to Chinese film theory of the New Era, and theoretical study has entered another stage.

The situation is not entirely bleak. Although the censorship, always systematic, has become increasingly cautious and strict, filmmaking in China continues to develop and mature. With the release of *Obsession* (Zhou Xiaowen, 1989), *Samsara* (Huang Jianxin, 1989), *Troubleshooters* (Mi Jiashan, 1988), *Puff and Blow* (Yie Daying, 1989), *Black Snow* (Xie Fei, 1990) and *Bloody Morning* (Liu Xiaohong, 1990), we can see that the entertainment genre now dominates the film market and that the overall quality of film continues to be refined. In addition, the Fifth Generation filmmakers continue to produce exceptional films. Wu Ziniu's *The Big Mill* (1990), after his *Evening Bell* (1987), and more importantly, Zhang Yimou's *Judou* (1990) and *Raise High the Red Lantern* (1991), both produced after *Red Sorghum*, have received international acclaim. We can feel assured that Chinese film will persist on its drive toward global recognition.

If the pursuit of film theory within the People's Republic has, since June 4, 1989, become somewhat more subdued and conservative, concentrating on the political and economic issues the country and the industry within it faces, we should also recognize the potential in the many young people who have left, and continue to leave, the country to study film and communications in the United States and elsewhere. They are beginning to leave their mark. Ma Ning, now in Australia, has already published significant new writings. Hou Jianping, Xia Hong and Chen Xihe, among the editors of the translations represented here and in our first volume, who continue to write and present their findings to the Society of Cinema Studies and the Asian Cinema Studies Society, have opened the door further. Wang Chun-Lei, from the China Film Archive; Wang Xiaowen, from the Beijing Film Academy; and Hu Yiyi, an actress from Shanghai, are beginning to produce work of the highest order. The formation of an Asian-American caucus at the 1992 SCS conference, through the efforts of Esther Yao, is another welcome aspect of this process. The literature continues to increase.

What is happening, in fact, if recent materials are a sign, is a renewal of energies. Most agree that the current stasis in China will not last forever. Through these knowledgable and enthusiastic young people, of whom China should be proud, the literature will continue to increase and mature. Though the influence of the West will become increasingly obvious, the results will continue to be theoretical materials which are at the least cross-cultural, but which maintain their significantly Chinese flavor. Where a few years ago Western film scholars were eager to explore Chinese film as a new frontier, they are now passing the banner on to the Chinese students who have come to study under them, and these young people will, in the long run, pursue the development of Chinese film theory and thereby further the development of Chinese film.

NOTE

1. Gao Honggu. "On the Subjectivity of the Entertainment Film," *Guangming Daily*, June 11, 1990.

Bibliography

Ai Mingzi, Li Tianji and Meng Senhui. "A Subject Never to Forget." *New Filmscripts*, February 1982.

Bai Jingsheng. "Throwing Away the Walking Stick of Drama." *Film Art Reference*, January 1979.

Bao Tianxiao. *A Reminscence about Chuanyinglou.* rev. ed. Hong Kong: Dahua Press, 1973.

Chen Huangmei. "Don't Forget Literature." *New Film Scripts*, January 1982.

Chen Lide. "Exploration and Innovation Must Originate from Life." *Film Art*, January 1980.

Chen Xihe. "Shadowplay: Chinese Film Aesthetics and Their Philosophical and Cultural Fundamentals." *Contemporary Cinema*, Spring 1986.

Cheng Jihua and Li Shaohai, eds. *History of the Development of Chinese Film.* Beijing: Chinese Film Press, 1963.

Dai Jinhua. "A Discussion with Shao Mujun." *Film Art*, December 1986.

————. "Reading Xia Yan's *Problems of Scriptwriting.*" *Contemporary Cinema*, Winter 1987.

Ding Yinnan. "The Change of Film Concept and the Demand of the Audience." *Explorations of Film Directing.* Vol. 2. Beijing: China Film Publishing House, 1982.

Gao Honggu. "On the Subjectivity of the Entertainment Film." *Guangming Daily*, June 11, 1990.

Gao Qing and Wang Zhongqian. "A Summary of the Discussion about the Dramatic, Literary, and Cinematic Characteristics of Film." *Film Art*, August 1983.

Han Xiaolei. "An Experiment of Truthfully Presenting Contemporary Youth." *Film Culture*, August 1983.

————. "Is Film Nationalization Scientific?" *Journal of Literature and Art*, July 1980.

Hou Yao. *On the Writing of Yingxi Scripts.* Nanjing: Taidong Press, 1926.

Huang Shixian. "Film Should Seek the Beauty of Its Form." *Film Art Reference*, no. 21, 1980.

Li Jie. "Xie Jin's Era Should End." *Wenhui Daily*, August 1, 1986.

Li Jisheng. "Theory, Reality and Styles of Study." *Film Art*, August 1988.

Li Shaobai. "My Understanding of Film Innovation." *Film Art*, December 1986.

————. "Scattered Thoughts on the Value of Film Theory." *Film Art*, January 1, 1988.

————. "Trivial Ideas on Film Nationalization." *Film Culture*, January 1981.

Li Shaobai, Rong Weijing and Li Shun. "Issues on Film Theory and Criticism." *Film Art*, February 1988.

Li Suyuan. "The Cultural Film: A Noticeable Change." *Contemporary Cinema*, no. 1, 1989.

Li Tuo, Zhong Dafeng, Zhou Chuanji and Hao Dazheng. "What Is Cinema? A New Look at the Question." *Film Art*, May 1988.

Lu Zhuguo. "Strive to Strengthen the Literary Quality of Film." *Screen and Audience*, August 1982.

Luo Yijun. "The Argument over Film Nationalization." *Film Art*, April 1985.

————. "The National Style in the Films of the 1930s." In *Cinematic Aesthetics: 1982*, Zhong Dianfei, ed. Beijing: Culture Association Publishers, 1983.

————. "Preliminary Research on the National Style of Film." *Film Art*, October and December 1981.

————. "The Style on the Screen in Beijing—the Ancient City." *Film Art*, October 1984.

————. "Three Problems of Film Nationalization." *Guangming Daily*, November 2, 1983.

Ma Zhonggai. "The Saying 'Film Nationalization' is also Imported." *Film Culture*, January 1981.

Mao Zedong. *Collected Writings of Mao Zedong*. Vol. 8. Tokyo: Chang-chang Press, 1983.

Ni Zhen. "After *Yellow Earth*." *Learned Journal of the Beijing Film Institute*, no. 1, 1985.

Rong Weijing. "On the Presentation of Nationalism through Film." *Film Art*, October 1986.

Semsel, George S., ed. *Chinese Film: The State of the Art in the People's Republic*. New York: Praeger, 1987.

Semsel, George S., Xia Hong and Hou Jianping, eds. *Chinese Film Theory: A Guide to the New Era*. New York: Praeger, 1990.

Shao Mujun. "About *A Corner Forsaken by Love*." *Film Art*, May 1979.

————. "The Argument over Similarity and Difference." *Film Art*, November 1985.

————. "Modernization and the Modernists." *Film Art*, May 1979.

————. "Notes on Film Aesthetics." *Film Art*, November 1984.

————. "Pure and Impure—An Analysis of the Direction of Contemporary Film Theory." *Film Art*, March 1988.

————. "A Response to the Issue of the Contemporary Entertainment Film." *Contemporary Cinema*, no. 2, 1989.

————. "The Road of Innovation in Chinese Cinema." *Film Art*, September 1986.

————. "Summary of Casual Thinking on Film Aesthetics." *Film Art*, November 1984.

Shen Jiming. "The Entertainment Film: Dialogue II." *Contemporary Cinema*, no. 2, 1987.

————. "The Entertainment Film: Dialogue III." *Contemporary Cinema*, no. 3, 1987.

Shen Yiaoting, Wu Yigong and Song Chong. "Film Art is Director's Art." *Wenhui Daily*, November 2, 1980.

Song Chong. "The Exploration of Contemporary Film Concept." *Film Art Reference*, August 1983.

Song Jianbo. "Thoughts on the Literary Value of Film." *Film Literature*, December 1982.

Tian Shen. "Film Should Belong to Literature." *Film Literature*, September 1982.

Wang Lian. "I'm all for 'Don't Forget Literature'." *New Filmscripts*, February 1982.

Wang Yuanlian. "Film: A Visual Form of Literature." *Film Literature*, September 1980.

Wang Zhongming. "On the Modern Consciousness of the Filmmaker." In *Film Aesthetics*. 1983. Zhong Dianfei, ed. Beijing: Culture Association Publisher, 1983.

Wu Yigong. "To Be a Loyal Artist to the People." *Film Art*, June 1987.

Xia Hong. "The Debate over *Horse Thief*." *Film Art*, July 1987.

Xia Yan. "About Chinese Film." *Research on Literature*, June 1980.

―――. *Problems of Screenwriting*. Beijing: China Film Press, 1959.

Xie Fei. "My View of the Concept of Film." *Film Art*, December 1984.

Xie Jin. "Speech at the Board Meeting of the China Film Association." *Film Art*, October 1986.

Xu Zhudai. "Shadowplay Is Drama." *Ming Xing Biweekly Special Issue*, no. 4, December 1926.

Yang Ni. "Film Is Film: A Response to Tan Peisheng." *Film Art*, October 1983.

Yang Yianjin. "No Nationalization in the Forms of Presentational Techniques." *Journal of Literature and Art*, July 1980.

Yao Xiaomeng. "The Entertainment Film: Dialogue I." *Contemporary Cinema*, no. 1, 1987.

Yao Xiaomeng and Hu Ke. "Film: A Myth with Hidden Ideologies." *Film Art*, no. 8, 1988.

Yie Dan. "Film Can't Separate from Literature." *New Filmscripts*, February 1982.

Yu Min. "Diversification, Not Prescriptions." *New Filmscripts*, February 1983.

Yuan Wenshu. "About Film Study." *Reference of World Cinema*, June 1980.

―――. "Film Tradition and Innovation." *Film Art*, June 1987.

Zhang Junxiang. "Essay Done in Film Terms." *Film Culture*, February 1980.

―――. "Film Is about Literature." *Film Communication*, no. 11, 1980.

―――. "A Letter to Comrade Xia Yan." *People's Daily*, November 3, 1986.

Zhang Nuanxin. "Exploration of the New Concept of Film." *Explorations of Film Directing*. Vol. 2. Beijing: China Publishing House, 1982.

Zhang Nuanxin and Li Tuo. "The Modernization of Film Language." *Film Art*, March 1979.

Zhang Wei. "Contemporary Chinese Entertainment Film: A Review of a Symposium." *Contemporary Cinema*, no. 1, 1989.

―――. "Query on the Literary Quality of Film." *Film Literature*, February 1982.

Zheng Dongtian. "The Aesthetics of *Neighbors*." *Film Art*, July 1983.

―――. "Only Seven Years: An Exploration of Middle-Aged and Young Directors (1979–1986)." *Contemporary Cinema*, January 1987.

Zheng Xuelai. "On Film Literature and Film Characteristics." *New Filmscripts*, May 1986.

Zhong Dafeng. "Also on the Traditional and Innovation of Film." *Film Art*, December 1986.

————. "A Historical Survey of the Yingxi (Shadowplay) Theory." *Contemporary Cinema*, no. 3, 1986.

Zhong Dianfei. "The Divorce between Film and Drama." *Film Communication*, no. 10, 1980.

————. "Film Form and Film's National Form." *Film Culture*, January 1981.

————. "Film Literature Should Make a Fresh Start." *New Filmscripts,* January 1983.

————. "Issues on Cinematic Aesthetics." *Research on Literature*, June 1980.

————. "A Letter to Ding Qiao." *Film News Report*, October 1980.

————. "Notes on Film Awards." *Popular Film*, June 1986.

————. "On Innovation in Social and Cinematic Ideas." *Film Art*, February 1985.

Zhou Chaunji and Li Tuo. "An Important School of Cinematic Aesthetics—About the Theory of the Long Take." *Film Culture*, no. 1, 1980.

Zhou Yu, et al. "The Inadequacies and Biases of Film Theory." *Film Art*. October 1987.

Zhu Dake. "The Drawback of Xie Jin's Model." *Wenhui Daily*, July 18, 1986.

Index

Contributors, Translators
and Editors

CHEN HUAIKAI, director, is a senior member of the directing staff of the Beijing Film Studio. Among his major works is *The Meeting of Two Heroes*.

CHEN XIHE, editor, has a B.A. in literature and an M.A. from the graduate college of the China Film Art Research Center. A research fellow of the China Film Art Research Center, he is completing his Ph.D. at Ohio State University. He is a columnist for *Beijing Huabao* and a special contributor to *Film Art*. His major works include *Film, Literature and Theatre*.

DAI JINHUA, critic, a graduate in Chinese language and literature at Beijing University, is a lecturer of film literature and criticism at the Beijing Film Institute.

FU BINBIN, translator, is a lecturer in English and translation at Beijing University. He is currently a doctoral candidate in English at Ohio University.

HAO DAZHENG, critic, is a senior fellow at the China Film Art Research Center.

HU KE, critic, is a research fellow at the China Film Art Research Center.

KONG DU, critic, is a professor of film history at the Beijing Film Institute. Much of his writing centers on Chinese film history.

LI CHAO, critic, works in the film theory and research section of the Changchun Film Studio in the northeast of China. He studied at the Beijing Film Institute.

LI SHAOBAI, critic, co-edited *History of the Development of Chinese Film* with Cheng Jihua. He is a senior fellow at the Institute for the Research of Chinese Art.

LI SUYUAN, critic, is a research fellow at the China Film Art Research Center in Beijing.

LI TUO, writer and critic, is deputy editor-in-chief of *Beijing Art and Literature*. Recently a visiting scholar at the University of Chicago, he is currently a visiting professor at the University of California in Berkeley. His works include numerous short stories and essays on literature and art.

LIU SHUSHENG, critic, is a research fellow at the Institute for the Research of Chinese Art.

MA NING, critic and theorist, is on the staff of the translation section of the China Film Corporation. A contributor to *Chinese Film: The State of the Art in the People's Republic* (Semsel, ed., 1987), he is completing his Ph.D. at Monash University in Victoria, Australia.

NI ZHEN, critic and screenwriter, is the chair of Center for Theoretical Studies at the Beijing Film Institute. He wrote *Raise High the Red Lantern* for Zhang Yimou.

QIAN JING, critic, is a research associate in the literature section of the China Social Science Institute.

RAO SHUGUANG, critic, graduated in Chinese language and literature at Sichuan University and is currently on the editorial staff of *Contemporary Cinema*.

GEORGE S. SEMSEL, editor, is a professor of film at Ohio University and is author/editor of *Chinese Film: The State of the Art in the People's Republic* and *Chinese Film Theory: A Guide to the New Era* (1990). Dr. Semsel, foreign expert at the China Film Corporation (1984–1985), was recently a Fulbright Scholar at Sukhothai Thammathirat Open University in Pakkret Thailand.

SHAO MUJUN, film critic and translator, is a research fellow of the China Film Association and the secretary of the secretariat of the China Film Association.

A graduate in English at St. John's University, Shanghai, and the foreign languages department of Qinghua University, his major works include *Survey of Western Film History* and *In the Sea of the Silver Screen* (a collection of essays).

SHEN JIMING, critic, was managing editor of *Contemporary Cinema* until June 1989. Her writings center on film marketing research.

SHI XIAOHUA, director, one of the major women directors in China, works at the Shanghai Film Studio. Among her films are *Spring Water Drips*.

SONG CHONG, now president of the Beijing Film Studio, is a former director of the Shanghai film studio. His films include *The Last Choice* and *Good Things Take Time*.

SUN JIANRONG, translator, is a doctoral candidate in education at Ohio University.

TIAN ZHUANGZHUANG, director, is one of the leading figures of the Fifth Generation. A graduate in directing at the Beijing Film Institute, his works include *The Red Elephant*, *September*, *On the Hunting Ground*, *Horse Thief*, *Traveling Players*, *Rock and Roll Kids*, and *The Last Eunuch*.

WANG XIAOWEN, translator, a graduate in English from Beijing University, teaches at the Beijing Film Institute. She is completing an M.A. in film theory at the Ohio University School of Film.

WANG ZHONGMING, critic, is president of the Beijing Young Critics Association.

WU YIGONG, director, is the head of the Shanghai Film Bureau and general director of the Shanghai Film Corporation. A graduate in directing at the Beijing Film Institute, his films include *Evening Rain*, *My Memories of Old Beijing*, *Sister*, *College in Exile* and *The Misfortune of the Young Master*.

XIA HONG, editor, a graduate of Fudan University and the Ohio University School of Film, is on the editorial staff of *Film Art* (*Dianying Yishu*), a theoretical journal published by the China Film Association. He was guest editor of the *Wide Angle* issue on Chinese film and one of the editors of *Chinese Film Theory: The New Era*.

XIE TIAN, director, is a well-known director of comedies at the Beijing Film Studio. Among his films are *The Guerrilla Force at Hong Hu*, *Teahouse* and *The Road of Fortune*.

XU YINGHUA, screenwriter, assigned to the Shanghai Film Studio, is the scriptwriter of *Narrow Lane* and writer and co-director of the remake of *Song at Midnight*.

YANG NI, critic, is on the editorial staff of *Film Art* (*Dianying Yishu*).

YANG YIANJIN is director of *Troubled Laughter*, *Narrow Lane*, and *T Province in 1984 and 1985*, and co-director of *Song at Midnight*.

YAO XIAOMONG, critic, is on the editorial staff of *Contemporary Cinema*.

ZHANG HUAXUN is a senior director at the Beijing Film Studio. His works, including *Wu Lin Zhi* and *Mysterious Buddha*, are kung fu and action films.

ZHANG RUI, scriptwriter and novelist, a graduate of Fudan University, wrote the script for *Horse Thief*.

ZHANG WEI, critic, a graduate of Nankai University in Tianjin and of the China Film Art Research Center, is an editor at *Contemporary Cinema*.

ZHAO BAOHUA, critic, is a research fellow at the theory and literature section of the Changchun Film Studio.

ZHENG DONGTIAN, film director and critic, is chairman and associate professor of directing at the Beijing Film Institute. His major works include the films *Neighbors* and *The Building for Couples* and the essays "Notes on *In the Wild Mountains*" and "After the Combination."

ZHONG DAFENG, a graduate of the China Film Art Research Center, is now chair of the film literature department at the Beijing Film Institute.

ZHONG DIANFEI, art and literary critic and theorist, is a research fellow at the China Film Art Research Center. He serves on the steering committee of the China Film Association and is president of the China Film Critics Society. His major works include *A Collection of Deep Thinking*, *Announcement of the Struggle*, "The Drum of Film" and "Strategies of Film." He has served as editor-in-chief of the annual *Film Aesthetics*.

ZHOU YU is a senior director at the Changchun Film Studio. His most widely known film is *At Middle Age*.